authentic FAITH

Also by Gary Thomas

Sacred Marriage

Sacred Pathways

authentic FAITH

The Power of a Fire-Tested Life

*What if life isn't meant to be perfect
but we are meant to trust the One who is?*

gary L. Thomas

GRAND RAPIDS, MICHIGAN 49530

ZONDERVAN™

Authentic Faith
Copyright © 2002 by Gary L. Thomas

Requests for information should be addressed to:
Zondervan, *Grand Rapids, Michigan 49530*

Library of Congress Cataloging-in-Publication Data

Thomas, Gary (Gary Lee)
     Authentic faith : the power of a fire-tested life / Gary Thomas.
        p. cm.
     Includes bibliographical references.
     ISBN 0-310-23692-4
     1. Christian life. I. Title.
   BV4501.3 .T47 2002
   248.4—dc21

20010056099

Interior design by Todd Sprague

Printed in the United States of America

---

02 03 04 05 06 07 08 /❖ DC/ 10 9 8 7 6 5 4 3

To Mark Rorem,
my fifth-grade teacher at Spinning Elementary School
in Puyallup, Washington.

People have frequently asked me when I got started on the "classics," and I was truly blessed to have a teacher turn me on to C. S. Lewis when I was just eleven years old—first the Narnia books, and then *The Screwtape Letters.* Thank you, Mark, for encouraging a young kid in his faith when other kids laughed at him, and for taking professional risks to nurture a private belief.

contents

acknowledgments

As always, I was well served by the people at Zondervan during the writing process, particularly John Sloan and Dirk Buursma—thank you so much for helping to get this message refined. And once the book was ready to go, John Topliff and Sam Hooks helped with the launch. You guys are great!

Several people read an earlier manuscript and provided many helpful comments. They include Jeromy Matkin, Bill Smith, Larry Madison, Evan Howard, Larry Gadbaugh, and Lisa Thomas. This book has been much improved because of their input. I also want to thank Mark Wilks, senior pastor at the First Baptist Church in Chehalis, Washington, for suggesting the tagline and for several comments he offered regarding the titling of this book, as well as Dr. Robert Stone, senior pastor at Hillcrest Chapel in Bellingham, Washington, whose sermons often seemed providentially timed as God used them to refine, confirm, and shape the message contained herein.

one

severe gifts

Fire-Testing Seasons from a Loving Father

The Church is the one thing that saves a man from the degrading servitude of being a child of his time.

G. K. Chesterton

"**D**id you hear about Mike?"

"No," I said. "What happened?"

When I arrived on Western Washington University's campus in 1980, Mike Dittman was perhaps the most dynamic Christian I had ever met. He was several years older than I was, and already a leader in the college ministry I attended. Mike had everything: a charismatic personality, great athletic ability, and a walk of integrity, as well as being a skilled worship leader and a good teacher. He could lead you into the presence of God like few I've ever met. I often sought him out at lunchtime to talk, and was later pleased to end up being in the small group he led.

Following his time at Western, Mike served as a campus pastor and then enrolled in graduate studies to become a counselor. He worked at a church for a number of years until finally an "intervention" of sorts took place. Men whom Mike respected and loved confronted him and said, "Mike, you're very competent. Very insightful. A dynamic leader. A guy who inspires admiration and respect. But you're also too blunt. You hurt people with your words. You lack compassion and empathy."

Mike was devastated, but in a good way. He realized that not one of the positive traits mentioned by these men was a "fruit of the Spirit," and he found himself praying, "God, I wish I was a little less 'dynamic' and a little more compassionate."

It was just a couple years later that a close friend told me the shocking news: After a morning workout, Mike's body dropped to the locker room floor. A brain hemorrhage almost took his life, but after a furious scare, doctors were able to keep Mike in this world—albeit, a very different Mike.

His Hollywood-handsome appearance was gone. Half of Mike's face now looks "fallen," pulled over to one side. He can't sing anymore or play his guitar, so there's no more leading worship. For a while his speech was slurred, so he couldn't teach. He was humbled in just about every way an ambitious man can be humbled.

After months of grueling therapy, Mike moved on. The devastating effect on his body was paralleled by an equally powerful—and wonderful—change in his spirit. Now, years later, Mike's ministry has never been more productive. He started a phenomenally successful department of counseling at the Philadelphia Biblical University, which has grown from a handful of students to hundreds of participants. People fly in to Philadelphia from all over the country to meet with Mike—pastors who have fallen, marriages that have broken apart, children who are rebelling. Mike's seen it all. Whereas before his focus was on the masses, Mike now specializes in healing hurting hearts, one at a time.

"The brain hemorrhage took a lot away from me," Mike told me recently, "but it gave me even more." Mike is now the type of guy whose spirit invites you to quiet your heart, get rid of all pretenses, and revel in God's presence. I think the main difference is that in college, when I was around Mike, I wanted to be like Mike. Now, after spending time with Mike, I want to be more like Jesus.

The amazing thing is that Mike's story, though inspirational, is not particularly unique. I have heard so many Christians tell me of a gut-wrenching season they walked through, only to hear them say, "In the end, I'm glad it happened. The fruit it creates far outweighs the pain and angst that come with it."

None of them would have chosen ahead of time to walk through such a difficult trial. But all of them are grateful, in hindsight, that the trial came. Such fire-testing seasons are severe gifts from a loving Father, though initially they are rarely received as such.

These seasons are necessary because we do not walk easily into maturity. At first, Christianity can be an intoxicating blend of freedom, joy, exuberance, and newfound discovery. Longtime sins drop off us with relatively little effort. Bible study is rich; we may feel like archaeologists finally coming across an unexplored cave as we become astonished at the insights that pour from the book in front of us. Intimacy, tears, and the assurance of God's voice and guidance mark our times of prayer.

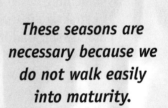

These seasons are necessary because we do not walk easily into maturity.

This "spiritual infatuation" phase is well known and well documented among spiritual directors and those familiar with spiritual formation. Just like romantic infatuation is self-centered, so spiritual infatuation tends to be "all about me." It *seems* as though it's all about God, but the focus of new believers' lives is still mostly taken up with how they're doing with regard to defeating sins, as well as cultivating the new joy and spiritual depth that come from walking with God. They're thrilled with what Christianity has done *for them.*

Eventually, God asks us to discard this infatuation and move on to a mature friendship with him. In a true friendship, it's no longer "all about me." It's about partnering with God to build his kingdom. That means, first, being "fire-tested" and, second, growing in ways that we naturally wouldn't be inclined to grow. This growth can be painful for us, but it's a growth that is necessary if we are to become the type of women and men whom God can use. Instead of focusing on our desire for God to answer our prayers, spiritual maturity leads us to yearn for faithfulness, Christlikeness, and others-centeredness. This is a painful process, a very real spiritual death that some have described as being "born again" *again*, except for the fact that it is never a onetime event.

> **The first sign that a believer has failed to move in a timely fashion past the spiritual infatuation stage is usually disillusionment.**

It is a mistake to ask someone to grow out of spiritual infatuation too quickly. Such a season has its place. There's no getting around the fact that babies need diapers and milk. But when a ten-, twenty-, or thirty-year-old still wears diapers and still acts as though the world revolves around his or her own personal happiness, something has gone wrong.

The first sign that a believer has failed to move in a timely fashion past the spiritual infatuation stage is usually *disillusionment*. Whereas before they thought of God as only kind, only merciful, and only loving, they now tend to view him as stubborn, severe, and unyielding. A wise spiritual director will seek to lay the groundwork for a new way of thinking during this stage. There's a place for this disillusionment, provided it effects the sea change that leads to mature friendship with God. If disillusionment remains, however, it ceases to motivate and eventually may bury the believer under its despair.

The second mark is an ongoing *what's in it for me personally?* attitude. We live in a "me-first" culture, and we often try to individualize corporate promises, largely because we're more concerned about what the Bible says to us individually than about how it calls us to live in community—that is, as those who are a part of the church. Peter tells us that, corporately, we are "a chosen people, a royal priesthood, a holy nation, a people belonging to God." Why? Not for any individual purpose, but for a corporate one that honors God: "that you may declare the praises of him who called you out of darkness into his wonderful light. Once you were not a people, but now you are the people of God; once you had not received mercy, but now you have received mercy" (1 Peter 2:9–10).

When God calls us to himself, he calls us to his church, to a purpose bigger than ourselves. This may sound shocking to some, but biblically, living for God means living for his church. There is a glory in the presence of Jesus Christ, seen when believers come together, that will necessarily be missing in an individual pursuit of God. When the gospel is turned from a community-centered faith to an individual-centered faith ("Jesus would have died for me if I had been the only one!"), we eclipse much of its power and meaning.

The new groundwork that needs to be laid is an authentic faith that is based on a God-centered life. Rather than the believer being the sun around whom God, the church, and the world

> *The new groundwork that needs to be laid is an authentic faith that is based on a God-centered life.*

revolve in order to create a happy, easy, and prosperous life, God becomes the sun around which the believer revolves, a believer who is willing to suffer—even to be persecuted—and lay down his or her life to build God's kingdom and to serve God's church. This is a radical shift—indeed, the most radical (and freeing) shift known in human experience—and it leads to a deep friendship with God.

friendship with god

In relationships, even our best intentions can go ridiculously awry. I read of one man who thought he had planned the perfect date with his wife: "For Valentine's Day," he wrote, "I decided to take my wife out for a nice romantic dinner, and all she did was complain. Next time I want to eat at Hooters, I'll go by myself." We can bring this same self-centeredness into our relationship with God. Much of what we say, or even think, we're doing on God's behalf is really being done for ourselves.

On a deeper level, I believe many of us are hungry and thirsty for a faith based on sacrifice instead of on self-absorption and simplistic denial. We don't want to become Christians in order to become an *improved* man or woman, but an *entirely new* man or woman—people who live with a different outlook on life, who find joy while others pursue happiness, who find meaning in what others see as something to simply be overcome or cured, who want to drink deeply of life—with its mountains and valleys, twists and turns—rather than to "rise above it."

This is an authentic faith, prescribed for a disillusioned world. It is a faith taught by Jesus, passed on by the ancients, and practiced throughout two thousand years of church history. It's our heritage, our birthright, and our blessing. It has been witnessed to as ultimately the most fulfilling life ever lived, though it is frequently a life of hardship and difficulty.

To embrace God's love and kingdom is to embrace his broken, passionate heart. It is to expose ourselves to the assaults brought on by the world's hatred toward God. The active Christian life is a life full of risks, heartaches, and responsibilities. God does indeed bear our burdens. Certainly, he blesses us in many ways, but this initial relief is for the purpose of assigning to us more important concerns than our own. Only this time, we weep not because our house is too small or because we have overextended our credit, but because we are taxed to the limit as we reach out to a hurting world. Yes, we experience peace, joy, and hope, but it is a peace in the midst of turmoil, a joy marked with empathy, and a hope refined by suffering.

> **To embrace God's love and kingdom is to embrace his broken, passionate heart.**

Ultimately, spiritual maturity is not about memorizing the Bible and mastering the spiritual disciplines. These are healthy things to do, but they are still only means to a greater end, which in itself is *learning to love with God's love* and *learning to serve with God's power.* In a fallen world, love begs to be unleashed—a love that is supernatural in origin, without limit, a love that perseveres in the face of the deepest hatred or the sharpest pain. It is a love that becomes silhouetted in a broken world, framed by human suffering, illuminated in an explosion of God's presence breaking into a dark cellar.

In a world where suffering and difficulty are certain, friendship with God frees us from being limited by what we don't have, by what we are suffering, or by what we are enduring. Mature friendship with God reminds us that our existence is much broader than our suffering and difficulty. God doesn't offer us freedom *from* a broken world; instead, he offers us friendship with himself as we walk *through* a fallen world—and those who persevere will find that this friendship is worth more, so very much more, than anything this fallen world can offer.

> *Friendship with God frees us from being limited by what we don't have, by what we are suffering, or by what we are enduring.*

In short, we are missing out when we insist on self-absorption, affluence, and ease over against pursuing a deeper walk with God. We miss out on an intimacy that has been heralded by previous generations, a fellowship of labor, suffering, persecution, and selflessness. It doesn't sound like much fun initially, but those who have walked these roads have left behind a witness that they have reached an invigorating, soul-satisfying land. These women and men testify to being radically satisfied in God, even though others may scratch their heads as they try to figure out how someone who walks such a difficult road could possibly be happy.

In a broken, fallen world, we really only have two choices: mature friendship with God, or radical disillusionment.

A classical faith

Today's self-oriented gospel is no stranger to the church. In fact, it is relatively similar to the faith that spawned the Christian flight to the desert in the fourth century, the spread of monasticism in the sixth century, the reform of monasticism in the Middle Ages, and then the spread of Puritanism in the seventeenth century. Throughout history, God has always left his witness of a "classical faith"— that is, a God-centered, authentic faith. Not the faith of the Pharisees, who majored on the minors and made legalistic obedience their god; not the faith of those who see God as their ticket to comfort and ease; nor yet the faith that sees Christianity as still another

> *In a broken, fallen world, we really only have two choices: mature friendship with God, or radical disillusionment.*

means to "improve ourselves" and become "more disciplined." God has served us and does serve us—but ultimately, classical, authentic Christianity is about glorifying, proclaiming, adoring, and obeying God.

If you've found yourself disillusioned in any way with Christianity or with your faith in God, make sure it's really Christianity you're disillusioned with and not some perversion of it that is only masquerading as faith. Check to see if you are caught in the crossroads of moving beyond spiritual infatuation, and being invited into the quieter—and, quite frankly, seemingly darker—waters of mature friendship with God. Authentic Christianity majors on a powerful display of God's presence, often through his people, in a world that is radically broken.

Authentic faith penetrates the most unlikely of places. This faith is found, for instance, when we die to ourselves and put others first (chapter 2). Such a faith is nurtured when we cultivate contentment instead of spending our best energy and efforts to improve our lot in life (chapter 9). Classical faith is strengthened in suffering (chapter 4), persecution (chapter 5), waiting (chapter 3), and even mourning (chapter 8). Just as surely as water seeks the lowest point in the land, so such a faith seeks the least of all people (chapter 6). Instead of holding on to grudges, authentic faith chooses forgiveness (chapter 7). Authentic faith lives with another world in mind, recognizing that what we do in this broken world will be judged (chapter 11).

The "authentic disciplines," as I call them, differ from the traditional spiritual disciplines in that the authentic disciplines are, for the most part, initiated outside of us.[1] God brings them into our life when he wills and as he wills. Just by reading about suffering doesn't bring you through suffering—you can't *make* these disciplines happen, as you can make fasting or meditation take place. This is a God-ordained spirituality, dependent on his sovereignty.

The traditional disciplines—fasting, meditation, study, prayer, and the like—are all crucial elements of building our faith, but let's be honest. They can also foster pride, arrogance, self-sufficiency, religiosity, and worse. Their benefit is clearly worth the risk, but that's why the authentic disciplines are such a helpful and even vital addition; they turn us away from human effort—from men and women seeking the face of God—and turn us back toward God seeking the face of men and women.

There's no pride left when God takes me through a time of suffering. There's no self-righteousness when I am called to wait. There is no religiosity when I am truly mourning. This is a spirituality I can't control, I can't initiate, I can't bring about. It is a radical dependence on God's husbandry. All I can do is try to appreciate it and learn from it. The rest—the duration of the trial, the intensity of the trial, the ultimate cessation of the trial—is almost always up to him.

When we live with such an authentic faith, in a mature friendship with God, we cultivate what I like to call a "defiant beauty."

Defiant Beauty

I once spoke at a married couple's retreat in southwestern Washington. To get there I had to travel through "tree country," miles and miles of tree farms planted by Weyerhaeuser, one of North America's largest producers of timber. Each farm had a sign announcing, "These trees were planted in 1988." "These trees were planted in 1992." "These trees were planted in 1996."

Interspersed among the tree farms were occasional stretches of clear-cut logging projects. I love trees, and perhaps because of that, I find few things more ugly than a clear-cut stretch of land. It looks devastated, broken, and abused. I know that, after planting, the land will come back, but it's still sad to see such brutal scarring of a forest.

As I drove up the highway, I passed yet another clear-cut stretch when my eye suddenly caught something that almost made me pull off the road. There, in a devastated patch of land, stood a startlingly beautiful maple tree in full autumn colors. Somehow, the loggers had missed it.

The contrast could not have been more stark and, for that reason, more beautiful. Beauty surrounded by beauty begins, after a time, to seem mediocre. Beauty in the midst of chaos or ugliness is stunning. It's onstage, and it seizes your attention. In a barren, broken stretch of land, this tree captured my imagination and told another story. Had it been in the midst of New Hampshire's White Mountains during autumn, it likely would have been missed—one stunning tree in a forest of stunning trees blends right in. Here, in a broken, hurting land, this glorious tree proclaimed a transcendent truth.

In the deepest part of us, we truly yearn, I believe, for such "defiant beauty." In a world where people live self-centered lives, where ugly things happen, where sin seems to spread unchecked, where daily assaults take their toll, we can point to the defiant beauty of a selfless life, seeking first the kingdom of God, putting others first, and even sacrificing ourselves in the process, if need be—all to proclaim a transcendent truth that is greater than ourselves.

> *In a world where people live self-centered lives, we can point to the defiant beauty of a selfless life.*

In this book, I'm going to invite you to develop a defiant beauty—the kind of defiant beauty that has shone through all generations of the church. At some points in our history, the beauty has been marred and partially hidden. But it's always been there. It's our legacy, and this is an invitation to pick it back up once again.

Authentic Faith

Following Lee's surrender to Grant at Appomattox during the waning days of the Civil War, the son of Henry Wise, an ex-Southern governor, told his father that he had taken the loyalty oath to the United States.

"You have disgraced the family, sir!" Henry Wise responded.

The son, a former captain in the Confederate Army, was mortified and pled his case: "But, Father, General Lee advised me to do it."

Hardly a moment passed before Wise recanted. "That alters the case," he told his son. "Whatever General Lee advises is right."

There may be some assertions in this book that, at first glance, don't seem right; they may lead you to ask, "Does Christianity really involve that?" My appeal to you is the same one made by Henry Wise's son: I ask you to consider who first said these words. I have purposely filled this book with more Scripture than any of my previous books, and I have worked just as diligently to root these thoughts and concepts in the precedence of the Christian classics, showing how each tenet was supported, affirmed, and taught by classical Christian writers throughout the centuries. [2]

Mine is not the role of a *pioneer,* much as this title sounds exalted for an author. To my chagrin, a far more honest description for what I'm doing is that of a *tour guide,* taking us through long-ago discovered truths and helping visitors discover their meaning for today. If at first these ideas seem to go against common sense, if some seem to be outdated or impossible to believe, my answer is to point back to these authorities.

What I hope you will find is an authentic faith that rings true throughout the ages. Some of the truths may sound hard, but they are the prescription we need in order to live a truly meaningful and productive life in Christ. And they are a sure remedy for the disillusionment that eventually arises whenever we discard God's truth for an immature, self-centered faith. Even more important, though, together they construct a time-tested pathway to a deeper and more mature friendship with God.

living beyond your self

The Discipline of Selflessness

Assurance is not to be obtained as much by self-examination as it is by action.

Jonathan Edwards

In late August 1992, Hurricane Andrew ripped through southern Florida, leveling many homes and buildings that had stood in its path. In the quiet aftermath, a young mother stepped out onto her porch to survey the damage with her little six-year-old boy named Timmy. The young woman looked at the community that used to be, amazed at the rubble that had replaced so many homes, and then she began to wonder, *What could be going through the mind of this young child, seeing such severe destruction?*

Timmy saw his mother looking down at him, and he got nervous, so before she could ask him, he piped up and said, "I didn't do it!"

It's human nature for a young child to survey devastating destruction and have his first thought be, "Don't blame me!" We grow up thinking of ourselves first: How does this affect *me*? What will this mean for *my* life? When we're at our selfish worst, world hunger could be solved, world peace could be ushered in, and cancer could be cured—all within the space of twenty-four hours—but if our hair doesn't do exactly what we want it to, it's an awful, horrible day.

If we fail to grow out of this self-obsession, it can become a character cancer, quieter and far more subtle than Hurricane Andrew, but ultimately no less destructive spiritually.

On the flip side, there's a clarity to our vision when we completely forget ourselves and concentrate solely on the task before us. It's an energizing feeling to be so focused on someone else that there is no thought of our own welfare or problems. Though it seems ironic, it's a blessed state, far more meaningful than when we are obsessed with our own trials and tribulations—but it's not one that naturally colors our spirit. In fact, I can think of many times when selfishness reigned in my heart.

"Hurry up!" I called out to my family once. "Get into the car! If we don't get moving, there won't be any good seats left!"

Our church has a problem that is simultaneously wonderful and frustrating: The services are packed, and if you don't get there early, you may have to sit in the overflow area. It was an Easter Sunday, and I had expected the services to be even more crowded than usual. My number one goal that morning was to get us to church in time to get decent seats.

> *There's a clarity to our vision when we completely forget ourselves and concentrate solely on the task before us.*

I gathered my car keys, only semipatiently waiting for my wife to finish drying her hair and my daughter to find her shoes. "I put them right by the door," Kelsey insisted. "Somebody must have *stolen* them!"

"Right, Kelsey," I answered. "Someone broke in last night, forgot about the TV, the VCR, and the computer, ignored my wallet sitting in the kitchen, and grabbed a used pair of little girl's size 7 shoes."

"Well, it's *possible!*" she hollered.

Walking out to the car, I had just a moment's pause when God's voice broke into my hurried, frenzied spirit. I realized that many of the people I wanted to "beat out" for a good seat would probably be visitors. Our church uses Easter to its fullest evangelistic effect, and God gently spoke to me about my selfish desire to enjoy good worship at the expense of a nonbeliever having the best chance to respond to the gospel. There's nothing wrong with trying to get to church on time, but my competitive nature spit into the face of what our church was trying to do that very morning.

> *Our fallen nature and the values of our culture collide with the force of an avalanche to push us ever further down the hill of self-centeredness.*

Self-centeredness can creep up on us in so many ways—including wanting to get good seats in church! Our fallen nature and the values of our culture collide with the force of an avalanche to push us ever further down the hill of self-centeredness, but authentic faith calls us back to the summit—and joy—of selflessness.

The Most Meaningful Life Imaginable

Many years ago, *The New Yorker* ran a cartoon in which a smiling woman was jabbering nonstop to a glum-faced companion. The smiling woman finally says, "Well, that's enough about me. Now let's talk about you. What do *you* think about *me?*"

The apostle Paul had an entirely different perspective. Instead of being preoccupied by what others thought of him, Paul learned the theme song of an authentic faith that is to be oriented around the needs of others: "We who are strong ought to bear with the failings of the weak and not to please ourselves. Each of us should please his neighbor for his good, to build him up. For even Christ did not please himself . . ." (Romans 15:1–3).

In fact, Paul took this line of thinking to a radical and somewhat shocking conclusion: "Though I am free and belong to no man, *I make myself a slave to everyone,* to win as many as possible"

(1 Corinthians 9:19, emphasis added). This is an astonishing statement when you consider the context behind it. Paul was a "king" in
his culture. Though he faced enemies, to be sure, Paul was often
treated with respect and adulation. In Lystra, he was even worshiped
as a god (see Acts 14:8–13). Furthermore, as a Pharisee Paul had
daily prayed the traditional prayer that went something like this:
"Dear God, thank you for not making me a Gentile, a slave, or a
woman." Before he met Christ, Paul spent every day of his life
thanking God that he wasn't a slave, and now he happily proclaims
to the Corinthians that God has turned him into one!

This is the defining difference in Paul's life. He didn't improve on
his morality after meeting Christ, because Pharisees went out of their
way to live blameless lives. Paul didn't pray more as a Christian,
because Pharisees were devoted to regular and public prayer. Paul
didn't fast more, because Pharisees were masters of spiritual discipline. The only real difference in Paul's
life is that he became centered on the
freedom of Christ's provision, which
enabled him to love God by serving
others instead of being obsessed about
his own religious achievements.

> **The only real difference
> in Paul's life is that he
> became centered on
> the freedom of Christ's
> provision.**

The extreme way in which Paul
adhered to this selflessness is, in fact,
shocking to modern sensibilities. He
tells the Romans that he wishes he
could cut himself off from salvation, if by doing so he might save
Israel (see Romans 9:3). Let's not quickly pass over this. Paul was
fully aware of hell's horrors—the physical pain, the emotional
angst, the spiritual alienation, separation from loving relationships
for all eternity—yet he proclaimed, "I wish I could be damned in
hell for all eternity, if, in the twilight before I enter hell, I can look
over my shoulder and see the nation of Israel marching into
heaven."

Moses prays roughly the same prayer in Exodus 32:32: "But
now, please forgive their sin—but if not, then blot me out of the
book you have written." Both leaders had such tremendous concern for the people under their charge that they would have placed

their own salvation beneath the people's welfare. The examples of Moses, Jesus (whose death *was* actually redemptive), and Paul safely make this a distinguishing mark of authentic faith.

Could you pray that prayer? I'm not sure I could. Could you willingly agree to spend eternity apart from loved ones and instead enter into an eternity surrounded by hatred, spite, jealousy, bitterness, and lust, separated from your children, grandchildren, parents, and close friends and existing entirely apart from the comfort, mercy, and grace of God? The very thought chills me to my core, yet such was Paul's love for others that he says he would gladly have made that trade.

Where did Paul get this selflessness? How could a man become so humble, so others-oriented, so willing to play the role of a servant? I believe it essentially comes down to this: Paul took the words of Jesus "It is more blessed to give than to receive" (Acts 20:35) literally, and he found that they were true! Throughout his letters, Paul is effusive with his thanks and affection for others. Clearly, his service on their behalf brings tremendous joy to his life: "I thank my God through Jesus Christ for all of you" (Romans 1:8; see 1 Corinthians 1:4). "For I wrote you out of great distress and anguish of heart and with many tears, not to grieve you but to let you know the depth of my love for you" (2 Corinthians 2:4). "It is right for me to feel this way about all of you, since I have you in my heart" (Philippians 1:7).

I confess to being somewhat in awe of Paul, particularly when I pause to think about how many communities Paul stayed in touch with and how many different churches he was genuinely concerned about. Paul's letters reveal an ongoing, passionate, and truly concerned relationship with churches spanning the Mediterranean Sea—from Rome to Corinth, Galatia, Ephesus, Philippi, Colosse, and Thessalonica (this in addition to maintaining fervid relationships with individuals such as Timothy, Titus, and dozens of women and men mentioned at the end of his letters—not to mention a lowly slave named Onesimus, on whose

> **Paul took the words of Jesus "It is more blessed to give than to receive" literally, and he found that they were true!**

behalf Paul took time, while in prison, to write a letter). It is truly amazing to see not just the depth, but the breadth of Paul's active love shown to so many different churches and individuals. One gets the impression that he couldn't have had much else going on in his life, for if he had, he wouldn't have had the emotional energy left to be actively compassionate, loving, and involved with so many people.

Yet nowhere does this affection seem obligatory. Paul's concern for others was real; the enjoyment he derived from serving them and sacrificing for them was tangible and at times intense. These are not the words of a man who only serves grudgingly. These are the words of a man who has found service to be the most meaningful life imaginable.

So we ask ourselves: Do we, as Peter urges us, truly "love the brotherhood of believers" (1 Peter 2:17)? I'm not talking about "love" in the all too American sense, offering a casual "how are you doing?" while not really caring about the answer. How concerned are we, truly, about God's church, and what sacrifices are we making on its behalf to give evidence to that love? Are we so busy with personal, individual pursuits that our passion for the church has dimmed?

The Christlike life is not simply about practicing impeccable morality and overcoming temptation and faithfully performing a few spiritual disciplines. All of these were done by the Pharisees far more faithfully than any of us will ever perform them, and yet Christ himself said these religious zealots had missed God's intention. To experience Christ's joy, passion, and fulfillment, we need to adopt an entirely new *mind-set* and *motivation*: We are invited to join our Lord in living for the glory of the Father instead of for our own reputation, and we are called to give ourselves over to the salvation and sanctification of Christ's bride, the church, rather than to be consumed by our own welfare. This holy self-forgetfulness is the most genuine mark of true faith, the evidence of God's merciful grace in our lives.[1]

Paul defiantly took his passion for God several steps further than modern society believes is healthy. He didn't just love Christ, he was nearly consumed by his commitment to his Savior and to the church. His goal and motivation are clearly laid out for us: "And [Christ] died for all, that those who live *should no longer live for themselves* but for him who died for them and was raised again" (2 Corinthians 5:15, emphasis added).

Everything Paul experienced was put through this grid. He even learned to rejoice in suffering, because by suffering "I fill up in my flesh what is still lacking in regard to Christ's afflictions, for the sake of his body, which is the church" (Colossians 1:24).

Paul didn't look at what hardship did to *him;* he was entirely preoccupied by what his suffering accomplished for *God's church.*

> **The key to experiencing Paul's joy is adopting Paul's mission, which is to become a champion of God's work on this earth. Selflessness seasons our faith with meaning and applies purpose to our pain.**

When he was imprisoned, Paul took heart in the fact that "because of my chains, most of the brothers in the Lord have been encouraged to speak the word of God more courageously and fearlessly" (Philippians 1:14).

The key to experiencing Paul's joy is adopting Paul's mission, which is to become a champion of God's work on this earth. Ironically, this attitude of selflessness actually creates a fountain of joy: "A generous man will prosper; he who refreshes others will himself be refreshed" (Proverbs 11:25). Selflessness seasons our faith with meaning and applies purpose to our pain. If we sacrifice, serve, and tirelessly work to build the kingdom of God in this world, we will find, as did Paul and the ancients, that the selfless life, though not an easy life, though filled with much pain, anguish, and heartache, is the most meaningful life that can be lived.

When you know you're doing something solely out of love for God and a desire to see his kingdom prosper on this earth, there's an unrivaled inner satisfaction that fills your soul. This satisfaction has been testified to for ages, beginning with the classical Christian writers.

The classical chorus

Augustine captured the spirit of Paul when he wrote that "God fashions us, that is, forms and creates us anew, not as men—for he has done that already—but as *good* men, which His grace is now doing, that we may be a new creation in Christ Jesus."[2] In other words, when God's Spirit transforms us and re-creates us, he does so with a view toward making us less selfish and more inclined to serve others—that is, to make us *good*. He doesn't just save us, but intends to *change* us. What else is the meaning of Paul's words, "For we are God's workmanship, created in Christ Jesus *to do good works,* which God prepared in advance for us to do" (Ephesians 2:10, emphasis added).

But here's the delightful irony: In Augustine's mind, acts of goodwill and charity, far from being a nuisance and a burden, actually promote true happiness: "Acts of compassion . . . towards our neighbors, when they are directed towards God . . . are intended to free us from misery and thus to bring us to happiness—which is only attained by that good of which it has been said, 'As for me, my true good is to cling to God' (Psalm 73:28)."[3]

Augustine had plenty of opportunities to apply this line of thinking. When he first became a Christian, Augustine's ambition was to become a quiet monk, living out his final days in prayer and contemplation. He had had enough of fast living, and he was ready to live the meditative life. His piety became noticed in high places, however, and church authorities soon asked Augustine to become a bishop, which led him into a very public life—the opposite of what he wanted. How many of us have felt this same tug. Perhaps you're a private person, called into a form of service and ministry you know God is leading you into, but it's something you would never choose on your own. That's the situation Augustine was in, and he responded in obedience.

Although this selflessness led Augustine into a life of great joy, meaning, and purpose, it also ultimately led him to his death. In 427, the Arian Vandals advanced into North Africa, where Augustine lived and ministered. Genserik, the Vandal king, specifically sought out Christian churches, as he had heard they were particularly rich with treasures. Refugees poured into Hippo, where Augustine was serving, and it wasn't long before Genserik had laid siege to Augustine's city.

The refugees not only brought heightened responsibilities for Augustine, they also brought disease. In the fifth century, so many

> **The ancients were not masochists; they wanted true joy like all of us do.**

people packed into so tight a space inevitably created a sick environment. At this point, Augustine had three choices: He could flee (as bishop, Augustine could have abandoned his people and his post and sought safe sanctuary elsewhere in the kingdom), he could stay holed up in his palace and ignore the needs of his people but perhaps preserve his own health, or he could go out, get his hands dirty, and risk becoming ill himself.

Augustine didn't know how to be a bishop from afar, so he kept up his active schedule, being present with the people—and paid dearly for his service. During the third month of the siege, in August of 430, Augustine developed a high fever from which he never recovered. This powerful man of God, whose books Christians still read because of their logic, power, passion, and faith, gave his last hours ministering to the most basic needs of a frightened flock.

God didn't re-create us to be men and women—he's done that already—but to become *good* men and women.

The literature of the classics is a veritable chorus of dying to self so that we might truly live. The ancients were not masochists; they wanted true joy like all of us do. Certainly, they sought fulfillment, and even happiness, but they discovered that happiness is best experienced in a selfless life, that self-centered living creates its own misery—and they were quite literally willing to bet their lives on it.

In *Beyond Personality,* C. S. Lewis writes the following:

> The principle runs through all life from top to bottom. Give up yourself, and you'll find your real self. Lose your life and you'll save it. Submit to death, death of your ambitions and favorite wishes every day and death of your whole body in the end: submit with every fiber of your being, and you will find eternal life.

> Keep *nothing* back. Nothing that you have not given away will
> ever be really yours. Nothing in you that has not died will ever
> be raised from the dead. Look for yourself, and you will find in
> the long run only hatred, loneliness, despair, rage, ruin, and
> decay. But look for Christ and you will find Him, and with Him
> everything else thrown in.[4]

This is why the self-centered "gospel" is so disillusioning. In the
long run, living only for comfort, pleasure, and ease—even using
religion to do so—leads only to "hatred, loneliness, despair, rage,
ruin, and decay." Dying to ourselves and living solely for God and
his kingdom, being enlisted to do good to others and focus on serving, gives us God, and in God we have everything.

Like Augustine, Lewis knew what he was talking about when he
spoke of the benefit that comes from selfless living. During the Second World War, Lewis took in numer-
ous children who were fleeing London
and other cities vulnerable to German
bombing. Bringing children into the
Kilns was a lot of extra work—not to
mention coping with the excess noise.
Be careful not to look at Lewis's sacrifice too lightly. As a writer, I work out
of my home, so I can imagine what it
would be like to try to prepare college

> *Dying to ourselves and
> living solely for God
> and his kingdom gives
> us God, and in God we
> have everything.*

courses and keep writing books and articles and respond to correspondence while there are unruly kids running around the house
(kids who miss their parents). Certainly, Lewis must have realized
that his work would take a severe beating. Yet, in actuality, this act
of sacrifice helped produce Lewis's most famous writings.

You see, one afternoon one of these evacuated children grew
interested in an old wardrobe and asked Lewis if, perhaps, there was
anything behind it. Thus was planted the seed for perhaps the most
beloved of all of Lewis's books, *The Lion, the Witch, and the
Wardrobe.* George Sayer, one of Lewis's biographers, writes of this
period, "Having children in the house benefited [Lewis] immensely.
He had been shy and ignorant of them, but he now gradually
acquired the knowledge and affection for them that made it possible

for him to write the Narnia books. Without their presence, it is unlikely that he would even have had the impulse."[5]

If you think selfless living is costly, you haven't honestly considered the even higher price we pay for living a selfish life. We may never know how many powerful times of ministry we've missed out on as we focused only on ourselves.

The Truly "Happy" State

Being a professional athlete makes you an object of love or hate. Rarely are you allowed to swim in the middle. When you're playing well, the fans love you. When you're having a bad season, the fans think you're an overpaid bum.

The precariousness of such a livelihood tempts many athletes to become extremely self-centered, but major league pitcher Orel Hershiser found a better way. In the late eighties and early nineties, Orel was about as accomplished as a pitcher can get. During one stretch, he pitched a major-league-record 59 consecutive scoreless innings—that's almost 7 straight games—an astonishing run by any measure. In 1988, he won the National League Cy Young Award (given annually to the league's outstanding pitcher) and was voted the World Series Most Valuable Player.

> *"From one big leaguer to another. See you back here soon."*

In short, Hershiser had a lot of "stock." Young players looked up to him as the model of what they wanted to achieve. Players can use this cache to either lord it over others or to serve, and Orel took the latter approach.

After the Los Angeles Dodgers spring training camp ended in 1992, a young, skinny pitcher felt devastated after being demoted to the minor leagues. When the young pitcher's head was turned, Orel quietly slipped a ball into his bag. On the ball, Orel had written, "From one big leaguer to another. See you back here soon."

Imagine being that discouraged pitcher, wondering if you'll ever get another chance, and then reaching into your bag when you get home and having the most accomplished pitcher of your day write,

"From one big leaguer to another." Even more encouraging, Orel showed his confidence in the young man's potential when he added, "See you back here soon."

Orel's words proved prophetic. That skinny pitcher's name was Pedro Martinez, now considered by many to be the best pitcher in all of baseball. At the time of this writing, he had the lowest earned run average in the entire major leagues.

Hershiser retired during the 2000 baseball season, but now that his own pitching career is over, he can take joy from the fact that he helped encourage a fellow player to not give up. In a sense, his influence lives on through a fiery pitcher who can often seem unbeatable.

When our happiness is dependent on what happens to us and when our self-focus determines our daily mood, our joy will necessarily be limited to whatever good thing happens to us. But when we learn to truly delight in the welfare of others and rejoice in what God is doing in their lives, the potential for increased joy skyrockets. Even when Paul was in prison, he could rejoice over what God was doing in Colosse. As death drew near, Paul took joy in the rise of Timothy's ministry. And as persecution followed upon persecution, Paul rejoiced at the strength and witness of the Philippians. Because Paul was so others-focused, nothing could get him down. There was always someone to rejoice about and to thank God for! This is the incredible miracle of joy that springs forth when an authentic faith governs our lives.

> *When we learn to truly delight in the welfare of others and rejoice in what God is doing in their lives, the potential for increased joy skyrockets.*

I remember my mentor J. I. Packer telling us in a class that this type of situation is the crossroads of true Christian living. "The happy state," Dr. Packer said, "which we know only rarely, is the unself-conscious state in which all our attention is being given to the people around us, to the situation outside us, and we're forgetting ourselves in the service of others. You see that to perfection in the life of Jesus."[6]

Rather than drink from the satisfying waters of selflessness, our culture has developed a dangerous appetite for the bitter drink of selfishness. I was asked to write an article on selflessness for a Christian magazine I highly respect. These people get it right far more often than not. After I submitted the article, I received an E-mail from the editor praising much of the article, then going on to make this request: "What we need now is for you to beef up the section on the rewards of selflessness."

> **Rather than drink from the satisfying waters of selflessness, our culture has developed a dangerous appetite for the bitter drink of selfishness.**

I understand what the editor was trying to do—the topic could appear very negative—but it seemed to me almost comically ironic that our culture is saying, in a sense, "I'm willing to be less selfish, but if I do that, *what's in it for me?* Where's my reward?" Even in our selflessness, we are prone to adopt a selfish attitude!

The great irony, of course, is that the ancients do testify to the many rewards of selflessness, making my editor's request not entirely inappropriate. But when you revisit Paul's astonishing statement in Romans 9:3, where he says he would choose damnation for the sake of others, you realize that "reward" as motivation to become less selfish can take us only so far; it will never usher us into the joyful self-abandonment experienced by Jesus, Paul, Augustine, and C. S. Lewis.

Keep in mind, this selflessness isn't reserved solely for mature Christians. Paul urges all of us to adopt it. "Do nothing out of selfish ambition or vain conceit," he tells the Philippians, "but in humility consider others better than yourselves. *Each of you* should look not only to your own interests, but also to the interests of others" (Philippians 2:3–4, emphasis added).

Spiritual health—in Paul's mind, at least—is marked by a vibrant, others-centered compassion and concern. Far from simply absorbing blessings, we are called to lavish God's love on others.

self-centered ministry

The joy of selflessness also affects *how* we minister. One day a Christian man invited me to lunch. After a short chat, he asked me how I handle temptations on the road. I had just written a magazine article on this very subject and was full of answers, anecdotes, and advice. For over forty-five minutes, I "blessed" him with my astounding wisdom, insight, and practical strategies.

I came home from that lunch quite exhausted—but also frustrated, feeling certain that I hadn't been any help to him at all. The next morning, as I prayed about what had happened during this lunch encounter, I realized why I had been unhelpful and why I was feeling frustrated. This brother's question, "How do you handle temptation on the road, Gary?" wasn't the question he really wanted answered. Certainly, that was the question he verbalized, but it wasn't truly what he wanted to know. The question burning in his soul was, rather, "Gary, how can *I* handle temptation on the road?"

Because he had framed the question with me as the subject, I went down the wrong trail. I was full of myself, and I gave him myself, but what he really needed was to encounter *God*.

In order to answer my friend's real question, I needed to listen before I spoke. I should have asked him questions rather than spewed out my answers. I should have sought the genesis of *his* temptations rather than assume they were the same as mine. And I should have helped him find *his* exodus rather than proudly display my own.

I rose from prayer, eager to see God destroy this cursed self-obsession. It is so easy to fall into such a focus—after all, my friend had invited me to do so—but so harmful. If I am to help people and lead a contemplative, God-directed life, the first thing I must do is die to myself. If I had relied on God during that lunch meeting, carefully and prayerfully seeking what the Spirit would do during our hour and a half together,

> *If I am to help people and lead a contemplative, God-directed life, the first thing I must do is die to myself.*

God would have led us to the real issues in this man's life. Instead, I was too eager to come up with principles and answers that were limited to my own experience, and not necessarily what this man needed to hear.

This is precisely why I long to mature in the faith. I don't fear that somehow my immaturity will keep me out of heaven. My destiny is secure in the finished, completed work of Jesus Christ. What my immaturity does more than anything is hinder God's work through me. Yes, he can work quite well in spite of my failings; but his ministry through me will become far more effective as I leave my old selfish habits and ways of relating behind. The immature might be on their way to heaven, but they rarely see deeply changed lives.

The danger is that we can become self-serving even in our service! Some might want to serve so that they can be admired and praised and feel wanted and needed. Precisely to counter this tendency, Paul stressed to the Corinthians that we should desire those spiritual gifts that *build up the church* and *edify others* (see 1 Corinthians 14:12). Even in the way God uses us, our motivation should be others-oriented, focused on the needs of our local Christian community.

Selflessness is far more a liberating truth than it is just another religious obligation, however. Going back through my journal one time, an entry caught my eye. I was feeling a bit overwhelmed and anxious about all that I had to do in the coming months, and I found solace in something I had written many months before: *God hasn't lost courage. God isn't wavering on endurance. God doesn't fear another day, another test, and God is standing behind me. He is making available for me all that he is. By grace, through faith, I have nothing to fear, no reason to feel defeated.*

> **Selflessness is far more a liberating truth than it is just another religious obligation.**

The words struck me as though someone else had written them. Clearly, this had come from prayer, and I had forgotten all about it, but just to be reminded of its truth felt like a late-afternoon explosion of sunlight into an otherwise dreary day. It was a spiritual bath, a refreshing liberation, when I remembered that ministry in its purest form is radically God-dependent and God-empowered. I was reminded of David's words, "I do not trust in my bow, my sword does not bring me victory; but you give us victory over our enemies, you put our adversaries to shame. In God we make our boast all day long" (Psalm 44:6–8).

> *The authentic faith of selflessness focuses our minds and hearts on serving God by serving others.*

Paul had this same mind-set when he wrote to the Corinthians, "But by the grace of God I am what I am, and his grace to me was not without effect. No, I worked harder than all of them—yet not I, but the grace of God that was with me" (1 Corinthians 15:10). You have this marvelous mix of Paul paddling furiously while he is carried down the river by God's great current. This is a sentiment Peter shared as well: "If anyone serves, he should do it with the strength God provides, so that in all things God may be praised through Jesus Christ" (1 Peter 4:11).

David, Paul, and Peter—three central characters in the Bible— and all three of them testified to learning the secret of working with God's strength, of leaning into the wind of God's Spirit and letting that Spirit enable them to do what they could never do on their own. The authentic faith of selflessness, then, focuses our minds and hearts on serving God by serving others. It affects not only where we minister and what we celebrate but also *how* we minister and *whose strength* we are dependent on.

Living beyond your self

How do we put all this into practice?

First, we must ask ourselves, How are we adopting Christ's passion for his body, the church? You may be doing everything seemingly right individually, but what is your role in Christ's community? God has blessed you. Wonderful! Now how are you going to use that blessing to bless and build up others?

Second, we must ask ourselves, How are we looking after others in our vocational and social lives? I told Orel Hershiser's story because most of us will not be called to make the kind of great sacrifice that Augustine made. Our selflessness will be played out on a much smaller scale, as Orel's was. Perhaps you'll find yourself coming into work early, at 7:30 A.M., to catch up on addressing 1,500 envelopes for invitations to a seminar that your group is sponsoring. You're hoping to have it done by 9:00, but just as you're getting up to speed, you notice one of the new secretaries over in the corner cubicle, someone who was hired just two weeks ago. She's bent over her typewriter, clutching a tissue to her face. Her shoulders are shaking, *but you're really busy.* What will you do?

Wherever we go—whether it's the golf course, a church conference room, a restaurant, or the local mall—we have the opportunity to open up our eyes to what is happening to others around us, to think thoughts bigger than those that concern only us, and to be used by God—if only just by *noticing* others—by caring, in large ways and small, and by getting involved.

> *Christians who let their weaknesses and inadequacies hold them back are just as self-focused as are believers who use their strengths to build self-glorifying kingdoms.*

Finally, we observed that selflessness means "God-dependence." Let's say your pastor and several trusted friends notice a gift you haven't been using—or perhaps they present an opportunity for service that sounds inviting and that fits right in with what you believe God has called you to do—but you're bothered with the nagging question, "Am I qualified to do that?" Christians who let their weaknesses and inadequacies hold them back are just as self-focused as are believers who use their strengths to build self-glorifying kingdoms. When will we learn that it's not about us? God is not impressed by our gifts, nor is he frightened by our inadequacies.

God-dependence also means that we will slow down in the midst of our ministry, making way for God's still, small voice, his gentle whisper, to guide us. The next time you're listening to someone pour out their heart or voice a complaint or ask for your advice, what well will you draw from? Whose shoulder will you lean on? As we engage ourselves on the front lines of ministry, let's check our hurry at the door, be fully present in the moment, and invite God to take the lead.

Authentic Faith

There's an oft-told story about a remarkable relationship forged during the terrible field battles of World War I. I like to read a lot of military history, and as best I can tell, the story is true.

World War I was a particularly bad war to be a part of, not that there is such a thing as a "good" war, I suppose; but if you were a grunt during World War I, you were likely to face the even more inhumane trauma of trench warfare. Trench warfare was characterized by an abundance of downtime, mixed in with moments of sheer, unadulterated terror.

During the downtime, two American soldiers bonded tightly as they talked about their families, what they wanted to do when the war was over, and even, on occasion, how they dealt with the fear of living so close to so many men whose only mission in life was to end theirs.

One night the order was given for the soldiers to leave their trench and attack the enemy. The fighting was fierce and desperate, and the two friends got separated. After a long and arduous battle, the call went out to retreat back to the safety of the trench. When the one soldier returned, he began asking about his buddy, finally discovering that his friend was still out there, wounded and bleeding. Without even considering the danger, he announced that he was going back to get his friend.

"Absolutely not," the commanding officer replied. "It's suicidal to go back out there, and it's not worth the risk. I've already lost more men than I can afford to lose."

The soldier waited until the officer's head was turned, then jumped out of the relative safety of the trench and crawled toward his wounded buddy. Immediately, he was forced to pay the price—the mind-splitting reverberations of the shelling, the smoke hacking at his throat and making him cough, and the bullets flying overhead, which had the added, gruesome effect of keeping his face smashed into the blood-and-gore-infested ground.

Still, he crawled on until he reached his friend, shared a few words, and then began pulling him back toward the trench. Somewhere between the time he reached his buddy and the time they both made it back to the trench, the wounded friend died. With great sorrow, the friend pulled a precious corpse into the trench.

> "When I reached him, he saw my face and said, 'I knew you'd come.'"

"So, was it worth it?" the officer barked, angry that his order had been disobeyed.

"Absolutely," the friend replied. "My buddy's final words made it all worthwhile."

"What could he have possibly said that made it worth risking your life to hear?" the officer shouted.

"When I reached him, he saw my face and said, 'I knew you'd come.'"

In a culture that celebrates the self, that calls us to be true to ourselves, there is a prophetic power released when people act with selflessness, when they learn to put others first and even to sacrifice themselves on another's behalf.

Τhαt εxcʄuciαtinɡ εxeʄcise

The Discipline of Waiting

I wait for the LORD, my soul waits,
  and in his word I put my hope.
My soul waits for the Lord
  more than watchmen wait for the morning.

Psalm 130:5–6

You're in a hurry, as usual. You jump into the elevator and feel the sweat trickling down the back of your neck. You punch a button for your floor, but the elevator stays open. You look at your watch. The elevator door is still open, so you furiously press the "close door" button several times. Finally, the doors close.

Surprise! You've just been had.

It's a little-known secret that many "close door" elevator buttons are merely mechanical placebos, put there to pacify impatient people by making them think they can speed up the elevator's programmed functions.

We are not a world that is ready to wait; we are a people who pride ourselves on how fast we move. This is not just a Western phenomenon, by the way—it is a human one. There is a restaurant in Tokyo, Japan, without any prices on the menu. Why? Because the owners don't charge you by what you eat—they charge you by how long you stay in the restaurant. And at lunchtime, there's actually a line to get in.

In his book *Faster: The Acceleration of Just About Everything*, James Gleick provides these and other telling anecdotes about the modern obsession with speed, including "one-minute bedtime stories," condensed so they can be read by a busy parent in one minute.

Our need for speed has become costly—and, ironically, quite time-consuming! The Surface Transportation Policy Project (a coalition of groups working for a more balanced transportation system) reports that an eight-year, $434 million construction project in Springfield, Virginia (just outside Washington, D.C.), is causing an additional thirty-minute delay on each rush-hour trip. After suffering through eight years of this one-hour-a-day delay, commuters will save somewhere between ninety seconds and two minutes in their daily drive. Salt Lake City, Utah, is spending $1.6 billion over four years to reconstruct I-15. The result? Drivers will be able to travel approximately one mph faster when the work is done.

> We are not a world that is ready to wait; we are a people who pride ourselves on how fast we move.

Once we arrive, we are no less anxious to get things done—even at the expense of our own health and well-being. In the summer of 2000, an up-and-coming computer publishing executive died at the young age of twenty-six. Aaron Bunnell was overwhelmed at the way the world was opening up before him. He was experiencing fantastic success and wealth, but in his desire to keep the ball rolling, he pushed himself a little too far and a little too fast. After Aaron's body was discovered in the Waldorf-Astoria Hotel, his dad, David Bunnell, publicly admitted that Aaron may well have been ingesting stamina-boosting drugs to "keep going and going. . . . He pushed it too far."[1]

The irony isn't hard to miss. In a desperate desire to keep things moving faster and faster and to boost his production just a little bit more, Aaron brought everything to a crashing halt. All his frantic efforts weren't just put on hold—they disintegrated in a premature and tragic end.

In spite of our obsession with instant results, we serve a God whose calendar moves by millennia, not minutes, and who thinks in terms of generations, not seasons. Unless we understand this about God—that he moves by millennia, not minutes—we will never understand his ways with us. Peter is very clear: "With the Lord a day is like a thousand years, and a thousand years are

> *We serve a God whose calendar moves by millennia, not minutes.*

like a day" (2 Peter 3:8). We are obsessed with where we are today and with what's going to happen in the next year, while God's plans for this world often take a long-term view.

called to wait

A retired missionary once told me with surprising confidence that China would eventually outlast the Communists. "They outlast everything that forces itself on them," he explained. "They're a patient people who will endure for centuries but eventually rise up when the time is right."

I remembered this prediction when I came across an excerpt from a book entitled *The Kissinger Transcripts: The Top-Secret Talks with Beijing and Moscow.*[2] During his negotiations with Chairman Mao, then-Secretary-of-State Henry Kissinger discussed the fate of Taiwan, and Mao said something very interesting. He explained that he didn't want Taiwan back: "If you were to send it back to me now, I would not want it, because it's not wantable [sic]. There are a huge bunch of counterrevolutionaries there. A hundred years hence we will want it . . . and we are going to fight for it. . . . And when I go to heaven to see God, I'll tell him it's better to have Taiwan under the care of the United States now."

China has survived because it thinks in terms of centuries rather than in four-year election cycles. Mao was patient beyond his own lifetime, thinking a hundred years ahead, and secure in his belief that eventually his country would get what it wanted under more favorable conditions.

Though his religious philosophy is anathema to Christian beliefs, his patience is a stunning example of orthodox Christian spirituality.

Abraham was a sprightly seventy-five years old when God promised him that he would be made into "a great nation"—a bold promise given to a childless man (see Genesis 12:1–5). A *quarter century* passed before Isaac was born, and a *full century* went by before the promise about the land took concrete shape.

Abraham's excruciating exercise of waiting marks the essence of the Christian life. The psalmist, though full of hope, recognizes that God's blessings do not always come with the speed of a bullet, but rather with the slow, steady approach of a glacier: "I wait for the LORD, my soul waits, and in his word I put my hope. My soul waits for the Lord more than watchmen wait for the morning" (Psalm 130:5–6).

> **God's blessings do not always come with the speed of a bullet, but rather with the slow, steady approach of a glacier.**

As Israel lay conquered, Jeremiah urged his countrymen, "I say to myself, 'The LORD is my portion; therefore I will wait for him.'. . . It is good to wait quietly for the salvation of the LORD" (Lamentations 3:24, 26). Jeremiah knew God would bring Israel back, but it would take time—a long time!

One thing is clear: God won't be rushed. Without a willingness to wait, we will be regularly frustrated with God and may become disillusioned with our faith. God never promises us that our present circumstances will always make sense. Sometimes, we'll have to wait until the present becomes the past before what we are going through becomes even remotely understandable.[3]

For example, the book of Psalms teaches us that waiting will be necessary in order for us to comprehend how "the wicked" seem to get away with everything. "Be still before the LORD and wait patiently for him," David writes. "Do not fret when men succeed in their ways, when they carry out their wicked schemes" (Psalm 37:7). Rewards and punishments, which we'll examine in chapter 11,

are not always immediate. God sees what's going on and he pronounces a judgment, but rarely does he carry it out within what
many of us would consider a normal time frame.

This waiting can be debilitating and suck our souls dry—unless
it is marked by hope in God. Waiting, for the believer, is not the
futile and desperate act of those who have no other options, but
rather a confident trust that eventually
God will set things right—even if he is
not operating within our preferred
time frame. "Those who hope in the
LORD will renew their strength," Isaiah tells us (Isaiah 40:31). It almost
goes without saying that there is no
reason for hoping if we already have
all that we want; this verse implies the
discipline of waiting.

Paul pictures the Christian life as
a type of "groaning in anticipation"
when he writes to the church in
Corinth: "Meanwhile we groan, long-
ing to be clothed with our heavenly dwelling. . . . For while we are
in this tent, we groan and are burdened. . . . We live by faith, not by
sight. We are confident, I say, and would prefer to be away from the
body and at home with the Lord" (2 Corinthians 5:2, 4, 7–8).

> *Waiting, for the believer, is not the futile and desperate act of those who have no other options, but rather a confident trust that eventually God will set things right.*

The natural state of the Christian is a person who *longs* for
what is to come, even to the point of groaning. A similar passage
appears in Paul's words to the Romans: "We ourselves, who have
the firstfruits of the Spirit, groan inwardly as we wait eagerly for
our adoption as sons, the redemption of our bodies. . . . Who hopes
for what he already has? But if we hope for what we do not have,
we wait for it patiently" (Romans 8:23–25).

This is by no means an easy waiting—as if we don't really want
it, or couldn't really care less about its arrival. On the contrary, it's
a passionate waiting: "Our citizenship is in heaven. And we *eagerly*
await a Savior from there, the Lord Jesus Christ, who, by the power
that enables him to bring everything under his control, will trans-
form our lowly bodies so that they will be like his glorious body"
(Philippians 3:20–21, emphasis added).

The spirit of waiting is the spirit of godliness; it's a combination of contentment, gentleness, and humility—three key Christian virtues. The plain truth is that we are not given all we want on this earth. Regardless of how much God blesses us in this life, if we are spiritually in tune with the Holy Spirit, we will live in perpetual waiting and anticipation, in a holy but peaceful anxiety for the better life that is to come in eternity. For us it is always just past Christmas Eve but never quite Christmas morning. We can smell the turkey basting, we can see the presents under the tree, we can anticipate the joy on our children's faces, but the full celebration is just minutes beyond our reach: "Here we do not have an enduring city, but we are looking for the city that is to come" (Hebrews 13:14).

Our response to this future city? "Be patient, then, brothers, until the Lord's coming. See how the farmer waits for the land to yield its valuable crop and how patient he is for the autumn and spring rains. You too, be patient and stand firm, because the Lord's coming is near" (James 5:7–8).

classical consolation

The Christian classics make it clear that waiting is an essential element of true Christian spirituality in two main areas—character growth and prayer. Personally, I've also experienced it in a third area, namely, my own vocation. Let's look at each of these.

Character Growth

I have a friend who in college was notorious for his brusque manner. He's pretty intelligent, and a quick thinker besides, so he became the master of the humorous and quick put-down. Then he married an unusually sensitive and amazingly empathetic wife. You couldn't find two people more opposite in that regard, and yet they have enjoyed almost two decades of a rich marriage.

Some time ago, my friend and his wife were under a mountain's weight of pressure. If you were to rate my friend on the stress scale—life events that contribute to stress—he would have been off the charts. One evening, he slipped back into his old style. He said something that ridiculed his wife. I missed it, but the next morning I received an E-mail from a very contrite friend. In the event that I had heard his unfortunate remark, he wanted to express how ashamed he felt, how sorry he was, how much he loved and respected his wife, and how much he wanted me to know that he wasn't the same guy he had been in college.

What amazed me is that his E-mail reminded me of what he had been like, but over the years, I had almost forgotten about that. God has so worked in this man's life that over time he has forged not a different personality but a more mature one. The same quick thinking and good humor remain, but they've been refined, "baptized" so to speak, and are usually put to good use rather than bad.

My friend didn't change overnight. He didn't change in one year; he didn't change completely in ten years. Change is a process. But where he is today is vastly different from where he was twenty years ago.

One of the keys to this man's story is that the growth took time. Habitual sins have to be "put to sleep." Faithful obedience, *over time,* weakens temptation's allure. As we begin to find new ways to deal with stress or insecurity or other "sin triggers" in our lives, we literally learn to live without the sin, which often has served as a crutch. One act of obedience doesn't put a sin to death. The fact is, we will have to choose obedience time after time until the sin loses its strong allure. And even after that, occasional lapses are not uncommon, but the force and general direction of our lives will have changed.

This is a reality well known to the ancients, who spoke often about the need to be patient when it comes to character growth. Sanctification (the Christian's holiness) has two elements—a declared holiness and a realized holiness. That's why the apostle Paul so frequently says, in effect, "Become what you already are." This dual reality accounts for the fact that waiting plays such a crucial role in our growth in righteousness. Paul tells the Galatians, "But by faith we eagerly await through the Spirit the righteousness for which we hope" (Galatians 5:5).

The Christian classics talk about a "soul sadness" or "inquietude" that comes about when we proudly demand a state of character development that we do not yet possess. Though pursuing holiness seems to be—and, in fact, is—a noble aim, and wanting to

experience greater depth in holiness appears to be—and, in fact, is—
a godly pursuit, it's possible that our desire for increased growth may
be fueled by pride, ambition, and self-interest—and our attitude as
we wait is often the best indicator of what our true motivation is.

The difference, according to Francis de Sales, well-known spiritual director from the seventeenth century, is that true holiness is
pursued with "patience, meekness, humility, and tranquility." If we
lack these qualities, Francis warns, we risk "fatiguing" our souls,
landing us in a season of great distress
and spiritual anguish. This spiritually
dangerous state, "instead of removing,
aggravates the evil, and involves [the
soul] in such anguish and distress,
with so great loss of courage and
strength," that we imagine ourselves
"incurable."[4] That is to say, because
we don't overcome a certain sin imme-
diately, or because one seems to keep coming back, we mentally
give up because of our impatience and a refusal to wait. We imagine it must be incurable because it isn't cured yet.

> *Our attitude as we wait is often the best indicator of what our true motivation is.*

While I have seen God miraculously deliver people from various addictions, it is far more common to see people lean on God as
he helps them walk away from a sin. Rather than experiencing a
sudden ejection of the sin, we often have to learn how to live without it. This can include fundamental Christian responses such as
repentance, vigilance, discerning the motivations behind the sin's
temptation, and addressing the secondary issues that feed habitual
sins. This latter approach takes hard work and cooperation with
God's Holy Spirit. There probably will be times of failure and seasons of setback. But the mature Christian will not give up; she will
continue to wait for the completion of God's work in her soul.

Impatience is a far more deadly enemy of spirituality than most
of us realize. It disguises itself as zeal when, in reality, it is nothing
more than a Trojan horse for pride. If we have spent ten, twenty, or
even thirty years pounding a sinful habit into our lifestyle, we
shouldn't be surprised if the residual elements take a long time to
be rooted out.

An overzealous pursuit of character transformation can actually work against us rather than for us. De Sales explains that the uneasiness and agitation we feel in our pursuit of holiness "proceeds from an inordinate desire of being delivered from the evil which we feel, or of acquiring the good which we desire: and yet there is nothing which tends more to increase evil, and to prevent the enjoyment of good, than an unquiet mind."[5]

> *The mature Christian will not give up; she will continue to wait for the completion of God's work in her soul.*

Francis is describing the person who wants to be holy, and who wants to be holy *now.* Such a believer has developed a demanding spirit, insisting that God fix every habit that the person himself has brought into his life—and insisting that God do it overnight. Do you see the trap? While thinking he is pursuing holiness, he is actually cultivating an offensive, vile attitude, accusing God for the consequences that he himself has brought into his life. Such a person doesn't realize that we live by grace through faith. Living as sinful people in a fallen world, we will never be finished with repentance. Ultimately, the Christian life is not about what *we* do, but about what Christ has already done.

Francis tells us that mature spiritual growth is more like that of a woman who conceives and *only after waiting* gives birth: "For you have conceived Jesus Christ, the noblest child in the world, in your soul, and until he is quite brought forth, you cannot but suffer in your labor; but be of good courage, these sorrows once past, everlasting joy shall remain with you for having brought him forth. Now you shall have wholly brought him forth, when you have entirely formed him in your heart and in your works, by an imitation of his life."[6]

You can tell if impatience is ruling your spiritual life by how much anger you harbor. John of the Cross, a medieval writer and monk, warns:

> [Some Christians], in becoming aware of their own imperfections, grow angry with themselves in an unhumble impatience. So impatient are they about these imperfections that they would want to become saints in a day.

Many of these beginners will make numerous plans and great resolutions, but since they are not humble and have no distrust of themselves, the more resolves they make the more they break, and the greater becomes their anger. They do not have the patience to wait until God gives them what they need when He so desires. Their attitude is contrary to spiritual meekness.[7]

Of course, it's possible to be *too* patient, and even complacent, about our spiritual growth. John of the Cross goes on to say, "Some, however, are so patient about their desire for advancement that God would prefer to see them a little less so." Just about any truth can be stretched too far.

> **Our pursuit of holiness should be a patient pursuit.**

However, in general, our pursuit of holiness should be a patient pursuit. We grow best living in a pool of spiritual serenity. Instead of a frantic and desperate clutching, we should adopt a patient waiting and a hopeful expectation: "Keep yourselves in God's love as you wait for the mercy of our Lord Jesus Christ to bring you to eternal life" (Jude 21).

Prayer

Waiting also plays a particularly important role for those who want to advance in prayer. Every reputable teacher of prayer I've ever read has warned that if you truly want to push forward in intimacy with God, you will invariably have to overcome some degree of boredom. It is not realistic to expect that you can fill your mind with endless diversion, static, and noise for twenty or thirty years, and then suddenly stop and pray for hours in rapturous delight.

Jeanne Guyon, who wrote a book on prayer in the latter part of the seventeenth century that eventually inspired the likes of John Wesley, François Fénelon, and Hudson Taylor, wrote, "If you set forth for the spiritual lands ... you must realize that times of dryness await you."[8] Guyon warns that in times of prayer dryness, we may be tempted to respond with an abundance of action. She urges a far different response: "You must await the return of your Beloved with *patient love*."[9] This is because, typically, the action is simply a way to end the boredom; it is not pure action, in that its ultimate end is not to serve God but to spare ourselves the pain of boredom. God sees through this ruse, and thus may ask us to wait for a long time.

Guyon asks a bold question: "What if the Lord called upon you to spend *your whole lifetime* waiting for His return to you? How would you conduct yourself if this were the lot the Lord should mete out to you for all the rest of your life?" Her advice is to "wait upon Him in a spirit of humility, in a spirit of abandonment, with contentment and resignation."[10]

Impatience with God seems to be a growing problem for today's Christian. We don't understand why he seems to move so slowly. Without the discipline of waiting, which I call "that excruciating exercise," we will experience great frustration in our prayer life and in our overall walk with God.

Vocation

"That's exactly what they needed to hear!"

Parent after parent came up to shake my hand after the commencement address. I knew that 99 percent of the kids wouldn't remember a thing I said, so I prayed about leaving them with a word picture that would stick with them.

I found it in my rejections box.

My wife and kids helped me staple and tape together over 150 rejection letters that I had received from publishers and editors over the years. The length of that roll was staggering, and each one represented a professional telling me my work wasn't wanted. When I told the young graduates that God's calling doesn't mean the way will be easy—without doubts and without rejections—I nodded to a few students who then began to unroll my rejection letters. Murmurs, laughs, and then gasps were unleashed throughout the auditorium as the roll grew longer and longer, ultimately stretching across the entire ballroom. I had been invited to speak as the author of numerous books and as one who travels nationally and internationally to speak—but I wanted the students to see the seminary graduate who wondered if anyone would ever want to hear what I believed God had given me to say.

Many Christians don't fail; they just quit before they get ripe.

Moses has always been a great example for me. He received what sounded like an impossible mission: Take a nation of slaves, with no government, no army—that means no captains, sergeants, privates, or weaponry—and no leverage, and break free from one of the most powerful regimes in all of human history.

> **Many Christians don't fail; they just quit before they get ripe.**

After some initial hesitation, Moses agreed. God had to perform a few "parlor tricks" (Moses became leprous, then was cured; his rod became a snake) to convince him to do it, but finally Moses approached Pharaoh and said, "Let my people go."

Of course, things went from bad to worse. Pharaoh increased Israel's workload, and as it turned out, Moses not only had Egypt to contend with, but the people of Israel now hated the very thought of him. Even so, Moses went back to Pharaoh, and once again he was unsuccessful. Pharaoh refused to let Israel go.

That's where the ten plagues *begin*. And there is no evidence at all that God pulled Moses aside and said, "Listen, Moses, there are going to be ten plagues. After the tenth one, you'll be out of here. Hang with me, though. This will play great in Hollywood. By the way, you'll be played by Charlton Heston, a famous actor who is going to be a lot better looking than you are. Put up with this, and together we'll make history."

All Moses knew was that God was sending him back to Pharaoh *one more time*. It wasn't until the twelfth confrontation that Moses actually succeeded in getting his people released.[11]

I've met too many young Christians who mistakenly think that if they're called, God will "open every door." What they mean by this is that the road will be easy, obstacles will be removed, and God will "bless" their obedience. They think there will be no waiting, or perhaps only a minimum amount of time between the promise and the fulfillment. Personally, I had to wait eight years from the time I believed God called me to become a writer before my first article was accepted by a national magazine. Being called is no guarantee of quick success. The writer of Hebrews tells us, "Let us run *with perseverance* the race marked out for us" (Hebrews 12:1, emphasis added).

The Bible is full of verses that stress the need to persevere: "We want each of you to show this same diligence to the very end, in order to make your hope sure. We do not want you to become lazy, but to imitate those who through faith and patience inherit what has been promised" (Hebrews 6:11–12). "You need to persevere so that when you have done the will of God, you will receive what he has promised" (Hebrews 10:36). "Blessed is the man who perseveres under trial, because when he has stood the test, he will receive the crown of life that God has promised to those who love him" (James 1:12).

> **Not only does impatience hinder our growth in holiness, prayer, and vocation, but it also inhibits our ability to love others.**

In fact, in the early church, perseverance and waiting were the hallmarks of being one of Christ's disciples. The apostle John wrote as "your brother and companion in the suffering and kingdom and *patient endurance* that are ours in Jesus" (Revelation 1:9, emphasis added).

Being called often means being asked to wait. It doesn't mean we remain completely passive, but it does mean we maintain an overarching attitude of patience and hope. I'm not suggesting that this is easy; waiting is one of the most difficult lessons I've ever had to learn, but it is essential as we travel this Christian journey. For not only does impatience hinder our growth in holiness, prayer, and vocation, but it also inhibits our ability to love others, as we'll see in the next section.

waiting: the backbone of love

If we are going to take seriously the call to follow Christ's love, we *must* learn to wait. If we don't, we will be overcome by the challenges of this fallen world.

I experience this regularly when I spend time with my friend, Scott Hope. Scott's life was irrevocably changed nearly three decades ago when, shortly before his high school graduation, a drunk driver plowed into his car. The injuries Scott sustained were severe. He spends his days in a wheelchair, and he has difficulty talking clearly.

Though I enjoy Scott's company, sometimes I have to admit there's sadness whenever I leave his small apartment, where he lives by himself. I wish he had a family to share his days with. I wish he could swing the clubs with me instead of just riding around in the cart when we go out on the golf course. I know he'd enjoy going on walks or accompanying our family to pick strawberries, instead of having to do the passive things we do together, like drive around and look at Christmas lights during the winter, or take in an occasional movie.

I ache over the daily challenges that Scott probably takes for granted now, but which I'm reminded of every time I realize I'm dropping him off, alone, in that tiny apartment, and I'm driving home, where I'll be met with a kiss from my wife and hugs from my kids. I think of this every time I grumble to Scott about my traveling schedule, forgetting that he is currently unemployed and would love the diversion of being out on the road—though in his physical condition, traveling by himself with no one to meet him on the other end, would be extremely difficult, if not impossible.

There's no cure to this sadness. The only way I can completely avoid it is to stop spending time with Scott, which isn't an option. Instead, I reinforce myself spiritually with the call to wait. One day, Scott will be healed. One day, he'll stand taller than I stand. One day, he won't need to lean on me for support as we stand together in the presence of God and worship before the throne.

Waiting is the portal of hope, a very necessary element of spirituality whenever we face the troubles of this world. If you work with people suffering from Alzheimer's disease, with people who have disabilities, with addicted people and dying people and imprisoned people—eventually love will require you to learn how to wait. You may have to wait for weeks while someone you're called to love recovers from a serious illness. You may have to wait for months as you patiently help a profligate spender climb out of debt. You may have to wait for years for an imprisoned but repentant person to be released from jail. You may have to wait for decades for a disabled person to finally be given a new "spiritual body." But one thing is certain: If you're called to love, you're called to wait. There is no love without patience, no love without waiting, no love without hope. John Climacus, author of the seventh-century classic,

> *Waiting is the portal of hope, a very necessary element of spirituality whenever we face the troubles of this world.*

The Ladder of Divine Ascent, called hope "the power behind love."[12] Waiting is the oxygen of love; it is the virtue that gives love its sustaining power.

Learning to wait

Perhaps God has given you a vision that burns in your soul. Initially, you received the call with excitement and enthusiasm, but now it's been several months, or even years, and you feel like the beginning of that work has never been farther away. What attitude will you have as time goes on? Will you take comfort from God while you wait, learning the lessons God wants you to learn, or will you begin accusing God of playing games with you? Remember this: God is not merely concerned with results but also with character—and few things produce character like learning how to wait. Paul's three cardinal virtues—faith, hope, and love—are all built on the foundation of patient waiting.

Perhaps you're in the middle of a difficult relationship, pleading with God for deliverance and answers and direction, and all you hear is, "Wait." That's the last answer you want to receive. You want God to move mountains on your behalf, and you want those mountains moving *now.* You've suffered long enough. Why can't the marriage be healed *today?* Why can't your child come back to her senses this weekend? I can't promise you that the relationship will *ever* be healed, but I can tell you that many, many people have written to me or have come over to speak to me after a seminar session, telling me how, over time, God has worked a mighty change. Nothing dramatic happened in any one week, but steadily, over the years, God brought a gentle healing. All families go through seasons; sometimes, we just have to weather the difficult ones.

> **God is not merely concerned with results, but also with character—and few things produce character like learning how to wait.**

Your waiting may involve someone you're caring for or someone you love. Perhaps a beloved parent you looked up to has been cut down by Alzheimer's disease; maybe a child you'd give your life for has been crippled by muscular dystrophy or multiple sclerosis; it's possible that a close friend has been stricken with cancer. You've prayed for healing, you've exercised your faith, but God has called you to wait. The healing, you now see, will come in eternity. What attitude will you embrace?

Your waiting might be more personal. Maybe there's an "obedience problem" that you truly wish to get rid of, but it has hung on with a dogged determination. This moral failing embarrasses you and frustrates you to no end, and yet you still occasionally fall back into it. Will you give up, or will you wait, maintaining your hope and relying on God's grace?

Waiting means, in part, pursuing refreshing recreation instead of soul-numbing narcotics. Impatience can lead us into any number of spiritually harmful activities. It can foster a spirit of rebellion that seeks immediate release—and this world offers many illicit releases. Waiting, on the other hand, can be restorative. For example, there's a tremendous difference between when I "recreate" by taking a walk outdoors and when I play solitaire on the computer. When I'm in reasonable spiritual and emotional health, the former leaves me with an increased zest for life, a sense of refreshment and renewal; the latter leaves me feeling zapped of my strength, listless, apathetic. One activity enlightens me; the other deadens my senses and dulls my spiritual sensitivity.

Growth is found by trading narcotics for inspiration. This is possible only when we realize that, living in a fallen world, a vague sense of uneasiness and disappointment is to be expected. We were made for heaven, but we are living on earth. We can't have heaven yet, so we can choose to dull the ache with a narcotic, or we can take the path of inspiration.

> **Growth is found by trading narcotics for inspiration.**

Find activities and thoughts that inspire you, and hold on to them. Gradually weed out those things that are just "passing time"—which in reality are actually killing time you'll never get back.

Authentic Faith

Sam Lacy's father was the first Black detective on the Washington, D.C., police force. As young boys, Sam and baseball great Jackie Robinson held back the loose boards for each other as they surreptitiously slipped into ballparks through the outfield fence.[13] While his friend Jackie went on to make baseball history by becoming the first major league baseball player of African descent, Lacy became the country's most celebrated Black sports columnist and editor. He accompanied Althea Gibson to her first tennis tournament and worked hard to give African-American athletes, including Olympian Wilma Rudolph, their due.

Though Sam felt the injustice of a prejudicial society, he maintained a sweet and steadfast spirit. Through the heyday of the "Black Is Beautiful" campaign, Lacy countered with, "An orchid is more beautiful. It's multicolored, like you and I." When the time was right, however, Sam wasn't shy about confronting unfair treatment. When he was introduced at a sportswriters' banquet as "the boy from the *Afro-American*," Sam pleasantly but firmly countered, "I'm the oldest sportswriter here. I'm just wondering, if you could tell me, when will I grow up to be a man?"

Born in 1904, Sam Lacy saw a century of change. He remembers how his wife used to have to sit in the "Jim Crow" section of the bleachers to watch ball games, while he, as a Black sportswriter, had to sit on the press-box roof. A few courageous Caucasian writers joined him. They told Sam they were "working on their tans," but as

Sam told the story when he was inducted into the Baseball Hall of
Fame in Cooperstown, these men had just come from Florida and
looked plenty dark to him.[14]

During the 1930s and 1940s, Sam Lacy worked tirelessly to
break the color barrier in baseball. He became famous for taking
on baseball commissioner Judge Kenesaw Mountain Landis. When
Jackie Robinson first donned his major league uniform, Sam was
forty-two years old—the same number that Jackie Robinson wore
and that has now been retired in honor of Robinson's ground-
breaking achievements.

As I write this, Sam, at 96, still works once a week, pounding
out columns with the same curiosity, tenacity, and insight that have
marked his life. But many things are no longer quite so shocking.
Black athletes now routinely get their fair share of victories and
recognition, with or without "Black writers." The sisters Serena and
Venus Williams are tearing up the pro tennis circuit that Althea
Gibson (with the help of Sam's columns) helped break open to
Black women. Muhammad Ali was widely heralded as the athlete
of the century during the making of many such lists. Even the last
bastion of athletic elitism, golf, is reaping the benefits of the incredible talents of one Tiger Woods.

If you were to go by generations, the most celebrated sports
stars are not hard to pick out: Muhammad Ali, Michael Jordan,
Tiger Woods. About 150 years ago, each one of these men might
well have been bought and sold. After countless prayers, the blood
sacrifice of hundreds of thousands of Civil War soldiers, deft political battling, and courageous leadership (which in many cases
resulted in death), African-Americans have made tremendous
progress. Many will say the struggle is far from over, that pockets
of prejudice still remain in many elements of society, but the great
human rights struggle has marched steadily onward. Tiger's father,
Earl Woods, sometimes had to sleep in different hotels and eat in
different restaurants while playing baseball for Kansas State University. His son, Tiger, now enjoys treatment that in previous ages
would have been reserved for royalty.

The advancement of African Americans has by no means been limited to athletics, of course. It's no longer headline news when a Black American becomes the CEO of a Fortune 500 company, and one of the most financially successful female entertainers of all time, Oprah Winfrey, is an African American. Politically, Blacks sit on the Supreme Court, have served as surgeon general, and take up positions in Congress and the Cabinet; one man, Colin Powell, perhaps could have been elected president if he had chosen to run, and he is now the first Black secretary of state in United States history.

None of this happened overnight. It took generations for ignorance to be replaced and prejudice, if not to be removed, at least to be rendered less potent. History's great struggles have often been played out over centuries, not decades.

> *Time rarely moves fast enough for those who are motivated by a true mission, but waiting is part of our human existence.*

It's never easy to wait. Time rarely moves fast enough for those who are motivated by a true mission, but waiting is part of our human existence. Waiting may not be the thread of our ministry, but it is certainly the warp and woof.

Always keep this in mind: We will never understand God and his ways unless we remind ourselves that throughout history he has moved by millennia, not minutes.

fragments of frustration

The Discipline of Suffering

In this world you will have trouble.

Jesus, in John 16:33

Join with me in suffering for the gospel.

Paul, in 2 Timothy 1:8

If we want to know whether a building will stand strong or not, we look at it when the wind is blowing hard. Similarly, we can list the reality of a man's Christian practice when he is under the trials of God's providence.

Jonathan Edwards

It was a short but severe run. I had gone about two miles when I made my way down a gently sloping trail that opens out onto a railroad track. While crossing the track, my foot caught a rail and all my weight came crashing down on my left wrist.

I heard it snap.

The pain was immediate, and the grotesque angle at which my wrist protruded from my arm left little doubt as to what had happened. I clutched the mangled limb to my waist and walked back up the slope, wondering how I was going to get back to my car. An elderly woman walking her dog saw me and asked, "Are you all right?"

We walked back toward her house, where she gave me a ride to my car. I had left my vehicle in a park, and I could hear the anxiety in my Good Samaritan's voice when she said, with obvious suspicion, "This seems like an awful long way to run."

I realized with sympathy that she was fearful I might be faking the injury so that I could get her in the park in the early morning hours and do who knows what, and I grieved that the world was such that good-hearted citizens must perform their kind deeds at such personal risk.

Although I didn't know it at the time, I think I'd started to go into mild shock. I kept making wrong turns on my way to the hospital, driving with one hand and trying to find the building that was then only three-quarters of a mile from my house. The giant hospital structure appeared to be hiding, but finally the signs led me into a distant parking lot. The pain was now fairly excruciating. I walked into the emergency room, and almost immediately my suffering was over.

The doctor took one look at my wrist and said, "I can't fix that. You're going to need surgery," but they pumped me up with so many drugs that I barely felt a thing. I was unconscious while the orthopedist operated, and I woke up with four long screws and a mechanical brace protruding from my arm. But the doctor prescribed Percocet, one of the strongest legal painkillers, and you love *everybody* when you're on Percocet. After I ran out of that bottle, he gave me Vicodin, and while you may not love everybody on Vicodin, the world is certainly a very pleasant place once that drug works its way into your bloodstream.

Breaking my wrist was certainly an inconvenience, but it was far from a tragedy. Modern medicine is such that an injury that would have permanently crippled me a hundred years ago is now a routine matter. The particular brace I wore, secured by four screws going into my bones, had just been invented a few years earlier. I was amazed by the effectiveness of the painkillers, which allowed me to "float" over a pain that earlier generations would have had to suffer through for weeks, if not months.

In so many ways, we have removed much of normal human suffering. The first time my wife gave birth, we followed the Lamaze method. The result was wonderful, but the process was ghastly. During the second birth, Lisa was forced to get an epidural. Suddenly, the pain was gone, completely gone. Lisa could actually enjoy the process, and I wanted to scream out, "Why in the world didn't we do this the first time?!" We don't ask people to "breathe through" appendectomies or broken arms, so why do so when having babies? "Natural childbirth," at least for the types of labor Lisa tends to have (long, slow, and hard), now has a decidedly malicious ring in my ears.

Even in the most severe situations, doctors can control most human pain. I wrote an article for *Christianity Today* some years ago that dealt with euthanasia and end-of-life care. "No one need suffer in a protracted way," Joanne Lynn of The George Washington University Medical Center assured me. "No one near death needs to be in pain. People find it hard to believe, but almost all patients can be kept conscious and out of pain. The rest can be kept sedated and out of pain."

> **Suffering is seen, almost exclusively, as an evil tormentor from hell, something to be cursed and avoided.**

I'm not denying that some cancer patients, as well as others, face constant pain and must learn to deal with it—but the percentage of people who live this way is infinitesimal compared with previous generations.

Because of these medical advances, the concept of patiently enduring suffering is not nearly as well developed—and certainly not embraced—as a spiritual discipline or practice in our culture. Suffering is seen, almost exclusively, as an evil tormentor from hell, something to be cursed and avoided.

The danger with this view is that some sort of suffering is guaranteed, even in a modern world, because this is still a *fallen* world. Jesus clearly warned his disciples, "In this world you will have trouble" (John 16:33), and the early apostles amplified this line of thinking: "We must go through *many* hardships to enter the kingdom of God" (Acts 14:22, emphasis added). Jesus said, "You'll have trouble," but the apostles promised we'd have *lots* of trouble.

In a mature view, we'll learn to take suffering and difficulty in the way Isaiah told Israel to take it: as "the bread of adversity and the water of affliction" (Isaiah 30:20), something that nourishes us even as it causes pain.

Maturity in the faith is no guarantee that we'll experience less suffering. In fact, it may well mean we will experience *more*. When I became familiar with the Christian classics as a young seminarian, I went through a difficult season of questioning my desire to draw closer to God, largely because the spiritual giants who wrote these books often lived bitterly difficult lives. Augustine died of a wasting disease while his city was under siege; Teresa of Avila suffered through years of intense migraines; Brother Lawrence never got over his chronic gout; Martin Luther died a difficult death following a long string of illnesses; the great Puritan writer Richard Baxter wrote one of his most famous works while a grotesquely large tumor protruded out of his body; Francis of Assisi, who loved to view nature as a way to adore God, was nearly blind as he wrote his famous "Canticle of the Creatures." God certainly seemed to ask more of these followers, not less, and I wondered whether I was willing to pay the price to enjoy such intimacy.

> *Maturity in the faith is no guarantee that we'll experience less suffering. In fact, it may well mean we will experience more.*

The biblical personalities had it just as tough. Jesus himself is described as a man "familiar with suffering" (Isaiah 53:3). "It was the LORD's will to crush him and cause him to suffer," Isaiah adds (53:10). Paul, who wrote much of the New Testament, lived with an ever-present "thorn in [his] flesh" (2 Corinthians 12:7). Elisha, the most powerfully and charismatically gifted of the Old Testament prophets, died of a protracted wasting illness (see 2 Kings 13:14). And this doesn't even begin to chronicle the lives of so many others, including Hosea, who was called to marry an adulterous and very difficult woman; Job, who lost everything but his life in one terrible blow; Deborah, who was forced to rule with cowardly men under her command; and Hannah, a pious woman who nevertheless suffered through years of infertility.

Getting close to God is by no means a guarantee of affluence, comfort, and serenity. On the contrary, getting close to God is to enroll in a difficult school where character is built out of persevering through difficult times.

Thoughtful Christians have understood the necessity of preemptively warning fellow believers about the difficulty and suffering that are inherent in this fallen world. When Christians are taught only that Christianity makes life easier, they become disenchanted when they find themselves or a loved one walking through cancer, unemployment, or other challenges. Worse, in some circles, facing sickness is seen as evidence of a lack of faith. I actually heard a well-known revivalist/faith healer say on television, "We must become as serious about fighting sickness as we are about fighting sin." He went on to suggest that just as faith overcomes sin, so true faith overcomes all sickness. Even my then nine-year-old daughter Allison saw through that one. She looked up from her puzzle and asked me—with skepticism dripping from her tongue—"Is that true, Daddy?"

We were able to look together at Galatians 4, in which Paul himself confesses he sometimes got very ill. "As you know," he writes, "it was because of an illness that I first preached the gospel to you. Even though my illness was a trial to you, you did not treat me with contempt or scorn. Instead, you welcomed me as if I were an angel of God, as if I were Christ Jesus himself" (Galatians 4:13–14). Far from Paul's sickness being a badge of shame, it elicited great honor and care. Not only did the Galatian believers not ostracize Paul, they treated him like Christ!

The same channel showcased another preacher who rebuked a woman who was asking honest and legitimate questions during her time of sickness. The preacher shouted out, "God has nothing to do with it! Show me one verse where God causes sickness!" I casually flipped to 2 Kings 15:3, 5: "[Azariah] did what was right in the eyes of the LORD, just as his father Amaziah had done.... The LORD afflicted the king with leprosy until the day he died, and he lived in a separate house."[1]

Out of good intentions, these teachers lead believers through a double crucifixion. Not only must these poor listeners bear their sicknesses, but they are also forced to endure an assault enacted by guilt, being taught that the only reason they're still sick is because they lack the faith to be well.

Sickness and suffering do not always evidence a lack of faith; if they did, then Paul, Augustine, Teresa of Avila, Francis of Assisi, Brother Lawrence, Martin Luther, and at least half of the Puritans have absolutely nothing to teach us— an absurd suggestion, to be sure. The fact is, my body belongs to God. If, in his wisdom, he can use physical suffering to strengthen my soul, that's a choice he can make because he is God. Because Christians live with an eternal worldview, temporal suffering is not necessarily evil if it creates a greater, long-term good.

> **Sickness and suffering do not always evidence a lack of faith.**

I remember seeing Larry King interview Billy Graham in the days after it was publicly announced that the evangelist was suffering from Parkinson's disease. "You pray not to be in pain, don't you?" Larry asked.

"Not at all," Graham responded. "I pray for God's will." Graham went on to explain how he was more than willing to suffer if God had another lesson for him to learn—this in his eighties! Billy Graham has led more people to the Lord than perhaps any other individual in all of Christian history. He has led a long and fruitful life, yet still he wants to learn, *even if his learning requires pain.* If Billy Graham has this attitude, how much more should we?

The "gifts" of cancer

As a former cross-country runner, my eyes were drawn to an article about Marty Liquori, who, until 2001, was the last high school runner in the United States to break four minutes in the mile—a feat he accomplished in 1967. Following an appearance in the 1968 Mexico City Olympics, Liquori opened a chain of athletic shoe stores, and then faced perhaps his greatest race ever: a battle against chronic lymphocytic leukemia, a cancer that attacks the blood supply.

Though Liquori has been successful in his bout against this disease, he is also realistic. "The key word is *chronic*," he explains. "[The cancer] will come back."

Today, he has reordered his life and has begun doing the things he truly enjoys, such as playing music. "It all falls under the heading of gifts that cancer can give," Liquori explains. "Once you have that wake-up call, you find you don't do things because they pay well or because someone says you should. Without the diagnosis, none of this would have happened."[2]

Gifts that cancer can give . . . I could never say something like this myself, having never gone through cancer, but it amazes me how frequently those who have faced cancer say something so similar. Lance Armstrong, a cancer survivor and three-time winner of the Tour de France, astonishingly writes in his book *It's Not About the Bike* that, knowing what he knows now, if he had to choose between winning the Tour de France and having cancer, he'd choose cancer.

I can honestly say that I learned some valuable lessons while breaking my arm. I don't know if God literally looked down on me that morning and told his archangel Michael that I needed a little pain to help me grow out of my complacency. "A broken wrist ought to do the trick, Michael—nothing too serious." While God is omnipresent, Michael isn't, so I'm sure the archangel is much too important to be called out on my behalf. Perhaps it was some junior angel still trying to get his wings. Whatever the case, should a conversation like that ever happen, I'd praise and thank God for loving me enough to let me go through his refining process. (Frankly, I'd settle for any explanation beyond that of my friend Rob Takemura: "Gary, face it. You're a klutz.")

Yes, God leads us to a place of spiritual abundance, but the road to that place is often marked with difficulty and suffering. The psalmist writes these words:

> *For you, O God, tested us;*
> *   you refined us like silver.*
> *You brought us into prison*
> *   and laid burdens on our backs.*
> *You let men ride over our heads;*
> *   we went through fire and water,*
> *   but you brought us to a place of abundance.*

PSALM 66:10–12

It has long been orthodox Christian teaching that difficulty "seasons" us. In fact, successfully walking through difficulty is a necessary part of becoming mature.

proven chαrαcter

In December of 1999, the heaviest rainfall in 100 years pelted Venezuela's northern coast, launching a devastating series of floods, mud slides, and rock avalanches. About 40,000 homes were annihilated, and estimates are that between 10,000 and 30,000 people died. With some areas buried under 22 feet of rubble, the true numbers will probably never be known.

Even more tragedy awaited two of the survivors. A nine-year-old girl had been visiting family relatives in Cuba during the disasters. Even though her parents' home had been destroyed in the disaster, they wanted their daughter to come home. It's a natural feeling after you've experienced such a terrible loss; you just want to hug your kids.

In this case, it was a hug that never happened. The young girl died in a plane crash on her way back home.

I can't even begin to fathom the depth of a parent's anguish upon learning that your child has died just days after you've lost your house and everything in it. The pain in this fallen world sometimes knows no bounds. Those who have suffered are by no means immune from even worse suffering.

> *God leads us to a place of spiritual abundance, but the road to that place is often marked with difficulty and suffering.*

The last thing I want to do is trivialize suffering. There's no way I could even begin to explain it away, and I'm sensitive to the fact that no matter what "good" comes out of such tragedy, it will undoubtedly seem like a poor trade to the parents. There is nothing on this earth I could imagine trading the life of my child for.

Having recognized this, the truth still remains that suffering is inevitable in this world. The question is not whether we'll suffer, but how we'll suffer, and, just as important, how we'll respond to suffering. "Endure hardship with us like a good soldier of Christ Jesus," Paul urged Timothy (2 Timothy 2:3).

Thomas Watson, a seventeenth-century Puritan pastor who ministered in London, wrote a book titled *A Divine Cordial,* in which, among other things, he lists the many ways that affliction works for the good of those who love God. It was part of his belief that Christians needed to see the bigger purpose behind our difficulties.

> *The question is not whether we'll suffer, but how we'll suffer, and, just as important, how we'll respond to suffering.*

Among his findings, Watson wrote that affliction works as our "preacher and tutor." He said that sometimes a sickbed can teach us more than a sermon. If we value wisdom more than comfort, we won't casually dismiss the role of suffering. Watson also said that in prosperity, we can be strangers to ourselves, but affliction teaches us to know ourselves, including the corruptions of our hearts. It's easy to be pleasant when all is well, when our finances are in order, and when we don't have a headache or back pain—but take away these comforts, and how patient are we then?

Watson goes on to call afflictions the "medicine that God uses to carry off our spiritual diseases," while they also conform us to Christ. They loosen our hearts from the world—an experiential crowbar, of sorts, reminding us that we are not to make our home here—and they even make us happy, if we respond to them by drawing nearer to God.

Watson's last point is one we'll explore in greater depth, as it is taught so well by the apostle Paul, namely, that afflictions work for our good in that they make way for glory. Paul describes a time-tested spiritual exercise in Romans 5:3–5a that emphasizes this truth: "We also rejoice in our sufferings, because we know that suffering produces perseverance; perseverance, character; and character, hope. And hope does not disappoint us."

Don't miss the stunning first half of this sentence: Paul *doesn't* say that he has learned to tolerate suffering, or even to wait patiently during suffering. On the contrary, he says he has learned to *rejoice* in his sufferings. Elsewhere, he says he has learned to delight in hardships and difficulties (see 2 Corinthians 12:10), because he wants to enjoy "the fellowship of sharing in [Christ's] sufferings" (Philippians 3:10). In Paul's mind, what suffering produces is so amazingly wonderful that it leads him to rejoice when suffering comes his way.

We can chart Romans 5:3–5a for a helpful and practical look at bedrock spiritual formation:

Suffering	➔	Perseverance
Perseverance	➔	Character
Character	➔	Hope
Hope	➔	Never Disappointed

First, let's be clear about the entryway. Suffering *hurts*. The Greek word used here *(thlipsis)* carries a sense of considerable oppression and affliction, not some minor inconvenience. There is no sentimentality buried in these words. To be blunt, Paul is talking about pain.

Without pain, of course, there is no need to persevere. We don't need to "keep pressing on" when we're enjoying something. A man sitting in his chair doesn't need to "persevere"; a man running a marathon does. Perseverance assumes discomfort.

It is only through discomfort, therefore, that we can ever learn to persevere. And it is only through perseverance that we can develop *character*. The Greek word here references a *proven* character, which is a thoroughly biblical concept. There is no such thing, really, as *potential* character. Character is forged only when we pass through the fire. If character is not tested, it's not really character—at least not in this biblical sense. This means that spiritual formation is achieved primarily when we learn to persevere through suffering, responding with biblical hope. Such a person will never be disillusioned or disappointed.

> **Let's be clear about the entryway. Suffering hurts.**

When Paul entered suffering on behalf of Christ, he thought ahead about four steps. Ultimately, he knew, suffering creates a hope that never disappoints. Suffering and affliction are but a doorway, not a house to dwell in, and the place they lead us is blessed indeed. Because of that, Paul actually welcomed them as friends.

> *Suffering and affliction are but a doorway, not a house to dwell in, and the place they lead us is blessed indeed.*

Paul was not a masochist. He didn't welcome suffering for the sake of suffering. He welcomed suffering *for the sake of hope,* a virtue that is infused with an eternal perspective, the promises offered to us in the gospel. Paul returns to this later in his letter to the Christians in Rome when he writes in Romans 8:18, "I consider that our present sufferings are not worth comparing with the glory that will be revealed in us."

Ancient Christians followed Paul's example. Basil wrote in the fourth century, "Good men take sickness as athletes take their contest, waiting for the crowns that are to reward their endurance."[3] Basil obviously believed that we gain a spiritual benefit from enduring even a common malady.

Listen to what Teresa of Avila taught: "When the Lord begins to grant greater favors here on earth, greater trials can be expected."[4] In her autobiography, Teresa confesses of herself, "I know a person who cannot truthfully say that from the time the Lord began forty years ago to grant the favor that was mentioned she spent one day without pains and other kinds of suffering."[5] The woman who through her writings has taught numerous generations of Christians how to enjoy a more intimate communion with God testifies that *not a single day* in her life went by without some form of pain and suffering to accompany it. When Teresa faced her migraines, she didn't have the benefit of Percocet or Vicodin. She didn't even have Tylenol or Bayer aspirin. Her medicines were of a far different kind: hope, endurance, and patience.

Thomas à Kempis reminds us that when we suffer, we aren't experiencing anything that everybody else doesn't also experience, in some way or other: "There is no person on this earth without some trouble or affliction. Who is it then who is most at ease in the midst of suffering? He who is willing to suffer some affliction for God's sake."[6] Thomas à Kempis is very practical here: Regardless of your theology, he says, you're going to suffer, because everyone does. The person who does best in this regard is not the person who lives in denial but rather the person who is willing to allow his or her suffering to be baptized in service to God.

> **Regardless of your theology, you're going to suffer, because everyone does.**

Am I saying it's wrong to pray for healing? Absolutely not. The Bible commands us to pray for healing (see James 5:14). Am I saying it's wrong to take pain medicine? No. I believe this world has enough suffering that we don't have to manufacture our own. What I am saying—and what I believe the biblical and classical writers are saying—is that when suffering is ordained on our behalf, we must be taught to endure it with hope and patience, valuing it for the spiritual benefit it brings.

social suffering

In a world mixed with free will and fallen humanity, suffering touches even the godliest of homes.

I once taught a weeklong course at Western Seminary in Portland, Oregon. On the fourth day of the course, we discussed discernment, and one of the class participants, Stephen Asonibare, talked about a particular situation in which he was trying to discern God's will.

Stephen lives in Nigeria. Just three weeks prior to our class, armed robbers raided his family's village. Stephen's wife and youngest son were severely beaten, and a neighbor woman was gang-raped by six men.

"What I'd like to do," Stephen offered, "is hold a thanksgiving service. As bad as it was, it could have been a lot worse. No one was killed. The problem is that I don't want to antagonize the robbers. If they hear about the service, they might come back and do something even worse."

"Is there any chance the robbers might be caught?" someone asked. It was a natural question.

Stephen shook his head. "Not likely. The new president is a Christian, and most of my country is Muslim. The police department wants the new president to look bad, so they aren't being very aggressive about stopping crime."

The choice was tough. On the one hand, Stephen wanted to bring spiritual care and nurture to a hurting village. On the other hand, he didn't want to bring further violence.

An immediate hush filled the room. We had been talking about discernment in the abstract situation of North American affluence—how we can help people listen for God's voice about buying a new home, getting a new job, choosing the right marriage partner—but now we were faced with a question of discernment that could literally be a matter of life and death.

What can make such suffering so difficult is the often senseless nature behind it. Stephen's village was not attacked because the inhabitants were Christian. They were attacked because some robbers wanted quick money and malicious sex. How does a pastor shepherd his people in such a world?

> **What can make such suffering so difficult is the often senseless nature behind it.**

There are certainly random acts of violence in this country as well—and not all of them at the hands of men or women. Two friends I had gone to college with were driving along a highway with a newborn baby in the car when a buck crashed into their vehicle. The animal went through a window and killed their baby.

As you work through such a horrific event, you are led to think, "God, couldn't you have delayed that buck for half a second? Couldn't you have delayed my friends' departure for five seconds? Why did this have to happen?"

While I think it is appropriate for us to talk about God's protection and the security we can have in him, I'm not so glib about it anymore. Terrible things happen in this world. If God had slowed that buck by three seconds, my friends would have a child now nearing adolescence, instead of a pile of painful photographs reminding them of their great loss.

We come back to the beginning: This is a fallen world, and terrible things happen in a fallen world. We dishonor our suffering sisters and brothers when we try to explain all of this away. The truth is, we are called to *suffer with them*, not—as some think we are called to do—to try to "cure" them of their suffering. Paul tells us to "carry each other's burdens" (Galatians 6:2), not try to explain the burdens away.

The Danger of refusing to suffer

Our refusal to suffer can lead to addictions and even physical breakdowns.

We know more about how the human brain works than we ever have before. Much remains a mystery, but the chemical reactions that lead to our body's functioning are becoming far more apparent.

In his book *Addiction and Grace*, Gerald May, a psychiatrist and trained spiritual director, explains how something as simple as nose drops can become addictive. The way our body works is to maintain chemical balance. This is hopelessly simplified, but in essence, when we take any chemical over a significant period of time, our body begins to count on that chemical in order to function—in other words, it adapts to the presence of the chemical. When our sinuses clog up, our brain releases another chemical telling our body to make the necessary adjustments for our sinuses to unclog—unless our body has learned to depend on an outside stimulant.

> **Paul tells us to "carry each other's burdens," not try to explain the burdens away.**

The problem is, sometimes our body doesn't respond fast enough—at least, not fast enough for our comfort. There is an initial period of suffering. If we immediately jump to the medicine, however, our body can become dependent on the decongestant to fight the sinus infection, no longer using the natural internal remedies present by God's design.

Using this analogy, May suggests that sometimes we will be healthier in the long run if we put up with minor suffering in the short run—within reason. Living in this world sometimes requires that we be uncomfortable. Our desire to live our lives free from pain can become a type of idol that leads us to rely heavily on non-prescription and prescription drugs.

Intriguing spiritual parallels lie behind this physical reality. If I am in a behavioral pattern and want to see it changed, there will be a time of suffering as I learn to live without the inappropriate behavior. Just talk to an alcoholic, a drug addict, or a person who has used pornography. If a person decides to stop depending on one of these crutches, he or she will normally experience times of extreme internal discomfort as he or she relearns how to endure internal tension without the use of a "spiritual narcotic."

In talking about holiness, it's important to stress the "desert of detachment." True holiness, according to the ancients, is experienced through such a desert. As far as emotional satisfaction is concerned, there may be a "dip" before there is a "rise," until we learn to live without the narcotic of sinful behavior or attitude. We usually engage in sin to meet some immediate demand or need. Merely stopping the sin does nothing to address the yearning that led to the sin in the first place, which is why we must pass through the desert to embrace the virtue of detachment. That is, we must separate ourselves from anything that takes the place of God in our lives. It takes time for us to be separated from our previous narcotics, and considerable suffering can be involved.

> **True holiness, according to the ancients, is experienced through a desert of detachment.**

This isn't the place for a full-blown discussion of sanctification, but, in short, the point I'm making is that holiness may make your life more miserable in the short run, though far more joyful in the long run. If you insist on avoiding suffering at all costs, you will never be free of your addictions. If someone is truly serious about spiritual growth or overcoming a long-term bad habit, he or she had better be prepared to go to war. A halfhearted effort usually won't suffice.

While an alcoholic can expect many difficult times ahead, he will also find that once the initial sharp urges have passed, he has far more time and energy than he ever imagined he could have. His initial suffering will produce tremendous long-term benefits that he can treasure. I once read an interview where a celebrity was asked what he valued most in life, and he responded in one word: "Sobriety." In all honesty, I have never treasured "sobriety," in large part because I've never been addicted to alcohol. But this man can now appreciate something in a way that I cannot, because he has suffered to attain it.

The point is that I must learn to accept some suffering as an inevitable part of living in a fallen world. These changes *hurt*. They are not easy. Suffering and change go hand in hand. If I refuse to suffer and refuse to face the discomfort of change, I will experience even more severe consequences as the idol increases its hold on my heart. I will be forever a stranger to experiential holiness. If I don't practice the virtue the ancients called "detachment," I will not live as a free man in the grace of Jesus Christ.[7]

enemy aversions

There is a lot of talk about addiction—talk that can, in fact, be dangerous. Gerald May warns that the concept of the "addictive personality" has been more harmful than helpful. Rather than talking about an addic*tive* personality, May prefers to speak of an addic*ted* personality. That is, the personality doesn't create the addiction; *the addiction creates the personality*. It is when we lose control that we feel a lack of self-esteem, an abundance of shame, and an all-consuming self-centeredness.[8]

The flip side of addiction is *aversion*. Whereas an addiction means we are drawn toward something, aversion means we are repelled by it. These aversions can be every bit as strong as addictions and can help explain some of the cruelty behind prejudice, racism, and the like. Dislike can become so intense that some people act with unimaginable malice and in profoundly evil ways.

Some of us have strong aversions to any kind of suffering. Even worse, some Christian teachers actually feed this aversion to suffering. They automatically assume that everything "negative" is "of the devil." ("Count it all *attack,* my brethren, when you face troubles of many kinds. . . ."[9]) There is no consideration that God can use temporary pain for eternal gain.

When we are ruled by our aversions, we are no less slaves than those who are riddled by addictions. Keep this in mind: Aversions direct and influence us every bit as much as addictions do, even though they rarely get spoken about. When we experience an occurrence of suffering, or financial scarcity, or physical pain, or rejection, or any kind of difficulty, we often pour into it all the experience that surrounded us the last time we felt a similar suffering. Suddenly, we're not just dealing merely with a colleague's good-natured ribbing, but a sibling's cruel chastising, a father's brutal ridiculing, a bully's malicious taunting—and we lose control. Our response is way out of proportion to the original offense. Everyone (including us) wonders, "Where did that response come from?"

> **Aversions direct and influence us every bit as much as addictions do.**

Frequently the answer is that someone has touched a buried aversion. Our current response is amplified by our past experience.

This is a natural process. If a healthy thirty-five-year-old woman feels tired for a few days, she probably thinks, "I need to get more sleep." If a recovering cancer patient feels a new weariness, his thought might be, "The cancer is back." The same feeling—weariness—is given two profoundly different interpretations and fears based on previous experience.

The journey to overcome our aversion to difficulty and suffering has to be an individual one. It's one thing for a man who has never been hungry to feel pangs while fasting; it is quite another for a man who grew up in real poverty and hunger and promised himself that once he became an adult he would never be hungry again.

I can't predict your aversions. I'm not even qualified to diagnose them! But you need to know they are there. When your reaction to an unkind but not necessarily cruel remark is way out of proportion, when you feel as though your world is falling apart just because an important relationship is experiencing tension, when you know there is a deep undercurrent to any reaction you might have to life's normal difficulties, it's time to pray and to perhaps discuss your feelings with a wise friend who can help you pinpoint the aversion so that it doesn't rule over you.

Why is this necessary? Because beyond our aversions and addictions, we yearn to belong completely and unreservedly to God. God will often walk us through paths that deliberately confront our attachments and prejudices and fears and aversions standing like roadblocks in our relationship to him. If we have an aversion to pain, hunger, rejection, insecurity, ridicule, or anything else, at that very point we are vulnerable to the worship of idols—whether our idol be comfort, fame, security, wealth, or acceptance. This is why God seems relentlessly bent on walking us through our worst fears.

> *Beyond our aversions and addictions, we yearn to belong completely and unreservedly to God.*

It's common sense that God would do this. I was throwing batting practice to my son one day, and Graham was hitting just about everything that crossed the plate. His confidence was soaring, and during one break, he said, "Now that I know I can hit a fastball, the only thing I'm worried about facing is a right-handed pitcher who throws sidearmed. That really throws me off."

What do you think I did as soon as we began playing again? That's right—I threw sidearmed, as hard as I could, until Graham could start hitting it. He needed to face his fears in order to grow as a hitter—just as we need to face our worst fears in order to grow as children of God.

Here's the key point: I threw sidearmed because I love Graham and want to help him grow, not because I enjoy being mean or malicious. Graham knew what I was doing. He even smiled about it, totally giving me the benefit of the doubt.

Will you do the same for God—give him the benefit of the doubt—if he chooses to take you past your worst fears?

Paul and the ancient saints seemed remarkably free of aversion. Paul found contentment in all situations. He didn't run *from* hunger, danger, persecution, or affluence and fame. He ran *toward*

God. In the Christian life, it's not so much where we *are* as where we *are headed* that signifies our maturity. Are we running *from* something else or *to* God?

seasoned by suffering

During the height of his writing years, C. S. Lewis cared for a very sick woman named Janie King Moore. On top of her protracted illness, Mrs. Moore had varicose veins, so whenever she called, Lewis had to go to her—and she called him many times a day. George Sayer, Lewis's biographer, explains: "[Lewis] would leave his work, go upstairs and do her bidding, and then return to his writing. There were two maids in the house, but they quarreled with each other and sometimes with Mrs. Moore, too. Jack's role was to try to make peace, over and over again."[10] Added to Mrs. Moore's illness was the constant irritation of Lewis's brother Warren's alcoholism, and Lewis's constant fears that he was about to go bankrupt.

As one who writes for a living, I can sympathize with the difficulty of continuing work amid so many interruptions, yet it was precisely under these conditions that Sayer says Lewis wrote "the best known and most widely loved of all his books"—*The Lion, the Witch, and the Wardrobe.* Sayer elucidates: "That the Narnia stories are full of laughter and the fact that they breathe forth joy does not mean that the years of their writing were happy for Jack. What it does mean is that his faith had taught him how to cope with difficulties and to rise above miseries that would have overwhelmed most men."[11]

Yet Sayer goes a step further, suggesting that the brilliance of the Narnia series was not achieved *in spite of* being written under such stress, but *because* it was written in a situation of human suffering. "If [Lewis] had lived the cloistered existence of a bachelor don, his writing would have suffered from a loss of warmth, humanity, and the understanding of pain and suffering."[12]

A life with no difficulty was not an ideal life in Lewis's mind, precisely because it tempted him to become what he despised: overly comfortable, complacent, and apathetic. In fact, when war was just breaking out between Britain and Germany in 1939, Lewis wrote to his friend Arthur Greeves, "I daresay, for me, personally, [the war] has come in the nick of time; I was just beginning to get too well settled in my profession, too successful, and probably self-complacent."[13]

Lewis's life was full of struggle. By the summer of 1949, the stress had reached such high levels that Lewis developed a severe infection. His symptoms included a high temperature, delirium, a splitting headache, a sore throat, and swollen glands. Lewis's doctor said the real problem was exhaustion resulting from his work and difficulties at home. Warren arranged for Jack to spend a month in Ireland, to which Lewis said, "It seems too good to be true."

Unfortunately, it was. Warren kept drinking his way into an asylum, ultimately requiring Lewis to forgo his own convalescence so that he could look after his brother. Lewis wrote, "It would be better that the door of my prison had never been opened than if it now bangs in my face! How hard to submit to God's will."[14]

All this prepared Lewis for his real test—going through the suffering of watching his wife die of cancer. During this ordeal, Lewis ruminated on a doctrine mentioned by George MacDonald, namely, "substitutionary sacrifice." Lewis wanted, like Christ, to put himself in Joy's place and take her suffering on himself. He actually prayed for his wife's pain to be transferred to him. Although some might question the theology undergirding this prayer, shortly after Lewis's prayer, Joy seemed to get much better, while Lewis suddenly endured such great pain that, according to a man who worked at his house, there was "screamin' and 'ollerin' and no sleep without dope."[15]

In reflection, Lewis said, "The intriguing thing was that while I (for no discernible reason) was losing the calcium from my bones, Joy, who needed it much more, was gaining it in hers."[16] Lewis's suffering was real. During this time he could hardly walk and was fitted with a surgical brace to support his weakened spine.

Lewis's work was seasoned with pain, true suffering, heartache, and tremendous difficulty. As we saw in an earlier chapter, the idea for The Chronicles of Narnia was spawned out of a selfless act of service; here we learn that the depth of that series was forged from a life of suffering. Yet out of this seemingly bitter stew emerged the

honey of a proven character, a seasoned soul, a stalwart defender
of the faith. This is Christianity in its truest and finest form, the
extension of Christ's own work—the One who suffered and died
that we might live.

Hanging our Hope

Jon Walker is a former editor at *HomeLife* magazine. In the January 2000 issue, he wrote about an excruciating choice he and his
wife, Sherry, had made. Their child was diagnosed with Trisomy 18,
meaning that there was no way the child would survive for more
than a few days after birth. A geneticist recommended an immediate abortion, which the Walkers rejected on moral grounds. Jon
told the doctor that he believed the baby was a creation of God and
therefore deserved "dignified treatment," informing him in no
uncertain terms that the child would be carried to term.

Jon and his wife had already lost three children in utero, so they
knew what they were talking about. "On this journey, where most
of our children have died on the womb side of life, we've learned
that 40 weeks or less in utero often is the breadth of one lifetime.
However short, it's always a life sent from the Creator and worthy
of celebrating."

The doctor was stunned, calling the Walkers the most mature
couple he'd ever met. In humility, Jon counters, "We know it's not
maturity, rather the Holy Spirit, and tomorrow, without God's
grace, we could fall apart." The doctor confessed that he was a
"nihilist," believing everything is random, all life is chance, and that
the Walkers "just got a bad roll of the dice."

In Jon's words, "Scripture teaches that nothing is random. 'The
die is cast, but its every direction is from the Lord.' Jeremy and his
quirky DNA and his spinal [sic] bifida—if we believe what we say
we believe—none of that was an accident. We've named him after
the prophet Jeremiah, to whom God said, 'Before I formed you in
the womb, I knew you.' Who says a life of 40 weeks is any less
valuable than one of 80 years?"

With understandable admiration, Jon calls his wife, Sherry, a
"hero," who literally sustained life "for one of God's more fragile
creations when the wise of this world suggested such a thing was

foolish. But then God's wisdom confounds the wise of this world, and young Jeremy is no less his wisdom than our beautiful, living son Christopher."

Jon admits, "The last 16 years haven't been easy, and I wouldn't be honest if I didn't tell you that some days I wonder why God keeps asking us to walk this road. It doesn't appear fair, but in those moments, I think about the prophet Jeremiah, who pleaded with God to let him go home and be quiet. He didn't like the life he'd been called to, but then again, he came to realize it was never his life to live. It was God's all along."

Jon's more remarkable words come near the end. He says, "My wife and I wouldn't trade the pain, the

> **"God's wisdom confounds the wise of this world."**

heartache or the difficulty of the last 16 years for anything if it meant abandoning God and his sovereignty in the process. We are better people because of the anvil he placed us on."[17]

Jon's story doesn't end there. I received an E-mail from him a few months after Jeremy died (you'll recall this is the fourth child he has lost). In addition to losing this precious child, in a twelve-month span Jon was rushed to the emergency room with severe abdominal pain (leading to a gallbladder removal), had a kidney stone removed and a hernia repaired, and underwent an operation on his writing hand.

The suffering he experienced was enough for a decade, yet God had permitted it to descend in one brutal year. Even so, Jon treasures 1999. "I have to tell you that I'm not at all defeated by these events," he wrote to me. "In fact, I've come to view this past year as perhaps the greatest of my life. I've learned that because God is in me, He's also in the middle of the mess, and I've learned that the mess is there to show me where I'm hanging my hope."

I love that line: *The mess is there to show me where I'm hanging my hope.* Perhaps life on this fallen earth is no longer meant to be perfect, but we were meant to trust the One who is. Suffering is God's tool to expose our false belief, and the mess is intended to drive us back to the only sure hope we can have.

Jon finds great solace in a much loved Christian classic writer: "Oswald Chambers once wrote, 'We are not here to prove God answers prayers; we are here to be living monuments of God's grace.' That means the issue is not whether God does what we ask when we ask in the way we ask—that's not what life is all about. Rather, it means we receive the grace of God each day and, knowing things are messy, knowing we're imperfect beings, we stand and show how God works through any and all of the circumstances in our lives." Even the "messy" ones.

> **Suffering is God's tool to expose our false belief, and the mess is intended to drive us back to the only sure hope we can have.**

So, as Jon asks, where are we hanging our hope? When a doctor's diagnosis comes back, and the news is decidedly less than good, will we take the path trod by Jesus, Paul, Teresa, C. S. Lewis, and Jon Walker, or will we hang on to our aversion to suffering? Prayer for healing is more than appropriate—it is, in fact, commanded—but what if God chooses to allow a period of suffering to season our faith?

When this fallen world's thorns penetrate our lives—whether it be a malicious storm, a drunk driver, or a terrible accident—will we seek the glory behind affliction, or will we allow ourselves to be buried in our grief? Grieving is more than appropriate—it is, in fact, commanded—but we don't grieve as those who have no hope (see 1 Thessalonians 4:13).

When resistance to sin becomes painful—when we honestly think we can't survive without that drink, that relationship, that old way of coping—will we embrace the suffering, endure the spiritual torment, and remain faithful to God, or will we collapse, once again, into the soft prison of our addictions?

Authentic Faith

As dawn broke over the Polish countryside on September 1, 1939, a nineteen-year-old acolyte helped his priest celebrate Mass in the heart of Krakow. Near the altar lay a silver casket bearing the remains of Saint Stanislaw, the patron saint of Poland.

Suddenly, but not unexpectedly, air raid sirens pierced the morning air. Antiaircraft fire shot into the sky, and German bombs pummeled the city. Peace was shattered, and chaos was unleashed. Hitler's grab for Poland—and after that, the world—had begun.

The people celebrating Mass fled, eager to find more secure shelter. But the young acolyte and his priest stood their ground and finished the Mass.

It was a tailor-made proving ground for the young acolyte, who was already familiar with suffering. He had lost his mother when he was just six years old. When he was twelve, he suffered through the death of an older brother. As an acolyte, he faced German occupation of his homeland. Two years later, his father died. Following the war, the Communists took over. This latter experience was hardly an auspicious start for a religious leader who was forced to lead his people in a land ruled by atheists.

When the archbishop of Krakow position became vacant, Communist party leaders backed this young priest, assuming that his youth would work in their favor by allowing them to control him. It was a grievous error—for their purposes—as Karol Wojtyla eventually ascended to the papacy, becoming Pope John Paul II, and from there he played a major role in the fall of Communism in Poland. Soviet boss Leonid Brezhnev warned Polish leaders not to let Pope John Paul II back into Poland, but the Communist leaders thought they could control what happened.

They couldn't have been more mistaken! In a once-in-a-century nine-day tour in 1979, Wojtyla's courage and charisma all but sounded the death knell for Communism at the same time that it preserved the future of the Solidarity movement.

It would be difficult to measure the uncertainty, pain, and suffering that the future pope experienced prior to assuming leadership of the Roman Catholic Church, and yet out of this crucible of a life—a life that no one addicted to comfort would ever choose—arose the character of a man who by many accounts really should have been chosen as the man of the century.

Pope John Paul II's biographer, George Weigel, quotes G. K. Chesterton (who was commenting on Saint Thomas More), to suggest that this pope "was, above all things, historic: he represented at once a type, a turning point, and an ultimate destiny. If there had not been that particular man at that particular moment, the whole of history would have been different."[18]

I write this as a confirmed evangelical Protestant. Obviously, I have theological issues with regard to some points of Roman Catholic doctrine, but few people who read widely would ever contest the positive social influence Pope John Paul II had on human history and events in the latter half of the twentieth century.

> *We are asked to cooperate with God's Spirit to forge lives of selflessness, compassion, and love. This transformation is impossible apart from suffering.*

We come back to where we started: All of us are born as selfish, arrogant, egocentric beings. Out of this beginning, we are asked to cooperate with God's Spirit to forge lives of selflessness, compassion, and love. This transformation is impossible apart from suffering. Don't be so quick to reject the very thing that will most help you become mature.

"We also rejoice in our sufferings, because we know that suffering produces perseverance; perseverance, character; and character, hope. And hope does not disappoint us" (Romans 5:3–5).

five

Titanic Testimony

The Discipline of Persecution

Everyone who wants to live a godly life in Christ Jesus will be persecuted.
Paul, in 2 Timothy 3:12

Many decades ago, Dick Gregory, at that time a well-known civil rights activist, grew weary of having to eat at greasy-spoon restaurants and sleeping in fleabag hotels, so he decided to order a nice dinner at a Whites-only restaurant, even though, because of his color, he wasn't welcome.

Surprisingly enough, his dinner was served, but just as he picked up his silverware, three light-skinned toughs came up behind him, and the biggest one said, "Boy, whatever you do to that chicken, we're gonna do to you." Dick put down his knife and fork, picked up his chicken, and kissed it.

Throughout history, standing against injustice has required creativity and courage, because the opposition is often fierce and violent. This has been no less true of our faith. After all, Jesus' entry into the world didn't inaugurate an earthly celebration, a world-wide holiday, or a festive parade. It does that now, of course, so sometimes we forget how much evil surrounded this magnificent act of God's charity. Instead of a party, Jesus' birth elicited a heartrending bout of infanticide. Dozens of boys two years and younger were ripped from their mothers' arms and slaughtered, all in an attempt to stop Jesus' young beating heart. For weeks on end, fresh blood stained the soil outside many Judean homes. Rags that were already drenched received even more tears from brokenhearted mothers.

> *Instead of a party, Jesus' birth elicited a heartrending bout of infanticide.*

The obscene measure of Herod's hatred of the Christ child was seen in this lesser-known fact: To try to ensure that Jesus was killed, even Herod's own son was slain under his edict. This heartless act, according to Macrobius, who wrote an ancient work entitled *Saturnalia,* led Caesar Augustus to declare the famous words, "I would rather have been Herod's hog than his son."[1]

We build churches now, put up large signs, even advertise in the paper: *Here we are. Come visit us!* There was a time, however—and we often forget it—when Christians were hated, hunted, and persecuted. The same struggle exists today, taking place in countries where Christians don't dare advertise, where they must view each visitor with a watchful eye rather than invite them to a "welcome to our church" introductory class, and where copies of a pastor's sermons are kept hidden for fear that someone's life will be forfeited if they are discovered.

Has God failed these believers—or are our ideas of what we should expect as Christians radically optimistic?

In fact, persecution has been unleashed on this earth from the very beginning. Abel—only the fourth person to ever live—was killed for one reason, and only one reason: He served God well, and his older brother, Cain, didn't—a fact that made Cain jealous, who then responded by murdering his brother. If faith-based persecution could be fatal with just four people on the face of the earth, how can we expect to avoid it with a world population of over six billion?

Many others have left their martyr's mark in Scripture: Zechariah son of Berekiah (see Matthew 23:35); King Joash, who rebuilt God's temple and "did what was right in the eyes of the LORD," but who still was assassinated (see 2 Kings 12:2, 20); and Uriah, who was "struck down with a sword" for prophesying the words of God to King Jehoiakim (Jeremiah 26:23). In the New Testament we read of Jesus, John the Baptist, Stephen, James the brother of John (see Acts 12:2), and Antipas, God's "faithful witness" (Revelation 2:13). Indeed, the book of Revelation records that John saw "the souls of those who had been slain because of the word of God and the testimony they had maintained" (6:9). Even more sobering, John was told that many more were yet to follow: "They were told to wait a little longer, until the number of their fellow servants and brothers who were to be killed as they had been was completed" (6:11).

> *Are our ideas of what we should expect as Christians radically optimistic?*

Still others weren't asked to give up their lives, but were severely persecuted as a result of their righteous ways. Joseph did the right thing in refusing to sleep with his master's wife, but he was still put in jail (see Genesis 39). Elijah was obedient, and as a result he received a death threat from Queen Jezebel (see 1 Kings 19:2). Hanani was jailed for speaking God's word to King Asa (see 2 Chronicles 16:10). Ahab put Micaiah in prison for his faithful prophesying, where he was forced to subsist solely on bread and water (see 2 Chronicles 18:26). Jeremiah was severely beaten and then put in stocks (see Jeremiah 20:1–2).

If your unwavering commitment to your faith has led people to lie about you, hate you, taunt you, torment you, and even threaten to kill you, take heart: You're living in marvelously good company. The good news is this: Hatred from the world often signifies friendship with God. That's why the saints of old discovered profound meaning whenever they faced faith-based opposition.

That Hunted and Hated Man

Imagine someone who ridicules everything you hold dear, who disgusts you, who you know will one day kill you and the members of your family, who exists only to challenge everything you live for. This man is utterly loathsome, the kind of person who sets your teeth on edge.

Now imagine you were accused of being this person.

Jesus came here to win back the lost from the clutches of Satan—the one who laid claim to this world with a vengeance. Satan stands for everything God hates. He hates everything God loves. Jesus was willing to bleed and to die in order to overthrow this foe.

> **Hatred from the world often signifies friendship with God.**

Imagine, then, how terribly hideous, how utterly shocking, it must have been when Jesus heard the Pharisees say, "It is by the prince of demons that he drives out demons" (Matthew 9:34). There is no worse accusation to make against our Lord than to suggest that he was in league with his mortal enemy.

When you love someone to the point of adoration, when your heart feels an almost physical ache at the mere mention of his name, when you love to sing worship songs to him and tears come to your eyes when you consider how much he means to you, how he is *everything* to you, it can be difficult to imagine him as being hunted and hated—but that's exactly what Jesus was throughout his entire life, beginning with his birth and extending to the time of his death.

Jesus accepted this hatred as inevitable, given his message: "The world ... hates me because I testify that what it does is evil" (John 7:7). In fact, Jesus even had to face opposition from the place where it hurt the most: his own family. Just as his public ministry was getting under way, some of his brothers accused him of being "out of his mind" (Mark 3:21).

This opposition to Jesus began shortly after he started his preaching ministry—well before it culminated at the cross. Members of the synagogue thought so much of Jesus' sermonizing that they attempted to throw him off the top of a cliff (see Luke 4:29–30). Jesus accepted all this with a resigned and surrendered heart: "Shall I not drink the cup the Father has given me?" (John 18:11). He valued obedience over comfort, the fulfillment of his mission over long life.

Those Hated, Hunted Followers

From the beginning, Jesus told his followers to expect the same kind of ugly treatment that he received: "All men will hate you because of me, but he who stands firm to the end will be saved" (Matthew 10:22). He even promises that if we were to leave every city where we are hated and persecuted, we would not run out of cities before his second coming (see Matthew 10:23). Imagine that promise—there will *always* be someone who hates us; we will never run out of places where we are not welcome. You don't see that one in too many "Bible promise" books!

And that's not all. Jesus also suggests that some of us will be killed by our own relatives solely because we trust in him. "Be on your guard against men," Jesus warns. "They will hand you over to the local councils and flog you in their synagogues.... Brother will betray brother to death, and a father his child; children will rebel against their parents and have them put to death" (Matthew 10:17, 21).

It is a rare moment in history when some type of persecution hasn't been going on. Even the earliest believers—those who followed Jesus before he died—were banished from the synagogue (see John 9:22). This may not seem so severe to us now, but keep in mind, being a first-century Jew banished from the synagogue meant you were torn away from your place in your culture's very identity. You suddenly became a spiritual alien and a social orphan.

Jesus never promises us absolute protection from bodily persecution. On the contrary, he warns us to expect it: "Do not be afraid of what you are about to suffer. I tell you, the devil will put some of you in prison to test you, and you will suffer persecution for ten days. Be faithful, even to the point of death, and I will give you the crown of life" (Revelation 2:10).

When God called Saul into service, he did so with a stern warning: "I will show him how much he must suffer for my name" (Acts 9:16).

It was a lesson Paul soon learned, so that when he later wrote to the Corinthians, he confessed that he risked death *daily* (see 1 Corinthians 15:30–31). What does this mean? Simply that Paul woke up not knowing whether he would live another twenty-four hours. Surprisingly, he didn't resent this opposition; he simply acknowledged it as a matter of fact: "A great door for effective work has opened to me, and there are many who oppose me" (1 Corinthians 16:9).

> **Jesus never promises us absolute protection from bodily persecution.**

Rather than be dismayed by this lack of assurance that believers will never face pain or even death, the apostles seemed to find shelter in it. The absolutely stunning fact is Jesus' followers took their Lord's words *literally* in Matthew 5:10–12: "Blessed are those who are persecuted because of righteousness.... Rejoice and be glad." And that's exactly what the early disciples did. After they were flogged—their backs slowly and methodically ripped open with thirty-nine lashes—the disciples didn't suffer a conflict of faith. There was no moment of second-guessing ("How could a loving God let this happen to us?"). On the contrary, they actually *rejoiced* that they had "been counted worthy of suffering disgrace for the Name" (Acts 5:41). If anything, this "negative" experience renewed their faith and led them into increased worship, praise, and thanksgiving.

Acts 14 chronicles a fascinating perseverance in the midst of sheer hatred. Paul's ministry in Iconium is not distinguished by a six-week revival meeting. It doesn't result in a new set of tapes (available in a packet of twelve for just $84.99, Visa and Master-Card accepted). Residents in Iconium didn't have to build a new sanctuary or tent to hold the new converts. In fact, Paul's stay ended when he and Barnabas fled town because they were afraid of being killed.

From Iconium, the two men went to Lystra, where Paul wasn't exactly welcomed with a book signing and tea in the back of the synagogue. On the contrary, he was stoned and left for dead. Paul picked himself up and went on to Derbe.

Then, in Acts 14:21, we're told that after Paul and Barnabas preached in Derbe, *they went back to Lystra and Iconium.* You'd think they wouldn't have dared to soil their sandals with the dirt of those towns, but no—they still had work to do. The believers in those two cities were understandably shaken by the treatment Paul had received. Not wanting to leave these new believers without a firm foundation, Paul returned to the place where he was a "wanted" man (in the worst way). These faithful witnesses encouraged the believers by saying, "We must go through many hardships to enter the kingdom of God" (14:22).

Because I've been on the Christian "speaking circuit" myself, I've heard plenty of stories about how on some occasions a certain celebrity and audience just "didn't get along." Invariably, the speaker will say, "I'll never go back there again." This certainly wasn't Paul's attitude. He went back to a place where people thought they had killed him—and presumably would try to kill him again.

Later, Paul and Barnabas are commended as true disciples to the Gentiles *because* they had risked their lives for the gospel (see Acts 15:26). Paul never anticipated anything *but* opposition. He once told the Ephesian elders, "I only know that in every city the Holy Spirit warns me that prison and hardships are facing me" (Acts 20:23). This opposition never affected what Paul set out to do—he never let personal danger deter him from fulfilling his duties as an apostle. When the prophet Agabus warned Paul that if he proceeded to Jerusalem, he would be bound and handed over to the Gentiles, Paul's companions wept and pleaded with Paul to turn back, but Paul said, "Why are you weeping and breaking my heart? I am ready not only to be bound, but also to die in Jerusalem for the name of the Lord Jesus" (Acts 21:13).

A human-centered gospel has no place for the enduring of such pervasive persecution. On the contrary, a human-centered faith believes God is "obligated" to never let such a thing happen to us. It's the kind of faith displayed by the early Peter, who was corrected by our Lord, "You do not have in mind the things of God, but the things of men" (Matthew 16:23). Jesus then reminds Peter that if we are to follow him we must take up our cross daily, and if we

want to save our life, we will lose it. Though we love to spiritual-
ize "whoever wants to save his life will lose it, but whoever loses
his life for me will find it" (Matthew 16:25), in context this verse
is explicitly addressing *martyrdom*. There is nothing metaphorical
about it. In fact, the word *martyr* derives from the Greek word for
"witness"—*martys*. That this word
came to be identified with those who
died on behalf of the gospel shows the
early association of witness and death.

> **A human-centered gospel has no place for the enduring of such pervasive persecution.**

Sadly, Jesus says in Mark 4:17
that persecution will turn many followers away. If all we're expecting
from our faith is affluence and ease,
we won't last when the persecution
starts. If our daily prayer is focused on our own benefit rather than
on the work of God's church, we'll crumble like a straw house
when the weight of pain is placed on our shoulders.

Because the early Christians expected opposition, persecution
strengthened them rather than weakened them. At least, that's what
happened to the Philippians. "Because of my chains," Paul writes,
"most of the brothers in the Lord have been encouraged to speak the
word of God more courageously and fearlessly" (Philippians 1:14).
Indeed, Paul talks about this aspect of the faith as a tremendous privilege: "For it has been granted to you on behalf of Christ not only
to believe on him, but also to suffer for him" (Philippians 1:29).

Rather than run from this truth, we are to accept it as a call to
intimacy, knowing that we are called to somehow "share" in
Christ's sufferings. Jesus told his disciples, "If the world hates you,
keep in mind that it hated me first. If you belonged to the world, it
would love you as its own. As it is, you do not belong to the world,
but I have chosen you out of the world. That is why the world hates
you. . . . If they persecuted me, they will persecute you also" (John
15:18–20). The irony is that people will persecute and even kill us,
thinking they are doing God a favor (see John 16:2). "I have told
you this," Jesus says, "so that when the time comes you will remember that I warned you" (John 16:4).

What can we say, then? As we serve God, we will be called many disgusting names. When we act out of love, we may be accused of hatred. When we proclaim a message of joyful life in Christ, we will sometimes be blasted with the charge of intolerance. When we seek to spread a message of salvation, we will occasionally be condemned. But lest any of us become tempted to pity our plight, let us remember that none of us will ever be more maligned or slandered than was our Lord. Regardless of what you are

> *Let us remember that none of us will ever be more maligned or slandered than was our Lord.*

called or how much your motives are mischaracterized, the injustice done to you will never equal what the Pharisees perpetrated on Christ, who was identified as being in league with his worst enemy.

Expect opposition. Expect to be ridiculed. Expect to have your good motives questioned. Assume that you will be called everything you find repugnant. Remember: Satan is the father of lies. His followers will not hesitate to unleash any charge, however baseless, if in doing so they can frustrate a work of God.

The Long Parade

I don't know how many lectures I attended at Regent College in Vancouver, British Columbia, but there are a few I'll never forget. Among them was the one Don Lewis gave as he surveyed a terrible but glorious time in church history when martyrs fell like branches in a storm. This was clearly no mere academic exercise to my professor. Dr. Lewis barely managed to complete the lecture, finally uttering Tertullian's famous phrase with an emotion-packed quiver, "The blood of the martyrs is the seed of the church."

Dr. Lewis left the room immediately, the only time I ever remember him not sticking around for questions.

Although many Christians today assume that faith will lead to affluence, blessing, and ease, the early church lived with the belief that holding to the faith could end your life well before your natural life span. Tradition tells us that every apostle except for John died a martyr's death.[2] Thomas, it is said, was slain with a dart. Simon, the brother of Jude, was crucified in an Egyptian city. Peter was crucified upside down (he considered himself unworthy to face death in the same manner as his Lord). Mark died in flames, while Bartholomew was beaten with sticks, crucified, and then beheaded (they must have *really* wanted him dead!). Andrew was crucified, which tradition says he welcomed, saying, "I would not have preached the honor and glory of the cross, if I had feared the death of the cross." Philip was crucified and stoned to death. James was stoned by a mob, and then finally felled with a severe blow to the head. Paul was likely beheaded under Nero.

> *The early church lived with the belief that holding to the faith could end your life well before your natural life span.*

The early church lived with these stories. These traditions shaped their expectation of what faith in God entails. In fact, an early church father, Jerome, said, "There is no day in the whole year unto which the number of five thousand martyrs cannot be ascribed, except only the first day of January."[3] Subsequent persecutions have removed January 1 from this honor!

Nor were these deaths "easy" deaths. Foxe writes, "Whatsoever the cruelness of man's invention could devise for the punishment of man's body, was practiced against the Christians—stripes and scourgings, drawings, tearings, stonings, plates of iron laid unto them burning hot, deep dungeons, racks, strangling in prisons, the teeth of wild beasts, gridirons, gibbets and gallows, tossing upon the horns of bulls." And yet, Foxe points out, "Notwithstanding all these continual persecutions and horrible punishments, the Church daily increased ... watered plenteously with the blood of saints."[4]

At certain stages in the church's history, martyrdom was so glorified that church authorities began to establish rules to prevent their members from frivolously throwing their lives away. In fact, Origen, an early church father, lived to be an adult only because his mother hid his clothes when he was a teen to prevent him from going outside to seek his martyrs' crown! Origin's early enthusiasm was based on a misunderstanding of Jesus' words in Matthew 16:24–26, giving a "salvific" effect to martyrdom—as though our souls could be saved on that basis alone.

The Letter to Diognetus (A.D. 150–200) described the early patterns of this curious group of people who were called Christians:

> Christians love all men, but all men persecute them. Condemned because they are not understood, they are put to death, but raised to life again. They live in poverty, but enrich many; they are totally destitute, but possess an abundance of everything. They suffer dishonor, but that is their glory. They are defamed, but vindicated. A blessing is their answer to abuse, deference their response to insult. For the good they do they receive the punishment of malefactors, but even then they rejoice, as though receiving the gift of life. They are attacked by the Jews as aliens, they are persecuted by the Greeks, yet no one can explain the reason for this hatred.
>
> To speak in general terms, we may say that the Christian is to the world what the soul is to the body.... The body hates the soul and wars against it, not because of any injury the soul has done it, but because of the restriction the soul places on its pleasures. Similarly, the world hates the Christians, not because they have done it any wrong, but because they are opposed to its enjoyments.
>
> Christians love those who hate them, just as the soul loves the body and all its members despite the body's hatred. It is by the soul, enclosed within the body, that the body is held together, and similarly, it is by the Christians, detained in the world as in a prison, that the world is held together. The soul, though immortal, has a mortal dwelling place; and Christians also live for a time amidst perishable things, while awaiting the freedom from change and decay that will be theirs in heaven. As the soul benefits from the deprivation of food and drink, so Christians flourish under persecution. Such is the Christian's lofty and divinely appointed function, from which he is not permitted to excuse himself.

We can and should be thankful that, for many of us living in more tolerant societies, Christians are not being put to death

> *Martyrdom is the ultimate statement that we are living for another world.*

(although there are many places around the world where this persecution continues unabated today).[5] But I hope that the legacy passed down by these women and men who were faithful even unto death will shape our own expectations about what faith in God entails. Martyrdom is the ultimate statement that we are living for another world. It is accepting the most severe earthly punishment possible in anticipation of receiving a glorious heavenly reward.

At the very least, we should be prepared and not caught by surprise if the social climate changes. In fact, it is clear that many storm clouds are approaching even now.

storm clouds

Perhaps I'm wrong, but I think a social watershed event occurred in 1998 when a young man named Matthew Shepard was murdered on the outskirts of a Wyoming city. Because Matthew was gay, the murder was labeled a "hate crime" and became a national fixation for several weeks, but that's not why I think it was a watershed event. Apart from the tragic loss of Matthew's life, the *social* significance of this murder can be found in the media's response.

A national reporter actually suggested that perhaps Christians such as James Dobson (he was mentioned by name) were at least somewhat responsible for Matthew's death. Dr. Dobson had publicly opposed political measures designed to give homosexual activists special rights while at the same time supporting political measures that denied affirmative action-like provisions based on sexual orientation. In the minds of some, this created a "climate of hate" that indirectly—if not directly—contributed to this murder.

For those of us who have listened to Dobson and derived great benefit from his books and video series, we see him as the type of man who, if he had been driving by during the incident, would have stopped his car and done all he could to prevent Matthew's murder (without asking questions about Matthew's sexual orientation). If there is a man I would trust with my wife, my daughters, and my son, it is certainly Dr. Dobson. The idea that he would in any way incite or condone murder is a vicious lie. It sounds ridiculous, until you realize that others took the charge seriously.

For me, the vicious and hate-filled backlash marked the possibility that we could once again face a society not unlike first-century Rome, which blamed Christians for social ills as an excuse totorture and exterminate them. Historically, it is only a small step from the time blame is cast and seriously debated until "punishment" is levied. The fact that presumably intelligent people debated Focus on the Family's culpability in a murder means that our culture has crossed a line; open season on Christians may not be far behind. In fact, these allegations made me wonder if we haven't arrived at the time foretold by Hosea: "Because your sins are so many and your hostility so great, the prophet is considered a fool, the inspired man a maniac" (Hosea 9:7).

> *Historically, it is only a small step from the time blame is cast and seriously debated until "punishment" is levied.*

The trend continued as I wrote this book. It's not my intention to sow political seeds in this book, but I think it's important to show that this growing hostility is not limited to a onetime media reaction; it has reached the highest levels. In December of 1999, a White House spokesman was asked about a Southern Baptist program designed to evangelize Jews, Muslims, and Hindus. The Southern Baptists were prepared to do what every Christian church is called to do—share the good news of the gospel. But in this day and age, that aim is seen by some as hateful. President Bill Clinton's spokesman declared this:

> I think the president has made very clear . . . how one of the greatest challenges going into the next century is dealing with intolerance, dealing with ethnic and religious hatred, and coming to grips with the long-held resentments between religions. So I think he's been very clear in his opposition to whatever organizations, including the Southern Baptists, that perpetuate ancient religious hatred.[6]

Did you catch that? The then president of the United States—himself a professing Christian—labeling the work of evangelism as "perpetuating ancient religious hatred."

Nor was it just a political leader who voiced his opposition. The Council of Religious Leaders of Metropolitan Chicago sent a letter to Southern Baptist Convention president Paige Patterson asking him to call off the evangelistic effort because it might "contribute to a climate conducive to hate crimes."[7]

At the risk of sounding pessimistic, I believe it's only a matter of time until this tinderbox explodes. Not only are we not allowed to speak out against sexual activities clearly denounced in Scripture, but now even sharing the gospel message that salvation is found solely in Jesus Christ is considered a hostile, hate-filled act—one that was publicly denounced from the White House.

We shouldn't act as though this is something new, however. Evangelism has never been particularly popular. Half a century ago, C. S. Lewis faced great hostility when he openly shared his faith at Oxford. His biographer, George Sayer, makes this observation:

> For many years, Christians had been passively on the defensive. You might encounter a man frequently without ever knowing that he was a Christian. It was unlikely that, in ordinary conversation, he would uphold Christian principles and almost unheard-of that he would make a vigorous, logical attack on nonbelievers from a Christian standpoint. Skepticism, tolerance, and even indifference were commonly thought to be the proper attitude toward Christianity. But, for the time being, Jack changed all that. He expressed his views, not only at the Socratic Club, but also at dinner and in the Senior Common Room afterward. This policy made him many enemies.
>
> Although he had transgressed an unwritten code, he persisted in behaving in a way that was intolerable and incorrect by the standards of Oxford society.... Jack's colleagues ... most especially could not forgive the fact that the man was serious in wanting to convert others.[8]

There is no getting around this truth: People hated Jesus, and they will hate us for preaching Jesus Christ. This is hard for some of us to believe. As I said before, the mere mention of Jesus' name can make our hearts melt; but for others, any mention of Jesus sets their teeth on edge and brings the taste of bile to their mouths.

In actuality, there is no escaping this hatred and resentment. Biblical truth is hard for a people pleaser like me. After I'm done talking, I love it when people affirm what I've said. But Jesus warned, "Woe to you when all men speak well of you, for that is how their fathers treated the false prophets" (Luke 6:26).

> **People hated Jesus, and they will hate us for preaching Jesus Christ.**

I was once asked to speak to a public high school class that was studying comparative religions. The teacher had brought in people of other faiths, and I was invited to speak as an evangelical Christian. I knew the question that would come up, and it did: "Why do you believe that only Christians go to heaven? How can Jesus be the *only* way?"

I used C. S. Lewis's own "Lord, liar, or lunatic" illustration, and then explained that ultimately, the judgment God makes on each individual is God's alone, and none of us should be so prideful as to casually assume we know someone else's destiny. However, according to the New Testament and the claims of Jesus Christ, the only way we can be *sure* someone has experienced salvation is by that person's confession of trust in God's Son, Jesus.

Afterwards, a mother told me how much her son appreciated what I had to share. Her son told her, "He answered tough questions in a way that people really couldn't refute," but then the mother admitted that one of her son's friends had said, "He's the kind of Christian I hate—the one who thinks everybody else is going to hell."

It's never easy to hear that anyone, even an adolescent, "hates" you, but there's really no getting around it. Lewis was hated for trying to convert others at Oxford, and we'll be hated for proclaiming the gospel at work, in schools, and in public settings. If we preach only to be patted on the back, our message will change with the times. As we enter a climate that is radically more wary and even, perhaps, hateful toward the gospel message, it is more important than ever to count the cost, lest our message be compromised.

friendly fire

One of the great ironics in the first century was that both Jesus and Paul were attacked *by the believing community of faith* for what were essentially religious arguments—in Jesus' case, that he was the Messiah; in Paul's case, for reaching out to the Gentiles (see Acts 22:21–22). In both instances, the secular authorities tried to save these men, but the so-called people of God warred against them!

> **Persecution comes to people who are gentle, as well as to those who are harsh.**

This is what we might call "friendly fire." People within the believing community will often say that those who are being persecuted "brought it on themselves," using the person's suffering to whittle away at his or her market share of influence. But the Bible teaches that persecution comes to people who are gentle and tolerant, as well as to those who are harsh and demanding. Jesus pointed this out when he said, "For John the Baptist came neither eating bread nor drinking wine, and you say, 'He has a demon.' The Son of Man came eating and drinking, and you say, 'Here is a glutton and a drunkard, a friend of tax collectors and "sinners"'" (Luke 7:33–34).

This same "friendly fire" is being lobbed at Christians today. I've had the privilege of working on two books with singer and composer Michael W. Smith. Michael has an enthusiastic heart and is the type of guy who makes you feel like a close friend just minutes after you meet him. After ten years as one of the best-selling Christian music artists in the industry, Michael released *The First Decade* album, a collection of previous top hits along with two new singles, "Kentucky Rose" and "Do You Dream of Me?"

Just after the CD was released, Michael was headed to his family's vacation home for some much-needed time off when Jennifer Cook, a vice president at his management company, called to let him know of a "little problem" with "Kentucky Rose."

"Kentucky Rose" is a fictional account of a respected preacher and farmer who lived in a tiny town in the foothills of Kentucky and who dies while saving a boy's life. Michael wrote the music and knew the words "Kentucky Rose" had to be in there, and Wayne Kirkpatrick filled out the rest of the story. The song ends with a poetic touch:

Now, on that hill one flower grows
They say it is the spirit of Kentucky Rose.

Keep in mind, this is one line, out of one song, on an album that signifies a decade's worth of writing and composing. Christians have been inspired and challenged by Michael's music for almost an entire generation—some worship songs, such as "Great Is the Lord" and "Agnus Dei," have become miniclassics—but these sixteen words created a firestorm of backlash.

One man read these lyrics and began faxing Christian radio stations all across the country, accusing Michael of going "New Age" for poetically referring to "the spirit of Kentucky Rose." The man never approached Michael about the true meaning of the words. He pretty much read them, passed judgment, and did his best to execute the sentence as soon as possible. At least he was creative, telling station executives, "There's a thorn in Kentucky Rose."

It's impossible to draw direct correlations, but the fact is, Christians can get very nervous when even ridiculous accusations are made. "Kentucky Rose" had by far the least successful radio-play of any single Michael has ever released.

What seems so unfair is that a man's entire career meant nothing to this critic in the face of sixteen words that could be interpreted in various ways. Michael has written some of the most moving worship songs in our day; his music has clearly been orthodox and affirmed by the widespread Christian church, but one line that wouldn't even make a heretic smile launched an all-out attack on his reputation and motives.

There are people who are determined to serve God, and there are people who live for nothing else than to attack people who serve God. If you speak out above a whisper, it's virtually guaranteed that someone will attack you with a shout.

Thankfully, Michael didn't waste time on this assault. Instead, he poured his energies into the next project and was soon blessed

> **If persecution is guaranteed to come, how should we face it?**

by a wildly successful year. His *Live the Life* album was enormously successful, and his subsequent album, *This Is Your Time,* became the all-time best-selling Christian record in first-week sales.

Sometimes, of course, Christians do bring persecution on themselves because of stupidity rather than because of their faith. Arrogant leaders can evoke great opposition, and in their pride they assume they are being persecuted when, in fact, they are being called to account. I've seen street preachers come through college campuses armed with arrogance rather than humility. Their message was based in hatred rather than in love, and the abuse they received was due not to their message as much as it was to their conduct, methods, and attitude.

But I've also watched godly, humble, and committed women and men be laughed at and ridiculed. Michael's story raises an important question: If persecution is guaranteed to come, how should we face it? What should be our response?

Attitude toward persecutors

One of the extraordinary things about the Gospels is that they do not condemn the executioners of Jesus.[9] There is no biblical record of vehement invective against Judas, Pilate, or any of the Jewish people who sought Jesus' death. There is no "enemy language," no calls for armed resistance. Though anti-Semitism certainly reared its ugly head later in church history, that type of thinking is foreign to the biblical record.

This is an important lesson to learn, for as Pascal ably warns us, "We never do evil so fully and cheerfully as when we do it out of conscience."[10] Jesus never allows the persecuted to become the persecutors. Self-righteousness is a deadly anesthetic that can deaden our conscience to the ugliness of our actions and attitudes.

Indeed, in one of Scripture's most amazing passages, Jesus actually calls the betraying Judas "friend"—even when Judas is in the very act of betrayal (see Matthew 26:50). Pascal explains why: "Jesus disregards the enmity of Judas, and sees only in him God's will, which he loves; so much so that he calls him friend."[11]

This is an attitude the apostles worked hard to emulate. Paul exhorted the Roman believers, "Bless those who persecute you; bless and do not curse" (Romans 12:14). Peter tells us to follow Jesus' example: "When they hurled their insults at him, he did not retaliate; when he suffered, he made no threats. Instead, he entrusted himself to him who judges justly" (1 Peter 2:23). Instead of reacting in surprise when we are persecuted, we've been given instructions for what to do: According to Jesus, we are to pray for our persecutors! (see Matthew 5:44; see also 1 Peter 3:9).

> *Self-righteousness is a deadly anesthetic that can deaden our conscience to the ugliness of our actions and attitudes.*

If we don't expect persecution, our natural inclination will be to respond with hatred and revenge. But when we've been warned—as we now have—we can pray that God would unleash his love through us, so that we can apply Jesus' words to love even our enemies.

I had a chance to practice this during the hearings on the nomination of John Ashcroft for United States attorney general. Because I had written a book with John, a Washington, D.C.-based reporter called me for some comments.[12] At the time, I was grieving over how a friend of mine, whom I know to be a man of integrity, deep faith, strong intellect, and impeccable character, was being maligned and mistreated by so many members of the media.

Immediately, I was on my guard. My first goal was to not say anything that could possibly be misconstrued. I spoke honestly, but I spoke very positively. Then the reporter baited me. There's a section in John's book where he talks about asking his father to anoint him before he was sworn in as Missouri governor and then as a United States senator. This is not a "freaky" practice—it has ample precedence in both Jewish and Christian circles, and the anointing John talks about is merely being touched on the head in a spirit of prayer with any available oil. Well, the reporter mentioned that John was being ridiculed for these "Crisco parties."

I was angry—at people's ignorance, arrogance, and antifaith bias. I was also sad that they would ridicule a humble man who, upon being elected to a very powerful position, simply wanted to acknowledge his need of God's guidance and assistance. To them, all this was mere sport, something to make fun of and to mock.

> We can pray that God would unleash his love through us, so that we can apply Jesus' words to love even our enemies.

"Hello!" the reporter interrupted my thoughts. "Are you still there? What do you say to that?"

"They're going to say what they're going to say," I offered—which seemed to me at the time (and still does) a pretty weak reply, but to be honest, I didn't trust myself to say anything more. I chose the way of silence, remembering that even when a man of integrity is being taken apart, it is our duty to, as Peter says, "not retaliate."

The only way we can learn to do this is to adopt Peter's description of Jesus' attitude, as Jesus entrusted each attack to "him who judges justly" (1 Peter 2:23). Wayne Grudem—one of my favorite commentators—has written, "This knowledge that God will ultimately right all wrongs is essential to a Christian response to suffering."[13] This is not a vindictive "You'll get yours!" because in fact, those who attack us can be forgiven if they turn to Jesus Christ and receive his substitutionary sacrifice. Grudem points out that the imperfect tense in this passage implies repeated action in the past—that is, Jesus "kept entrusting."[14] It's neither venting nor suppressing our anger, but rather "repeatedly and continually committing the situation into God's hands."[15] We seek shelter in the fact that, one way or another, God will set everything right.

Personally, I take great satisfaction whenever I sing a worship song that quotes the biblical truth, "Every knee will bow, and every tongue confess . . ." Ultimately, the day will come when God is proven right and when faith in Jesus is rewarded. I don't have to be insecure about defending either my own belief or God's claim to our allegiance. Instead, I can humbly, but without apology, present the truth declared in the gospel, and people will respond as they will.

giving a Titanic Testimony

Imagine this: You're a student, or an employee standing around the teaming table, who thinks of yourself as reasonably intelligent and thoughtful. During a group discussion, the question comes up, "Do you *really* believe that everyone came from Adam and Eve? You don't honestly think there's a heaven and hell, do you? You can't be serious, right?"

> **Will we rejoice that we have been counted worthy to suffer for his name?**

When your heart starts pounding and your palms start sweating, will you choose to stand with your Lord, the apostles, and two thousand years' worth of faithful witnesses, or will you sell your soul in a vain attempt to impress one cynic and to spare yourself a little mocking laughter?

When a family member or employer gives you an ultimatum—shut up, or be cut off—will you rest in eternal glory, or grasp at earthly comfort? I'm not talking about being obnoxious, but just as C. S. Lewis was resented for being a persuasive witness, we can expect that we, too, will be resented. And sometimes we'll have to pay the price.

Most difficult of all, let's say a fellow believer mocks you, lies about you, and seems obsessed with destroying your reputation. For the sake of your ministry, you may need to set matters right and speak the truth[16]—but internally, how will you respond? Will you keep entrusting the matter to God's judgment, or will you lower yourself to that person's level, retaliating with an equal vengeance?

Finally, when persecution does come—as it surely will—what attitude toward God will we adopt? Will we rejoice that we have been counted worthy to suffer for his name? Or will we resent God and accuse him of not protecting us?

Authentic Faith

C. S. Lewis calls it "a literary and spiritual masterpiece." John Owen, the man who systematized Calvinism, calls it a "masterpiece of Christian devotion." Patrick Henry hailed it as a "veritable

Christian classic." Charles Spurgeon read it more than a hundred times, and D. L. Moody frequently used it to get primed for his famous evangelistic services.[17]

I'm speaking, of course, about the great Christian classic *Pilgrim's Progress*. Although John Bunyan is now revered the world over for his momentous work, his writings were far from appreciated in his own day. Following the restoration of the monarchy, religious practice was restricted to state-sponsored churches. Rightly understanding that when the gospel is well preached it carries enormous political and social ramifications, government authorities were determined to stamp out "unlicensed" or "unauthorized" preaching.

Bunyan was not ordained, and he paid dearly for his decision to continue proclaiming the gospel in his small, nonconforming church. He was arrested so many times that, for the first twenty years of his marriage to Elizabeth (his second wife), he spent less than three years actually living at home. Elizabeth was no less a saint, for in those days family members were solely responsible to meet the food and clothing needs of jailed relatives. Not only did Elizabeth care for John's children from his previous marriage, but she had to make regular trips to prison to care for John's personal needs.

Pilgrim's Progress, the work that has inspired, challenged, and instructed so many generations of Christians, was conceived and partially written during a six-month confinement in 1675, after Parliament had issued the Test Act. The story of Christian so closely mirrors that of Bunyan that it almost seems autobiographical. In their book *Best Friends,* George and Karen Grant describe it this way:

> Despite the fact that he was helped from time to time by a whole host of heroic characters such as Evangelist, Faithful, Good-will, Hopeful, Knowledge, Experience, Watchful, and Sincere, the hapless pilgrim had to struggle through one difficulty or distraction after another. Again and again he was forced to decide between compromise or faithfulness, between accommodation with the world or holy perseverance, between the wide way to destruction or the narrow road to glory.[18]

Today, in the center of Bedford, England, stands a statue of Bunyan that marks the place where he was imprisoned for so many years.

What is even more extraordinary than the statue, however, is the little bronze plaque at its foot, on which are engraved the words of Bunyan's prosecutor, spoken when John was sentenced in 1673: "At last we are done with this tinker and his cause. Never more will he plague us: for his name, locked away as surely as he, shall be

> *Enduring persecution creates a titanic testimony, a vibrant marker, of an authentic faith.*

forgotten, as surely as he. Done we are, and all eternity with him."[19]

The man couldn't have been more mistaken. Bunyan's reputation has only grown, while this prosecutor's name has fallen out of history. He remains, as the Grants point out, "unnamed and unremembered."

As I read this account, I thought of Tertullian's famous phrase, "The blood of the martyrs is the seed of the church." So many times throughout history, governments and church authorities seek to wield the final, silencing blow, only to realize that their efforts are simply planting the seeds for a new harvest.

Jesus described this as the ultimate love: "Greater love has no one than this, that he lay down his life for his friends" (John 15:13). Enduring persecution creates a titanic testimony, a vibrant marker, of an authentic faith. The shots—either verbal, financial, emotional, relational, or literal—will come. Some will bounce off us. Others will wound us. A few might cripple us, and the rare bullet may even kill us, but through it all, Jesus tells us this: "Love your enemies and pray for those who persecute you, that you may be sons of your Father in heaven" (Matthew 5:44–45).

sIX

тhe people
of god's нearт

The Discipline of Social Mercy

"He defended the cause of the poor and needy, and so all went well.
Is that not what it means to know me?" declares the LORD.

Jeremiah 22:16

In the early 1970s, few places on this earth were marked by more
human misery than Calcutta, India. Franklin Graham, now president of Samaritan's Purse, once told me about his first visit there.

Though Franklin has been in some of the world's most violent
places—Lebanon, Somalia, Kosovo—Calcutta may have been the
most difficult, the type of place that makes you want to leave as
soon as you set foot on its soil. Calcutta may not have been as violent as the other places Franklin has been to, but its abject poverty
was just as deadly. Every morning a truck went through the streets,
gathering the corpses of people who had died the night before. The
bodies were stacked like cords of wood and then taken to the outskirts of town and burned. As Franklin recounts it:

> It's a ghastly sight to watch those bodies burn. As soon as the stiffened corpses hit the flames, the muscles, sinews, and tendons contract, many times grotesquely lifting the bodies into a sitting position, as if the dead were rising in front of you. The flames begin licking and then blackening the corpses' skinny limbs. The fire consumes the hair first, then collapses the skin, until the body falls back over. It was a chilling sight.[1]

Franklin knew he was in a place where hygiene was an afterthought when he saw one man urinating in the gutter; half a block away, downstream, another man was using the "water" in that same gutter to brush his teeth.

Franklin was traveling with Bob Pierce, founder of World Vision and Samaritan's Purse. They stopped off to visit Mother Teresa, an Albanian-born nun who left her home to live and work in the slums of Calcutta.

I want you to place yourself in Mother Teresa's position. You're being visited by Bob Pierce, who founded World Vision, one of the most influential Christian development and relief ministries in the history of Christianity. Along with him is Franklin Graham, who would one day become head of Samaritan's Purse but who even at that time, as the son of Billy Graham, represented the doorway to millions of dollars' worth of aid. When you run a charity dependent on others' good favor, you need money to continue your work, and here were two of the most influential gatekeepers in the world.

Yet when Franklin and Bob stopped in to announce their arrival, one of the sisters returned to say that Mother Teresa would be happy to greet them just as soon as the dying man she was caring for had breathed his last breath.

Today, nobody knows who the dying man was. His name has been forgotten, lost among the thousands of seemingly insignificant casualties that took place every day in Calcutta. Yet for a few hours, that man was more important to Mother Teresa than two men representing some of the biggest religious influences from the United States.

Throughout history, an authentic faith has been marked by a compassionate response toward those the world tends to forget. Whether these persons are poor, imprisoned, disabled, sick, or mentally challenged, we are called to dignify them by caring about their condition and, whenever possible, reaching out to them on God's behalf.

A Different Nation

God's vision for Israel is stunning. The society he regulated through Moses was never fully lived out, but the promising ideal should challenge all of us to this day. There's no mistaking Moses' forcefulness: "There should be no poor among you" (Deuteronomy 15:4).

Because he understood reality, however, Moses went on to regulate how the poor should be treated so that they needn't *stay* poor.

> If there is a poor man among your brothers in any of the towns of the land that the LORD your God is giving you, do not be hardhearted or tightfisted toward your poor brother. Rather be openhanded and freely lend him whatever he needs. . . . Give generously to him and do so without a grudging heart; then because of this the LORD your God will bless you in all your work and in everything you put your hand to. There will always be poor people in the land. Therefore I command you to be openhanded toward your brothers and toward the poor and needy in your land.
>
> DEUTERONOMY 15:7–8, 10–11

The Bible is replete with verses calling us to reach out to the disenfranchised in our society. Deuteronomy tells us that God defends the cause of the orphan, widow, and alien (see Deuteronomy 10:18). A portion of the Israelites' tithes was to be set aside for these three groups (see Deuteronomy 14:28–29). We are told to take an *active* role in defending the cause of the poor: "Speak up for those who cannot speak for themselves, for the rights of all who are destitute. Speak up and judge fairly; defend the rights of the poor and needy" (Proverbs 31:8–9). This means our spiritual obligation isn't fulfilled simply by *not doing harm*, but only by *actively getting involved* to confront and challenge injustice.

> **Throughout history, an authentic faith has been marked by a compassionate response toward those the world tends to forget.**

Even business dealings were to take the poor into consideration. Leviticus 23:22 tells the Israelites not to reap the edges of their fields but to leave those for the poor and for the alien. The Israelites were ordered not to return refugee slaves (see Deuteronomy 23:15) and were told they would be "cursed" if they withheld justice from the alien, the fatherless, or the widow (see Deuteronomy 27:19). Ezekiel forbids the practice of lending money at excessive interest (see Ezekiel 18:8).

> *Religious duty apart from concern for the poor is entirely unacceptable in God's mind.*

Early on, the Old Testament connects our spirituality with our works of kindness. According to the biblical record, a truly spiritual person is a truly caring person. The book of Proverbs suggests that God's willingness to hear our prayers is contingent on our willingness to hear the cry of the poor (see Proverbs 21:13). If we stop up our ears to the cry of the poor, God stops his ears to our own prayers of petition.

Solomon tells us that "he who oppresses the poor shows contempt for their Maker, but whoever is kind to the needy honors God" (Proverbs 14:31). In other words, our *attitude* toward God is defined by our *actions* toward the less fortunate.

Religious duty apart from concern for the poor is entirely unacceptable in God's mind. We can have perfect church attendance, set records for fasting, have the longest quiet times, listen to the most sermons and praise tapes of anyone in our circle of friends, and avoid scandalous sin, but if we are missing this part of our religious obligation, namely, social mercy, we are missing God entirely:

> *Is not this the kind of fasting I have chosen:*
> *to loose the chains of injustice*
> *   and untie the cords of the yoke,*
> *to set the oppressed free*
> *   and break every yoke?*
> *Is it not to share your food with the hungry*
> *   and to provide the poor wanderer with shelter—*
> *when you see the naked, to clothe him,*
> *   and not to turn away from your own flesh and blood?*
> *Then your light will break forth like the dawn.*
>
> ISAIAH 58:6–8

In God's own words concerning King Josiah, authentic faith is looking out for the least: "'He defended the cause of the poor and needy, and so all went well. *Is that not what it means to know me?'* declares the LORD" (Jeremiah 22:16, emphasis added). Righteousness always has a social justice element: "Renounce your sins by doing what is right, and your wickedness by being kind to the oppressed" (Daniel 4:27).

Given this biblical witness, I was somewhat astonished to hear the story of Gene and Helen Tabor.[2] The Tabors traveled to the Philippines with a Christian evangelistic ministry and started helping Filipinos develop small, self-supporting farming and business operations. Gene thought it was important to minister to economic needs as well as spiritual ones, but apparently his mission organization didn't agree, saying that Tabor was "wasting valuable time" that could be spent evangelizing. Tabor was given what seems to me an absurd ultimatum: Quit helping the poor, or quit the "Christian" organization.

Tabor sided with hundreds of years' worth of authentic faith, quit the organization, and started his own work, now called REACH Ministries. Twenty-five years later, REACH has helped give birth to twenty thousand new Christians in twenty-one locations throughout the Philippines, India, and Hong Kong. This astonishing record of evangelism has been buttressed by social efforts. The Tabors have targeted the academic community by offering scholarships in tandem with discipleship programs.

> **We must beware of the warped spirituality that separates "the spiritual life" from our life of caring for others.**

They also offer small loans to help the very poor begin home-based businesses. Apparently, we don't have to choose between social mercy and evangelism. The two can be, and are, complementary.

We must beware of the warped spirituality that separates "the spiritual life" from our life of caring for others. In a self-based Christianity, faith is almost entirely about how we learn to overcome our sins, grow in the spiritual disciplines, and build healthier, happier families. These are all wonderful things, but authentic faith urges us to take our newfound victory over temptation, our strong character forged by practicing the disciplines, and the stability offered by having a strong family, and then *put them to use* by reaching out to those who need God's love the most.

This others-focused faith is not a new teaching. It is the model that our Lord himself taught and practiced.

messiah's methods — and message

When Jesus stood up in the synagogue and read a Messianic passage from Isaiah, proclaiming that this Scripture was fulfilled in their hearing, he read a passage (Isaiah 61:1–2) that focuses on the socially challenged. The Messiah was sent, Jesus read, to preach to *the poor.* He came to proclaim freedom for *prisoners,* restore the sight of *the blind,* and to release *the oppressed* (see Luke 4:16–21).

It wasn't just the miracles that marked Jesus as the Messiah; it was also his care for the most unfortunate. At least, that's the "evidence" he provided John the Baptist's disciples when they came to ask Jesus if he was really the Messiah. Jesus' answer is intriguing. Notice the objects of his outreach: "Go back and report to John what you hear and see: The *blind* receive sight, the *lame* walk, *those who have leprosy* are cured, the *deaf* hear, the *dead* are raised, and the good news is preached to the *poor*" (Matthew 11:4–5, emphasis added).

Jesus' ministry was focused intensely on the disenfranchised, the down-and-out, the leftovers of society. These are the groups Jesus reached out to, the very groups he says validate his ministry as the Messiah.

Many of us think of holiness in terms of what we *don't* do; it's been an issue throughout history, going right back to the Pharisees. Jesus taught a positive ethic—what matters most, he said, is what we *do* do. When one of the Pharisees judged Jesus for not washing before a meal—a ceremonial

> *Jesus' ministry was focused intensely on the disenfranchised, the down-and-out, the leftovers of society.*

concern, at best—Jesus lifted holiness to a new level: "Give what is inside the dish to the poor, and everything will be clean for you" (Luke 11:41).

Those of us who live in affluent societies may find it hard to take seriously the truly radical nature of Jesus' teaching, but I'd urge us to consider, at least as it comes to expression in one community, the priorities that often mark our lives.

If you walk through the wealthier sections of Los Angeles, two things mark the prosperity: dogs and domestics. Rosa Diaz came to the United States from El Salvador, at the time I write this, less than a year ago. As a housekeeper, Rosa is struggling with her humble situation. "It's still very strange that I'm doing a job like this," the well-educated young woman told reporter Doug Saunders. "I once thought that I would end up having a domestic worker, but now I am one."

In addition to following Rosa the domestic, Doug also followed Custer, a Los Angeles dog owned by a successful Hollywood screenwriter. The comparisons are astonishing.

Rosa's salary is such that she can afford just $50 a week toward rent, so she shares a small two-room apartment with three other adult women. Custer was staying at Canyon View Ranch, "a canine spa, boarding retreat and training center that advertises itself as a 'country club for dogs.'" This pet luxury comes at a steep price: Custer's owners pay $70 a day or $490 a week for the privilege— almost ten times the cost of what Rosa pays for her lodgings. Custer's owner explains, "It costs a little more, but it means that when we go away we can truly have a vacation without guilt. Just ask the dogs—you can tell how excited they are when they come here."

Rosa gets $225 a week to work from dawn until late evening. Some domestics get paid more, of course. A few of the "lucky" ones get $450 or even $500, but Rosa also knows of some who start out at $80 to $100. Compare this to your average dog walker in Los Angeles, who is typically paid about $200 a week.

Rosa's tight salary allows her to spend about $50 a week on groceries. Custer eats pretty well. Though the "standard" Canyon View Ranch meal contains lamb and rice, most owners leave special instructions. A Canyon View worker explains: "We get every kind of special food request you can imagine, and then some. We get vegetarian diets, and raw foods, and we get up to six supplements at a time that have to be crushed and mixed up and blended. And some people want the food heated up." Several owners also ask for "dog gravy" to be poured over the top of their dog's dinner.

Custer's owner explains, "The joy of golden retrievers is their wonderful personalities, but the downside is that they are known for their sensitive stomachs. We have [Custer] on a special diet, and it costs us a pretty penny."

Custer is treated to a monthly $40 shampoo; Rosa makes do with a bottle purchased at a drugstore. Los Angeles dog owners typically pay $100 a month in vet fees, even for healthy dogs. Rosa's salary doesn't include any insurance, medical, or dental coverage. Custer gets to ride in a car or limo; Rosa rides to work on the city bus.

Saunders ends his article with a report of the *Los Angeles Times* coverage of the trial of a California man charged with killing a woman's small white dog in an act of road rage. In the aftermath local residents were furious, and they raised $175,000 to find the dog's killer. This unleashed several weeks' worth of front-page stories on animal abuse.

The day before this story broke, Saunders notes, the Human Rights Watch released a report of their own, challenging the "widespread physical abuse and economic mistreatment of thousands of domestic workers in diplomatic households." Not a single Los Angeles paper chose to carry it.[3]

While caring for pets can be considered a sensitive act—after all, pets are God's creatures, too—we have to guard against priorities that treat dogs better than humans. I'm not suggesting we should be cruel to animals, but I am asking us to reflect on whether we are as kind as we might be to humans.

According to Jesus, such kindness is essential for authentic faith. In the Gospels, Jesus stresses two things: (1) God's generosity and (2) our corresponding obligation to show the same generosity rather than to hoard God's blessing. Social mercy begins with the freedom we have because God is so generous: "Do not be afraid, little flock, for your Father has been pleased to give you the kingdom." It continues with the corresponding invitation: "Sell your possessions and give to the poor. Provide purses for yourselves that will not wear out, a treasure in heaven that will not be exhausted, where no thief comes near and no moth destroys. For where your treasure is, there your heart will be also" (Luke 12:32–34).

This verse follows the well-known "don't worry about what you will eat or wear" passage. Jesus wants his followers to know that God's kingdom is theirs. We are going to inherit unimaginable wealth. Our response shouldn't be to put on airs, but to give away what we do have, knowing that abundance awaits us in the future.

> **Social mercy begins with the freedom we have because God is so generous.**

If we fail to live up to this ethic, the punishment will be severe. Jesus' teaching about "the sheep and the goats" has one clear strain: The sheep are rewarded for their good *deeds*—feeding the poor (humans), visiting the sick and imprisoned, clothing the naked. And the goats are punished for what they left undone—ignoring those already mentioned. All judgment is based on what the respective individuals did or didn't do for hurting human beings (see Matthew 25:31–46.)

Because of this truth, Jesus stresses that our parties need to be the kind that will reap heavenly rewards. He tells his disciples that when they have a banquet, they shouldn't invite rich people or their own relatives. Otherwise, they'll be repaid and lose any reward. Instead, they should invite the poor, the crippled, the lame, and the blind (see Luke 14:12–14).

I think about this when Lisa and I plan activities. When I take my kids to a movie, they know I'm going to invite my friend Scott. Do you have a friend who just needs to get out of the house? Do you know of someone who needs an extra hand? If not, why not? Maybe it's time to make a new friend, Jesus-style.

Jesus completely rejects any notion that "religious obligation" can be used as an excuse to ignore the poor or needy—including church building programs. He chastised the Pharisees for telling people to give money to the temple instead of to their needy parents (see Mark 7:9–13). He said that teachers of the law who specialize in long, showy prayers but who "devour widows' houses . . . will be punished most severely" (Luke 20:46–47). There is an increasing interest in Christian spirituality today, including the prayer life, but any growth in prayer without a corresponding concern and demonstrated compassion for the down-and-out is a sham, according to the teachings of Jesus.

But perhaps the most poignant moment of Jesus' teaching on social concern comes as he hangs dying on the cross. We know that Jesus was beaten virtually beyond recognition. The pain he felt, both physical and emotional, was eclipsed only by the spiritual anguish of having the entire sins of the world placed upon his perfect soul. No one had a more important mission to perform than Jesus. No one was more "busy" in that sense. And no one has ever had a better excuse to think about other things.

> *Any growth in prayer without a corresponding concern and demonstrated compassion for the down-and-out is a sham.*

But even in the midst of this agony, Jesus focused his compassion on his widowed mother, who was watching her oldest son die. There was one piece of unfinished business, which Jesus nobly dispatches as he looks down from that cross, dripping with blood. He summons up his last vestiges of strength to say, "Dear woman, here is your son," and to John, "Here is your mother" (John 19:26–27).

Some of the last words Jesus uttered on this earth were spoken to make sure a widow would be cared for after he was gone. Once that was accomplished—and *only* after that was accomplished—he could finally say, "It is finished."

ancient concern

There's no getting around the fact that even biblical characters could at times disagree with each other (see Galatians 2:11), but there was one aspect of the Christian life that they all held to be an essential element of the gospel.[4] Paul tells the Galatians that as he, James, Peter, and John discussed Paul's work among the Gentiles, the one thing the "pillars" of the church made sure to stress was that Paul "should continue to remember the poor, the very thing I was eager to do" (Galatians 2:10). The writer of Hebrews concurs, stressing that we should "remember those in prison as if you were their fellow prisoners, and those who are mistreated as if you yourselves were suffering" (Hebrews 13:3).

John goes so far as to question the sincerity of anyone's faith and the reality of their conversion if they stubbornly stop their ears to the cries of the needy: "If anyone has material possessions and sees his brother in need but has no pity on him, how can the love of God be in him? Dear children, let us not love with words or tongue but with actions and in truth" (1 John 3:17–18). In John's mind, compassion for the poor is one of the primary ways we build assurance of our faith. To the verses we've just read, he adds, "This then is how we know that we belong to the truth, and how we set our hearts at rest in his presence whenever our hearts condemn us" (3:19–20).

The early church soon became known for putting Jesus' and his apostle's instructions into practice. The pagan emperor Julian the Apostate worked feverishly to crush Christianity in the fourth century, though he admitted to a fellow pagan that doing so would have severe repercussions: "The godless Galileans [Christians] feed not only their poor but ours also."[5] Given what we spoke about in the previous chapter, this is almost funny. Here we have a wicked emperor bent on destroying Christians, yet torn because these hated believers for the most part comprise his country's only means of helping the poor!

The classic Christian writers acutely understood the need for social mercy. Ambrose of Milan wrote, "If thou clothe the naked, thou clothest thyself with righteousness; if thou bring the stranger under thy roof, if thou support the needy, he procures for thee the friendship of the saints and eternal habitations. That is no small recompense. Thou sowest earthly things and receive heavenly."[6] Teresa of Avila sternly warned, "As God's stewards we share our wealth among the poor and must give a strict account for the time we keep a surplus in our coffers, while delaying and putting off the poor who are suffering."[7]

Great Christian thinkers not only taught this, they lived it out as well. C. S. Lewis was among them. Even after enjoying great success, Lewis didn't leave behind the principle of reaching out to the downtrodden. His literary production between 1942 and 1946 is, as his biographer George Sayer puts it, "astonishing." Consider how many classics he wrote in this four-year span: *A Preface to Paradise Lost, Beyond Personality, Out of the Silent Planet, Perelandra, That Hideous Strength, The Abolition of Man,* and *The Great Divorce.* In addition to writing books,

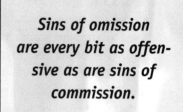

Sins of omission are every bit as offensive as are sins of commission.

he continued writing his letters and papers and performing his academic tasks (he was working full-time as a tutor and lecturer). Yet in the midst of all this, Lewis still took time out to spend many hours trying to teach a mentally retarded boy to read and write.[8]

Some of the world's greatest novelists (both Tolstoy and Dickens immediately come to mind) often used their talents to highlight the plight of the needy. Dickens has given us a legacy of compassion through his stunningly beautiful book *A Christmas Carol.* The best literature always highlights truth in a new light, and Dickens certainly knew how to awaken hearts that had grown callous to human suffering.

The point is that sins of omission are every bit as offensive as are sins of commission: "Anyone, then, who knows the good he ought to do and doesn't do it, sins" (James 4:17). Authentic faith calls us to express our belief by reaching out to the poor, the needy, and the hurting.

One caveat is in order: The ancients—beginning with Paul—urge us to be *discriminating* in our giving. Though some gave without reserve or even judgment (arguing that we are responsible to give, and the recipient is responsible for his or her motives and actions), many adopted the rule that Paul gave when he wrote, "If a man will not work, he shall not eat" (2 Thessalonians 3:10). Basil (A.D. 329–379), an early church bishop, made this distinction: "Experience [is] needed in order to distinguish between cases of genuine need and of mere greedy begging. For whoever gives to the afflicted [the truly needy] gives to the Lord, and from the Lord shall have his reward; but he who gives to every vagabond casts to a dog, a nuisance indeed from his importunity, but deserving no pity on the ground of want."[9]

It's a tough lesson to learn, but seeing somebody in want doesn't necessarily mean they are in need. There's a guy in Bellingham, my hometown, who stands near a busy intersection. One day his sign read, "Homeless vet, anything helps, God bless you." The next day his sign read—I swear I'm not making this up—"Why lie? I need beer." Apparently, that approach wasn't too successful, because two days later he had gone back to, "Homeless vet, hungry, please help."

Determining who is truly needy and who is merely lazy isn't always easy to do, but I don't believe either Scripture or the tradition of the Christian classics obligates us to support every panhandler we come across; to do so might, in fact, cause us to support any number of drug habits and other wasteful spending habits. At times, of course, God may indeed lead us to give to panhandlers— to, in fact, give far more than simply a dollar bill—by offering some time and conversation and perhaps pointing them in a direction where they can receive even more substantial support.

contemporary compassion

On the east bank of the Columbia River in Washington State, on a plot of land situated between Priest Rapids at Sentinel Gap and a small town called Mattawa, time hasn't moved very fast. In September 1998, author David Guterson took a journalist's tour of Washington's apple country and discovered a makeshift village of migrant apple harvesters. These laborers—the vast majority of them from Mexico—exist in broken-down cars that double as hotel rooms and in tiny shelters constructed out of cardboard, old tents, and tarps. The population is seasonal, but even during the harvest, it changes by the day. The land is actually owned by the Grant County Public Utility District, which seems to have accepted the squatter's claims. The county provides trash bins and portable outhouses, but that's about it. The only visible means of recreation is an old hubcap with its center ripped out. It's been nailed to a tree, approximately ten feet off the ground, and serves as a basketball hoop.

There is no electricity and no plumbing—little of the things that most of us take for granted. When workers want to bathe, they use the Columbia River. Many of the men are here without their families. The wages are poor by our standards (about $60 to $70 a day), but high by theirs, and many of their goals are simple. One man told Guterson he hoped to make enough money so that he could install electricity in his family's home. Another said that one month of picking fruit will support his family for three months. Guterson did his best to elicit stories of misery, but the men had another take: "This is an adventure," one man said. "And we are making very good money."[10]

The next day, Guterson's tour took him into the Yakima Valley, where he once again crossed the Columbia River (to drive through eastern Washington is to cross the Columbia every fifty miles or so) and made his way to the Broetje Orchards, virtually a sea of apples with its astonishing 4000 contiguous acres of fruit.

Ralph and Cheryl Broetje are Christians, and they own one of the state's largest apple orchards. What marks them as different, however, isn't the sheer quantity of apples they provide or the high number of workers they employ (1000 or more), but Vista Hermosa, one of the few housing complexes in the state privately built for migrant laborers.

Vista Hermosa did not come cheap. The Broetjes "have spent $5.5 million to build eighty homes; twenty-eight apartments; a school, gym, and day care center; a laundromat, gas station, and convenience store; a chapel and a post office." This is all private land, not a municipality, but the housing complex reminds Guterson of the "clean, tidy, stuccoed look of a suburban development in Phoenix or Albuquerque." The homes are adorned with green lawns, flower gardens, even barbecues. Workers have to pay to live here, but the rate is very affordable: $350 a month for a three-bedroom house (with a single-car garage), or $400 for one with four bedrooms. For just $25 a month, parents can send their children to the private school, and that $25 includes two daily meals and a snack.

The chapel offers worship services, and a community center holds Bible classes as well as an annual "Christian Talent Contest." Housing leases stipulate that there will be no consumption of alcohol outside the house, no garbage left in the driveways or yards, no abandoned vehicles anywhere, and no fighting. With such regulations, Vista Hermosa will never degenerate into a slum.

Another astonishing fact is that the Broetjes are committed to nearly year-round employment for their workers. Most orchards hire only seasonally, but the Broetjes realize that it's difficult to make a living when you only work a few months a year.

You'd think that offering seasonal workers year-round employment and the construction of a multimillion-dollar housing complex would suffice for any family's social conscience, but not the Broetjes! They have a larger vision, and thus participate in World Vision's child sponsorship program.

When Guterson probed Ralph Broetje to find out why he would spend millions of dollars on workers who, just miles away, fend for themselves in a makeshift village at zero cost to orchard owners, Broetje admitted that, while it might increase productivity by cutting down on turnover and building a more motivated workforce, "if you just look at the bottom line, it doesn't make financial sense to spend so much on Vista Hermosa. But it does make human sense."

This admission might explain why some rival growers call Broetje an "evangelical fanatic." I think of him as a prophetic Christian, faithfully living out the truth of the gospel. Spending over $5 million on such a project is an amazing sum by any measure, but Vista Hermosa is right in line with what the most mature Christian writers and teachers have called us to uphold, beginning with Jesus himself.

realistic compassion

As you begin to reach out to the hurting, it's important to check your sentimentality at the door. Some Christians who have never worked in the trenches may initially have an idealized view about the socially needy. They assume that such people are naturally lovable. Such is often not the case. The poor, diseased, and dispossessed can be as arrogant, ungrateful, bitter, and cruel as anyone else.

Directors of crisis pregnancy centers have on occasion found that some who come in to help as counselors are somewhat surprised by this. These well-meaning Christians want to help young women who are in trouble, but they may not realize that the reason they are in trouble is because they're troubled! Many expect to see young women who resemble their daughters and granddaughters. They expect to be thanked and appreciated—and sometimes they are. But they also meet their share of "just give me the pregnancy test and I'm out of here" type of women.

Cesar Chavez had to work through this "romanticism of the needy" with the idealistic college students who volunteered to work with his farmworkers. When many of these farmworkers fully supported American involvement in Vietnam, the college students were surprised, as if the fact of having experienced suffering would suddenly turn the poor into pacifists.

Chavez immediately dispelled any such notions: "I told them to understand that farm workers are human beings. 'If you don't understand that, you are going to be mighty disappointed. You have to understand that you may work very hard, and the day will come when they will just boot you out, or they don't appreciate what you are doing.' And I warned them not to have any hidden agenda."[11]

> **Social mercy is based on obedience to God and depends on God's love for his failing children.**

My wife volunteered to work with a weeklong camp that reached out to inner-city children from troubled backgrounds. She soon learned what she was up against. Any romantic notions she might have secretly harbored about what the week would be like were quickly dispelled when the trainer taught them how to respond to a kid who is biting you. (Rather than pull your arm back—which allows the child's teeth to set—you should push your arm into the child's mouth until the child stops biting. When the arm is pushed in, it's far more difficult to receive a hurtful bite.) At the end of the camp, I joined my wife for a luncheon given in recognition of the camp workers. A young man actually received an award for being the most patient in the face of the most abuse. He had been kicked, hit, pummeled, even spit on.

I think it's important to mention this, because after reading a chapter like this, some people might jump headfirst into compassionate service, when in reality it's something we need to do with our eyes fully open. It's helpful for Christians who are eager to get their hands dirty to first do a motivation check. Are you doing this to be loved in return? Are you doing this to save a life? What if the person doesn't want to be saved? What if the addict refuses to quit?

What if the crisis pregnancy center client gets pregnant again? Will that make you quit?

Social mercy is based on obedience to God and depends on God's love for his failing children. We cannot maintain or manufacture a false love. Sentimentality won't last you until lunchtime if you're in a real ministry. Nothing short of God's supernatural care and concern will suffice.

But behind this pain is an unparalleled, almost otherworldly, pleasure. J. I. Packer once told a class of seminary students, "As you serve the Lord, you hurt. And as you serve the Lord, your hurt, which feels sometimes like a death experience, gives way to a joy which feels like a resurrection experience. The Lord makes it happen."[12]

political programs

Well-known writer, speaker, and inner-city ministry advocate Tony Campolo came to speak at my hometown in 1998. He addressed a large, refreshingly multigenerational crowd on the campus of Western Washington University. When Tony gave an impassioned plea to reach out to the poor, when he talked about how the essence of Christianity is its care for the disenfranchised, I could scarcely contain my "amens." He was dynamic, powerful, and persuasive. I was delighted to have him address our community. But every time he then applied that concern to a political position, I cringed. I couldn't disagree with him more on some issues.

Both of us have had our sensitivity to the downcast sharpened by the same Scriptures, but as soon as we both tried to apply how that concern can be best expressed in today's society, we quickly parted company.

It's the same with evangelism. Most Christians agree that it must be done. As soon as we begin promoting various strategies ("seeker-friendly churches" or "contact evangelism"), the fights erupt. With missions, there is a raging debate regarding whether we should focus on sending missionaries who must learn the language, or whether we should put increasing effort into supporting indigenous workers who can minister for a fraction of the cost—but who sometimes "take the money and run." And what do we do when there is no indigenous evangelist?

As soon as policy or strategy comes into play, disputes break out. While this lack of agreement can be extremely frustrating for those of us engaged in it, it just might be that the cause of the poor is better served through a variety of approaches. Social compassion is not owned by Democrats or Republicans, conservatives or liberals. When I disagree with another believer politically, I can at least respect what he or she is trying to do *in principle*. The average Southern Baptists and United Methodists may well find themselves lobbying on opposing sides of any one bill, but even this is to be preferred over apathy. To ignore the poor and to do nothing is the sin that brings down Scripture's most heated rebukes.

I was particularly impressed when I had the privilege of meeting Franklin Graham, president of Samaritan's Purse and now CEO of the Billy Graham Evangelistic Association (BGEA). The BGEA has about as much integrity as a Christian organization can have; there's no way Franklin can improve on what is nearly a perfect record. Once Billy Graham retires (which probably won't happen until God takes him home), Samaritan's Purse will join forces with the BGEA as Franklin assumes his father's leadership. The future joining

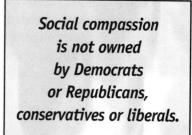

Social compassion is not owned by Democrats or Republicans, conservatives or liberals.

of the country's most celebrated and historic evangelistic outreach with perhaps our most strategic and effective ministry of compassion to the world's disenfranchised is a profoundly significant merger, perhaps even a prophetic example of God's providence.

While working on a project together, Franklin and I spent a number of days getting to know each other. Hearing his story and seeing how God is using him in so many hot spots around the world was a highlight experience for me. Franklin took what was a relatively tiny ministry and with God's blessing built it into a force for good that has saved literally millions of lives. What's more, Samaritan's Purse prefers to work through local churches, so that the people who are reached connect with this local expression of faith rather than with a distant American organization. It's a brilliant plan, prophetically heeding the call to share our faith while at the same time meeting our neighbor's needs.

Franklin knows that no one can replace his father, and he would never try to do so. He is definitely his own man. Yet, after spending time with Franklin, I walked away amazed as I realized that, due in part to the social compassion ministry he has overseen for many years, he may well *improve* on his dad's legacy. He may yet offer an even fuller expression of Christian care and concern for the whole person. Fifteen years ago, who would have ever believed such a thing was possible?

called to care

Regardless of where we live—whether in the suburbs of the Midwest, the elite societies of the East, or the rural South—or what we do, as a laborer or business owner, we are all called to care. If there is no evidence of social mercy in your life, if there isn't a single poor person, prisoner, man or woman with a disability, or refugee who can stand up and testify that you have lived out and continue to live out your faith with compassionate care, then know this: Scripture, the Christian classics, and contemporary faith all stand in one accord to challenge the sub-Christian religion that you have adopted.

This might seem like a harsh statement, but you cannot read Scripture with any honesty, you cannot read very deeply in Christian history, and you cannot live with open eyes in contemporary Christianity without being challenged by how central a compassionate outreach to the poor and needy is to the gospel message.

The late Klaus Bockmuehl challenged me in seminary, "Living for yourself is too notoriously small an aim for any human soul." If your faith begins and ends with you—your victories over sin and temptation, your ability to pay the bills, your family's health—you are missing the truly profound experience of working with God to make a difference in a needy person's life.

In your financial plan, besides retirement, are you investing in those who are less well-off than you are? Brady Bobbink, one of my early mentors, earns a relatively low salary as a campus pastor, but he made a pledge over fifteen years ago that each year he and his wife would add one more World Vision or Compassion child to their budget. On a limited income, they are looking at eventually sponsoring two-dozen children.

Maybe you're the coach of a soccer team. One boy is being raised by a single mom and seems eager for more male influence in his life. That boy is the same age as your son. Will your interest in that boy extend beyond the season, or will it stop as soon as he can't score goals for you anymore?

Perhaps your church has a strong outreach to teens, young married couples, and middle-aged profession-als—but elderly men and women keep getting ignored. Their income is lim-

> *If your faith begins and ends with you, you are missing the truly profound experience of working with God to make a difference in a needy person's life.*

ited and many of them can't make it to church because of physical constraints, but they still need spiritual and sometimes physical care. Will they be forgotten, or will you go out of your way to remember them? The integrity of a church is often seen most clearly in how it treats the people who seemingly can offer the least in return (although the truth is that many seniors are great sources of wisdom and guidance).

As our young people form their life plans, choose their majors in college, and begin preparing for their vocations, will we urge them to go after just the top-paying jobs, or will we encourage them to lay their gifts at the feet of Jesus and see where he leads them? They may still end up on Wall Street—but some may also be called to inner-city Los Angeles.

Authentic Faith

Gary Haugen picked up a skull and called out, "Male."

"Cause of death?"

"Machete."

Haugen picked up another skull. "Child," he said.

"Cause of death?"

"Machete."

As part of Haugen's work for International Justice Mission, the Harvard Law graduate directed the United Nations' genocide investigation in Rwanda during the late 1990s. It was his job to go through mass graves to determine the number that had died and how. "It's just filthy, disgusting," Haugen admitted in an interview with *Beyond* magazine.

If anything was worse than picking up the dead, however, it was talking to the living, particularly the children with whom Haugen had to maintain eye contact as he listened to them describe the most brutal of massacres. Further adding to Haugen's sobriety was the fact that at least half of the massacres took place in churches because that's where people ran for sanctuary.

As a Harvard graduate, Haugen had the opportunity to choose where he wanted to work and where he wanted to live. There was no necessity to "get his hands dirty," either literally or figuratively. He had the background that would have provided affluence and comfort, but he chose to enter work that eventually led him—of all places—to Rwanda, and that decision has had a profound impact on his sense of intimacy with God.

> **"If you want to know what God is like, you need to know something about where He's been."**

"If you want to know somebody," he says, "you want to know where they come from, what they've been through. And if you want to know what God is like, you need to know something about where He's been. I think it's hard for us living in comfortable North American communities to think that God has been in some of the places that He has been. Because that's one of the hard things for me to think about: what it was like for God to endure all those people gathered in these churches who clearly were crying out to Him in the midst of all that."

Haugen's perspective is extraordinary and profound. Imagine, indeed, what it must have been like as God personally heard the cries of children, women, and men who cried out to him as they were hacked to death with bloody machetes, on the very same spot where they had sung songs of worship and danced before his name.

"God was right there through every minute and hour of the genocide that was going on in that church. He's there every minute for the child prostitute who is being raped again tonight. He's there sitting by the bonded child laborer who spends 12 or 14 hours a day spinning silk or rolling cigarettes for 50 cents a week on a debt that will take him through his entire childhood even though it's only $35. Jesus sits right beside that child all day long.... And the difference that makes helps you

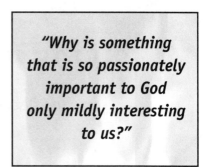

"Why is something that is so passionately important to God only mildly interesting to us?"

understand why God hates injustice so much. If you had to be there, day in and day out, and sit and watch it and hear it and smell it, you would hate it, and you would want it to stop.

"It's not a side issue, that His people address suffering and injustice. It's not one of those extra credit options, that if you do everything else, then maybe you can do something on behalf of those who are victimized by the abuse of power. It's the thing that breaks [God's] heart. And then we have to ask, why is something that is so passionately important to God only mildly interesting to us?"

In Haugen's mind, if we truly desire to know God, we will go where the suffering is greatest. "My friends can't understand what it's like to interview a child survivor of one of these massacres, or what it's like to roll over the corpse of a mother who clearly has thrown her body over the child to protect it. I can't explain in any way that someone can totally understand what that is in terms of understanding me, but a person who really does want to know me ... wants to sit down with me, wants to know where I've been and what I've seen. And likewise, if we want to know God deeply, it just requires some measure of willingness to understand the places where He's been."[13]

If you truly want to experience an authentic faith, go where people are hurting the most and get involved in their lives. You'll not only see God at work, you'll also gain his heart and very likely become transformed in the process.

seven

giving up the grudge

The Discipline of Forgiveness

If forgiveness is a whitewashing of wrong, then it is itself wrong.
Nothing that whitewashes evil can be good. It can be good only if it
is a redemption from the effects of evil, not a make-believing that the
evil never happened.

Lewis B. Smedes

If religion forbids all instances of revenge without any exception, 'tis
because all revenge is of the nature of poison.

William Law

July 4, 1826. John Adams was close to death in his Massachusetts home. He had lived a full life—an original signer of the Declaration of Independence, the first vice president and second president of the United States, father of the nation's sixth president—and he had enjoyed a rich, deep marriage. His final thoughts, however, were particularly intriguing. Some of his last words concerned his longtime political rival and onetime archenemy Thomas Jefferson. As Adams lay dying, several people nearby heard him whisper, "Thomas Jefferson still survives."

In fact, unknown to Adams, Jefferson had died hours earlier in his home in Monticello, Virginia.

By all accounts, both Adams and Jefferson lived complete lives. Not only had both men served as president, but they also worked together on the Declaration of Independence. Historian David McCullough calls Jefferson the "pen" of the Declaration of Independence and Adams its "voice."[1] The two men literally shaped a burgeoning republic with their own opinions and beliefs and presidential administrations.

If we think today's partisan politics are unprecedented, we haven't read much history, for the dispute between Adams and Jefferson was unusually intense—ultimately leading to a duel in which Aaron Burr fatally wounded Alexander Hamilton in 1804.

Jefferson's victory in the 1800 election kept Adams from serving a second term; as just the second president, Adams had no precedent for a defeated officeholder to follow. Adams had served his country long and well and sacrificially; the electoral defeat hurt him and made him angry as well as bitter. The pain of his loss was intensified by the fact that the man who was replacing him was his opposite in just about every way:

> The differences in physique, background, manner, and temperament could hardly have been more contrasting. Where Adams was stout, Jefferson was lean and long-limbed, almost bony. Where Adams was nearly bald, Jefferson had a full head of thick, coppery hair. . . .
>
> Jefferson was devoted to the ideal of improving mankind but had comparatively little interest in people in particular. Adams was not inclined to believe mankind improvable, but was certain it was important that human nature be understood. . . .
>
> It was Jefferson's graciousness that was so appealing. He was never blunt or assertive, as Adams could be, but subtle, serene by all appearances, always polite, soft-spoken, and diplomatic, if somewhat remote. With Adams there was seldom a doubt about what he meant by what he said. With Jefferson there was nearly always a slight air of ambiguity.[2]

Jefferson, of course, had his own issues with Adams. After he took office, Jefferson accused Adams of furiously appointing many "midnight judges" on his last day in office, with the intent to hamstring the enactment of Jefferson's policies (though most appointments had taken place before that, and it was to be expected that Adams would appoint people from his own party). Jefferson later wrote in a letter to Abigail Adams (John's wife) that he considered these appointments "personally unkind."[3]

There was certainly no amicable transfer of power—Adams didn't even bother to show up for Jefferson's inauguration! The second president chose to leave town in the early hours rather than personally witness his enemy receiving the honor of his own former office. This disappointed Adams's supporters as much as it did Jefferson's followers.

Following two short letters about some unfinished business, over eleven years would pass before the two men would write or speak to each other again. Interestingly, though, there was a somewhat heated correspondence between Abigail and Jefferson, in which Jefferson made mention of Mr. Adams's "personal wrath."[4]

Benjamin Rush, a mutual friend, eventually urged Adams to write to Jefferson. Rush called Adams and Jefferson the "North and South Poles of the American Revolution" and argued that two men who both played such pivotal roles in the founding of a nation should not die in acrimony.

An astonishing correspondence followed. Fifty letters went back and forth over the next twenty-four months.[5] Though Adams wrote far more frequently than did Jefferson, there was clearly some degree of respect, if not admiration, for the work each had done. Even so, their disagreements continued. In one letter, Adams wrote, "Whether you or I were right, posterity must judge. I never have approved and never can approve the repeal of taxes, the repeal of the judiciary system, or the neglect of the navy." In another, Adams chided, "Checks and balances, Jefferson, however you and your party may have ridiculed them, are our only security."

True to his irascible nature, Adams seemed to want to continue the now good-natured quarrel. "My friend! You and I have passed our lives in serious times," he wrote to Jefferson. "You and I ought not to die before we have explained ourselves to each other."

Jefferson refused to be drawn in, not wanting to rehash old arguments. "To me then it appears that there have been differences of opinion, and party differences, from the establishment of governments to the present day.... Nothing new can be added by you or me or to what has been said by others, and will be said in every age."

But to characterize the letters as only a renewal of old debates would not do them justice. The men discussed their daily habits and what they were reading, and they often sent their best wishes. In one letter, Jefferson spoke of how, in spite of their disagreements, they had still been working toward the same general end: "Laboring always at the same oar, with some wave ever ahead threatening to overwhelm us and yet passing harmless under our bark, we knew not how we rode through the storm with heart and hand, and made a happy port."[6]

One of Adams's friends was astonished to hear of this reconciliation. He asked Adams how he could possibly be on such good terms with his old rival after all the abuse he had suffered from him. Adams replied, "I do not believe that Mr. Jefferson ever hated me ... but he detested my whole administration. Then he wished to be president of the United States and I stood in his way. So he did everything that he could to pull me down. But if I should quarrel with him for that, I might quarrel with every man I have had anything to do with in life. This is human nature.... I forgive all my enemies and hope they may find mercy in Heaven. Mr. Jefferson and I have grown old and retired from public life. So we are upon our ancient terms of goodwill."[7]

Adams may never have known that the last letter Jefferson wrote to him was written beneath a plaster bust of John Adams, which Jefferson kept on a shelf in his office. And Jefferson surely never knew that his onetime rival died with Jefferson's name on his lips.

Whereas these men could easily have died bitter deaths, they were enriched in their final hours not just by their family but by thoughts of another man who had once been a sworn enemy. Their character was seen not just in their political accomplishments but in their willingness to forgive and move on.

God wants to save us from ourselves. The message of the gospel is that, from a human perspective, the first person served by forgiveness is the one who does the forgiving. From a broader perspective, God's glory is served. In both cases, the discipline of forgiveness marks a truly authentic faith.

poisoned Hearts

Early on, the Old Testament offers some startling pictures of forgiveness, perhaps the most poignant of which is Joseph's forgiveness of his brothers for selling him into slavery (see Genesis 45). Joseph, stuck in a hole, had heard his siblings discuss his fate (see Genesis 37:26–27). He knew that their original plans were to kill him and that their decision to spare his life and sell him off as a slave was purely economical—why rub out your brother when you can gain a few bucks by selling him off? Yet, even armed with this knowledge, Joseph chose to look at the larger picture in the end.

"You intended to harm me," he told his brothers, "but God intended it for good to accomplish what is now being done, the saving of many lives. So then, don't be afraid. I will provide for you and your children" (Genesis 50:20–21).

Joseph could so easily have made his brothers pay. Instead, he took the noble path of authentic faith and not only refused to harbor a grudge but actually provided generously for the very brothers who had treated him so terribly. It's one thing to not strike back; it's something else entirely to respond by blessing someone who has hated you.

> **The first person served by forgiveness is the one who does the forgiving.**

The Wisdom literature in Scripture is replete with verses that talk about the agony and brutality that result from our taking offense at others and refusing to forgive: "Better a dry crust with peace and quiet than a house full of feasting, with strife" (Proverbs 17:1). Living in contention, Solomon suggests, is the height of stupidity, the domain of fools: "It is to a man's honor to avoid strife, but every fool is quick to quarrel" (Proverbs 20:3).

I've seen strife rip families apart. Two people, crazy enough about each other to pledge before family and friends that they will live together in sickness and health until they are parted by death, ten years later find themselves absolutely hating each other. What happened? In many cases, the simple lack of forgiveness, compounded by cultivating grudges, has erupted into raw emotional and relational wounds that never healed. These wounds and hurts became infected with bitterness, and two people make each other miserable because they allowed strife to take over.

At the heart of unforgiveness is obstinacy—a stubbornness that refuses to let up, that marches relentlessly toward mutual destruction: "An offended brother is more unyielding than a fortified city, and disputes are like the barred gates of a citadel" (Proverbs 18:19). In contrast, the picture of wisdom and refinement, biblically speaking, is learning to overcome the baser part of our nature that is easily offended and that demands immediate revenge: "A man's wisdom gives him patience; it is to his glory to overlook an offense" (Proverbs 19:11).

> *At the heart of unforgiveness is obstinacy—a stubbornness that refuses to let up, that marches relentlessly toward mutual destruction.*

This is a crucial quality in the workplace. It is inevitable that people will let us down, sin against us, and maybe even deliberately malign us. If we spend our energy trying to get back at and ruin the other person, we debase ourselves; even worse, we become like the very person we despise. It is a glorious thing to respond to sin with forgiveness, grace, and mercy. Any simpleton can respond with hatred; it is the mark of one who possesses a truly authentic faith to respond with gentleness, understanding, and forgiveness. When you can respond that way, you know Jesus is operating within you.

Being unwilling to forgive means that we hold everyone around us to a standard of perfection—something that we ourselves will never achieve. In wisdom, we learn to forgive because we know that we, too, have sinned—often in the same way that others have sinned against us: "Do not pay attention to every word people say, or you may hear your servant cursing you—for you know in your heart that many times you yourself have cursed others" (Ecclesiastes 7:21–22).

I hate to be gossiped about; it hurts when I hear that someone has ridiculed me or put what I said in a bad light or made humor at my expense. But if I'm honest, I know I've done the same thing to others. By God's grace, we can respond to such revelations by trying to become more sensitive to our own tendency toward this sin rather than continuing to sin by gossiping about the person who gossiped about us. Having felt the sting of gossip, we can say, "That hurts; I don't want to do that to anyone else," rather than perpetuating the mutual spiritual destruction.

Another reason the wise person learns to forgive is because the Old Testament makes it unequivocally clear that vengeance belongs to God: "Do not say, 'I'll pay you back for this wrong!' Wait for the LORD, and he will deliver you" (Proverbs 20:22; see Leviticus 19:18; Proverbs 24:29).

The New Testament makes clear that offering forgiveness to others is a Christian obligation. Paul tells the Ephesian Christians to forgive each other, "just as in Christ God forgave you" (Ephesians 4:32). In fact, mature believers are told to forgive beyond count (see Matthew 18:21–22). Paul is adamant: Revenge is not for Christians; on the contrary, we should care for our enemies rather than seek their harm (see Romans 12:17–21), just as Joseph fed his brothers instead of putting them to death.

The shocking truth about Christianity is Scripture's insistence that forgiveness is not an option but an obligation, a duty. Refusing to forgive has serious repercussions. Jesus warned that God will treat us unmercifully if we refuse to forgive those who sin against us (see Matthew 18:35). He even suggests that our forgiveness from God is contingent on our willingness to forgive others: "And when you stand praying, if you hold anything against anyone, forgive him, so that your Father in heaven may forgive you your sins" (Mark 11:25). Jesus is even more resolute in Matthew 6:14–15: "For if you forgive men when they sin against you, your heavenly Father will also forgive you. But if you do not forgive men their sins, your Father will not forgive your sins." This sounds so unlike the gospel that some theologians expend a multitude of words trying to convince us that this doesn't mean what it clearly sounds like it means, namely, if we refuse to forgive, we will not be forgiven. Augustine had no such reticence.

> **Forgiveness is not an option but an obligation, a duty.**

About this verse he has written, "The man whom the thunder of this warning does not awaken is not asleep, but dead; and yet so powerful is that voice, that it can awaken even the dead."[8]

But beyond this clear biblical obligation, forgiveness offers a tremendous personal blessing. In *Shoah,* Claude Lanzmann's documentary on the Holocaust, a leader of the Warsaw ghetto uprising speaks of the bitterness that remains in his soul over how he and his countrymen were treated by the Nazis: "If you could lick my heart," he says, "it would poison you."

> *Social scientists are discovering that forgiveness may lead to victims' emotional and even physical healing and wholeness, releasing the "poison" of resentment and bitterness.*

Researchers are finding that this Holocaust survivor's sentiment is not necessarily metaphorical. While the biblical practice of forgiveness is typically preached as a Christian obligation, social scientists are discovering that forgiveness may lead to victims' emotional and even physical healing and wholeness, releasing the "poison" of resentment and bitterness.

Psychologist Glen Mack Harnden is enthusiastic about the personal benefits of forgiveness that have been demonstrated through numerous academic studies: "[Forgiveness] not only heightens the potential for reconciliation," he says, "but also releases the offender from prolonged anger, rage, and stress that have been linked to physiological problems, such as cardiovascular diseases, high blood pressure, hypertension, cancer, and other psychosomatic illness."[9]

Robert Enright, professor of educational psychology at the University of Wisconsin-Madison, is president of the International Forgiveness Institute. Together with philosopher Joanna North, Enright has written extensively about the benefits of forgiveness:

> It is an obvious fact that we live in a world where violence, hatred, and animosity surround us on all sides. . . . We hear much about the 'social' causes of crime—poverty, unemployment, and illiteracy, for example. We sometimes hear about the need for tolerance and cooperation, compassion and understanding. But

almost never do we hear public leaders declaring their belief that forgiveness can bring people together, heal their wounds, and alleviate the bitterness and resentment caused by wrongdoing.

Enright and North believe that "forgiveness might be useful in helping those who have been affected by cruelty, crime, and violence, and ... might play a valuable role in reconciling warring parties and restoring harmony between people."

> **When we are sinned against, how will we respond?**

Since we live in a fallen world where we are surrounded by sinners, it is certain that we will be sinned against. Some of those sinning against us will be strangers. They may be passing in a car, someone we have never seen before and will never see again. Some will be our family members or our closest friends. A few may even be our role models or pastors. When we are sinned against, how will we respond? What will our faith call us to, and why? According to Harnden, Enright, and North, forgiveness is a life-giving, protective strategy whose time has come.

The Taste of Bitterness

In 1990, a young mother of three pleaded for her life after being confronted by an assailant wearing combat fatigues.

"Please don't shoot me," she whimpered.

The murderer coldheartedly fired anyway, fatally wounding the woman.

The assailant made so many mistakes in covering up her crime that had the situation not been so tragic, it would have been comical. She sloppily disposed of her clothing and weapon and left enough signs pointing to her that the Colorado Springs police had her in custody within twenty-four hours. Shortly thereafter, they also arrested the victim's husband after determining that the shooter and the husband had been having an affair.

Sydna Masse, a friend whom I met when she worked at Focus on the Family,[10] lived behind the murdered woman. When Sydna heard about the killing, she responded with (in her own words) hatred and rage. "I had a dead friend and now lived behind three motherless kids," she told me. "I felt I had every right to hate the murderer who caused this."

Sydna grew "physically hot" when the murderer's name—Jennifer—was even mentioned or her picture was flashed on television. "For a while I couldn't even read the newspaper articles," she admits.

Sydna's hatred wasn't a solitary affair. "The whole city and state hated her," she says. Jennifer's life sentence did little to diminish Sydna's passion. "There was no relief in her sentencing. That's the thing with hatred and bitterness—it eats you alive. Every time I passed the house, I missed Diane and became angry all over again."

Shortly after Jennifer was sentenced, Sydna began going through a Bible study that included a chapter on forgiveness. Sydna prayerfully asked God whom she needed to forgive, and, in her words, "Jennifer's name came right to my head. I literally did a whiplash and protested, 'No way I can forgive her. She killed my friend! She killed a mother of three!"

As happens so often with the spiritually sincere, God's persistent conviction outlasted Sydna's reluctance. Sydna finally yielded and wrote a carefully crafted letter to Jennifer, expressing her forgiveness. She was caught by surprise by what happened inside her. As soon as Sydna dropped the letter into the mail, "a weight lifted. I felt like I was losing twenty pounds. That's when I learned that anger, bitterness, and unforgiveness keeps you from experiencing the depths of joy."

Sydna experienced a truth made more widely known by Fuller Seminary professor Lewis Smedes, whose 1984 *Forgive and Forget* is a seminal book on the topic of human forgiveness. As Smedes reflected on the gospel, it occurred to him that "forgiving fellow human beings for wrongs done to them was close to the quintessence of Christian experience. And, more, that the inability to forgive other people was a cause of added misery to the one who was wronged in the first place."

Smedes found that, in the past, "human forgiveness had been seen as a religious obligation of love that we owe to the person who has offended us. The discovery that I made was the important benefit that forgiving is to the forgiver."

This doesn't negate the fact that forgiveness is a Christian obligation, but it should help us to embrace the call to forgive, because to do so is ultimately an act of self-defense. Smedes presents a real-world view of forgiveness. Rather than seeing the aim of forgiveness as exclusively reconciliation, it becomes a matter of self-preservation. "Ideally," Smedes says, "forgiving brings reconciliation, but not always. Reconciliation depends on the response of the person who injured someone and is forgiven. But that person may tell the forgiver to take his forgiveness and shove it down the toilet. Indeed, there is never a real reconciliation unless the wronged person first heals herself by forgiving the person who wronged her."

> **To embrace the call to forgive is ultimately an act of self-defense.**

Does that render forgiveness invalid? "Not at all," says Smedes. "The first person who gains from forgiveness is the person who does the forgiving and the first person injured by the refusal to forgive is the one who was wronged in the first place." Smedes believes that "untold pain is brought about in the world by people's unwillingness to forgive and the corresponding passion to get even."

A patient process

Though Sydna Masse forgave Diane for murdering her friend, she did so initially out of a sense of obligation. "What I didn't expect was what I got in return," she says today.

Just days after mailing her letter to Jennifer, Sydna received a response. "I'm sorry for killing your friend," Jennifer wrote.

When Sydna read those words, it hit her "like a thunderbolt." "I didn't realize I needed to hear that," she says.

But she did.

A pen-pal relationship developed, and Sydna eventually realized that what she once viewed as an obligation—forgiving Jennifer— ended up ministering to her own heart in some profound ways. She admits that if she hadn't forgiven first, Jennifer never could have expressed her repentance to her, because Jennifer didn't even know that Sydna existed.

Ironically, Jennifer began ministering to Sydna through her letters. "For some reason, her letters always came on dark days for me. Jennifer became one of my greatest encouragers."

Over time, Sydna began to consider Jennifer a friend "just as much as I had considered Diane a friend."

If forgiveness is so powerful, how do we experience it? How do we learn to let go of bitterness and resentment?

L. Gregory Jones, dean of the divinity school and professor of theology at Duke University, points out that forgiveness is a process. "Forgiveness is not an all-or-nothing affair," he told me. "It involves the healing of brokenness, and it involves words, emotions, and actions. If persons continue to have feelings of bitterness toward another, there may not be the fullness of forgiveness, but that doesn't mean there is no forgiveness. Rather, the persons are involved in *a timeful process*."

When I remember that forgiveness is a process, it helps me when feelings of anger and bitterness return. It is a mistake to assume that "letting go" is always going to be a onetime event. Far more often, it is an ongoing *commitment*.

The process of forgiveness involves overcoming negative emotions (such as resentment), thoughts (such as harsh judgments), and behaviors (such as revenge seeking) toward the person who did the wrong, and substitutes instead more positive emotions (such as wishing them well), thoughts (such as remembering that

> ### *If forgiveness is so powerful, how do we experience it?*

all of us have sinned), and behaviors (such as doing something to "bless" them). It is the "art of substitution": wishing well instead of wishing ill, blessing instead of cursing. Forgiveness thus involves the total person—everything, in fact, that makes us human.

This is the opposite, of course, of what happens so often when parents insist that their children say, "I'm sorry," and the child replies, "Sooorrrryyyyy" with all the sincerity of a 3:00 A.M. infomercial. True forgiveness calls us to address our feelings, our thoughts, and our actions—in other words, the total person.

As part of this process, it's important to address the issue of justice. Robert Enright and two other researchers suggest that forgiveness is distinguished from justice "in that the latter involves reciprocity of some kind, whereas forgiveness is an unconditional gift given to one who does not deserve it." Sometimes we hesitate to forgive because it seems so antagonistic to our sense of justice, but Glen Mack Harnden points out that "forgiveness does not preclude the enforcement of healthy and natural consequences on the offender. . . . Whenever an individual offends another, the offender gives up a certain degree of power in determining his or her own destiny, with the power being given over to the offended."

> **Sometimes we hesitate to forgive because it seems so antagonistic to our sense of justice.**

This is something with which Lewis Smedes would agree: "Some people view forgiveness as a cheap avoidance of justice, a plastering over of wrong, a sentimental make-believe. If forgiveness is a whitewashing of wrong, then it is itself wrong. Nothing that whitewashes evil can be good. It can be good only if it is a redemption from the effects of evil, not a make-believing that the evil never happened."

This distinction between justice and forgiveness became blurred during a particularly sad chapter in the history of the United States, the impeachment trial of President Bill Clinton. Robert Enright explains, "In many instances where President Clinton was asking for forgiveness, I think he was asking for legal pardon, and those are very different concepts. There was a confusion that then arose by many people that when we forgive we can let go of all the legal ramifications. That's a misunderstanding of forgiveness."

This is not to suggest that forgiveness doesn't have a place in the political arena. On the contrary, it was put to remarkably good use in Yugoslavia.

Arresting the violence

"It's one thing to believe in miracles, it's another to be part of one," says Roy Lloyd, a founding board member of the International Forgiveness Institute and the broadcast news director for the National Council of Churches. Lloyd was part of a fifteen-member delegation that traveled to Yugoslavia during April of 1999 in a successful attempt to get three captured American soldiers released.

The rescue mission, though portrayed by some as a Jesse Jackson media stunt, was co-led by Jackson and Joan Brown Campbell, then the general secretary of the National Council of Churches. Some years back, Roy Lloyd and Campbell had had several discussions about the role of forgiveness in healing social wrongs in the wake of church burnings.

One young man who had been convicted of setting fire to a church was visited by several pastors during his imprisonment and ultimately made a profession of faith in Jesus Christ. Upon his release, he returned to the church and publicly asked for forgiveness. The church members surrounded the man and prayed for God to bless him.

Following this experience, both Campbell and Lloyd were eager to apply the principles of forgiveness research to the problems in Yugoslavia. The delegation to that country transcended religious lines—mainline Protestant Christians, Roman Catholics, Jews, Orthodox Christians, and Muslims all took part.

"A number of our basic premises were very important," Lloyd says. "All throughout the trip you heard people from our delegation saying that the cycle of violence needs to be broken and that past injuries shouldn't dictate the present or the future. Forgiveness is first of all a gift that you give to yourself. You shouldn't allow something that happened to you or your ancestors long ago to continue injuring you. The most important thing is wishing the best for yourself as well as for others. In that process, you and those with whom you interact are freed from what has been and can envision what might be."

Lloyd heard both Joan Brown Campbell and Jesse Jackson voice these sentiments on several occasions, but he became disillusioned by a media that he describes as "narrow-minded and lazy." On one occasion, Jackson urged reporters to pay careful attention to a rabbi within the delegation, but as soon as Jackson stepped away from the microphone, "the television lights went off. They had their sound bite and didn't want anything more, even though they were missing a major part of the story"—namely, the role forgiveness played in helping to address the problems in Kosovo. Roy Lloyd described it this way:

> In meetings with the foreign secretary of Yugoslavia and other political leaders, we made points about how the violence needs to stop in Kosovo. We applied the principles of forgiveness research—that people are responsible, but that we shouldn't look at others as enemies, but rather as friends if we want to break the cycle of violence. Forgiveness of deeds long past needs to take place rather than repeating them. We need to envision the best for ourselves and for others, and in that everyone will find a peaceful future.

When members of the delegation met with the then Yugoslav president Slobodan Milosevic, they were well aware that negotiations for the release of the American soldiers weren't really possible. "We had nothing to offer," Lloyd admits, "other than a religious, spiritual, and humanitarian approach." Without political leverage, the leaders spoke of the importance of forgiveness and doing the right thing. "Our delegation told Milosevic that he was treated so poorly in the press because of what he had done. If he wanted to change the press, he had to change his ways."

> **Without political leverage, the leaders spoke of the importance of forgiveness and doing the right thing.**

According to Lloyd, all nine of Milosevic's top advisers (several of whom had met with the Campbell-Jackson delegation) spoke with one voice: "Let the soldiers go." Milosevic ultimately agreed with his advisers, but then it was his turn to practice forgiveness.

"On the very day [Milosevic promised the soldiers' return], a busload of ethnic Albanians was hit by a bomb while crossing a bridge, killing dozens," Lloyd remembers. "And then [NATO] bombed the ambulance that was going out to help them." In spite of these events, Milosevic stayed true to his word.

Lloyd says that the released soldiers practiced their own brand of forgiveness. "Each of the three young soldiers was very religious," he points out, "and one of them, Christopher Stone, wouldn't leave until he was allowed to go back to the soldier who served as his guard and pray for him."

In spite of the political realities surrounding the delegation, Lloyd says the fifteen members called themselves "the Religious Mission to Belgrade." When Jesse Jackson finally received the news of the soldiers' impending release, he held off reporters long enough to gather the delegation for group prayer.

Researchers are finding that a practice taught by Jesus Christ nearly two thousand years ago may be our most effective tool and response.

While Lloyd advocates forgiveness, he still believes that justice needs to be done in Yugoslavia. "Milosevic has done terrible, evil things," he says. "One can forgive him, but one can also call for him to indeed be tried in the Hague for crimes against humanity."

Stories such as this one also reinforce Glen Mack Harnden's belief that forgiveness has great potential to solve many social problems, including crime. Retaliation or pursuing vengeance, he says, "often leads to the perpetuation of increasingly a more severe retaliatory, violent response." At an American Psychological Association meeting, Harnden suggested that forgiveness, not retaliation, "represents the most strategic intervention in reducing violence in our society."

Harnden quotes from research conducted by former Union Theological Seminary president Donald Shriver when he says that from the 1500s to the 1800s—a period of four centuries—a total of 34.1 million persons were killed in war. In the last century alone (the 1900s), almost three times that many (107.8 million) have been similarly killed. "Forgiveness stops the ongoing cycle of repaying vengeance with vengeance that appears to contribute to the perpetuation of an increasingly violent society," Harnden says.

Thus, for international, national, and even personal situations, researchers are finding that a practice taught by Jesus Christ nearly two thousand years ago may be our most effective tool and response.

ancient witness

Forgiveness was certainly at the heart of the ancients' message of a true spirituality. William Law, a post-Reformation Anglican mystic (1686–1761), shows that Lewis Smedes's "discovery"—that the first person served by forgiveness is the person who does the forgiving—is by no means a new one. Law wrote about this some 350 years ago:

> If religion forbids all instances of revenge without any exception, 'tis because all revenge is of the nature of poison, and though we don't take so much as to put an end to life, yet if we take any at all, it corrupts the whole mass of blood and makes it difficult to be restored to our former health.
>
> If religion commands a universal charity, to love our neighbor as ourselves, to forgive and pray for all our enemies without any reserve, 'tis because all degrees of love are degrees of happiness that strengthen and support the divine life of the soul and are as necessary to its health and happiness as proper food is necessary to the health and happiness of the body.[11]

Do you want to strengthen "the divine life" of your soul? If so, Law says, you must avoid the poison of bitterness and revenge, and learn to forgive.

But how? Law prescribes prayers of blessing to help us overcome a lack of forgiveness. Instead of giving in to the "first approaches of resentment, envy, or contempt toward others," we can intercede for those who sinned against us and let God redirect our heart toward charity and grace.[12] In effect, Law says, if you're having a difficult time letting go of bitterness toward someone, begin praying for them. Instead of fuming, bless them and ask God to do a new work in their hearts and to make all things well with their soul.

> *If you're having a difficult time letting go of bitterness toward someone, begin praying for them.*

The great Protestant Reformer John Calvin has helped me deal with the need to call people to justice and repentance in light of the corresponding call to forgive. He teaches that if the offender remains "deaf to our reproofs," continues to flatter himself, stubbornly resists any admonitions, "or excuses himself by hypocrisy," then "greater severity is to be used toward him." But once the offender is repentant and "trembles under the sense of his sin," we should immediately respond with grace, mercy, and pardon.[13]

This approach is helpful to me, because it shows that the ancients didn't view forgiveness as the whitewashing of sin. We are to be very clear about the offense, and how it is an offense against justice, but as soon as repentance is genuine, we must be *just as eager* and *just as quick* to offer forgiveness as we were to point out the original fault.

Calvin stresses that we have a special duty to forgive fellow believers: "If we have been injured by the members of the Church, we must not be too rigid and immovable in pardoning the offense." He writes that, while forgiveness is generally urged on us toward all persons, we are "harder than iron" if we are not especially eager to forgive members of God's own family.[14]

In light of a multitude of church fights today, the body of Christ would do well to take these words to heart. For some reason, we seem more reluctant to forgive fellow Christians than non-Christians, and we are often the most reluctant to forgive pastors and Christian leaders. This makes us, in Calvin's words, "harder than iron."

giving up the grudge

Do you, like Sydna, have a neighbor—or maybe a family member or friend—to forgive? Are you allowing a past deed to poison your spiritual life, dampen your witness, and ultimately make you miserable?

Maybe you had a rough time growing up. Kids teased you unmercifully. Even the teachers didn't treat you fairly. The mere mention of your former school's name makes your insides churn and burn. Is this bitterness serving you, or is it destroying you? Are you willing to consider initiating the process of letting the resentment go through the spiritual discipline of forgiveness?

You might also have a longtime rival or enemy, a John Adams to your own Thomas Jefferson. Is it possible to revisit that relationship, offer words of grace and healing, and not be burdened in your final days with grievances that are decades old?

> **Protect yourself and honor God by embracing the fullness that forgiveness offers.**

Perhaps you've tried to forgive someone, but a new offense, or perhaps a recovered memory, has short-circuited the process. Remember: Forgiveness requires perseverance. Press on to complete the work God has given you to do. Consciously apply grace to the offense. Begin interceding for and spiritually blessing the offender. Protect yourself and honor God by embracing the fullness that forgiveness offers.

Authentic Faith

In January of 1972, tensions were high as Ohio State got set to meet Minnesota in an NCAA basketball game. Back then, you had to win your conference to be invited to the national tournament. Ohio State was ranked third in the nation and Minnesota was ranked fourth, but only one of them could make it out of the Big Ten conference.

The press didn't help things by playing the racial card. Most of Minnesota's players were black; the majority of Ohio State's players were white. The media hype, the stakes for which the teams were playing, and the intensity of the moment created a tinderbox that could explode at the slightest spark.

In the last minute of that contest, the spark ignited.

Before the game, Minnesota's coach had told his players that the key to victory would be to neutralize Luke Witte, Ohio State's center. If they could take Luke out of the game, the coach reasoned, their chance of winning was good.

With about a minute to go, Ohio State was leading by six points. Witte yanked down a defensive rebound, and Minnesota stayed downcourt to put pressure on the ball handler. Luke escaped to the other end of the court and was all alone under Ohio State's basket when he got the ball. In a furious catch-up chase, Minnesota player Clyde Turner raced up the court and hit Luke with a roundhouse across his face as Luke went up for a left-handed layup. Luke dropped to the floor, dazed, but as he looked up, he saw a hand come down to pick him up. Luke thought it was a friendly hand, but he couldn't have been more mistaken.

Corky Taylor helped Witte get halfway up, and then he kneed him in the groin. Luke dropped back to the floor, nearly unconscious from the pain. Minnesota player Ron Behagen—who had fouled out earlier and thus had been sitting on the bench—rushed onto the floor and kicked Luke in the head three times.

A near riot ensued as another Ohio State player was badly injured, and the entire Ohio State contingent huddled in the middle of the floor, unsure of what would happen next.

The next thing Luke knew he was lying in a University of Minnesota hospital room, one of his teammates in the bed next to him. He had no recollection of the horrific abuse he had received the night before. When his brother called to ask him how he was, Luke still wasn't sure what had happened. His contacts had been taken out, so he couldn't see well. He remembers stammering, "Well, my head is covered with bandages, I have a patch over one eye, and I feel like I was drug behind a truck, but other than that, I guess I'm okay."

When Wayne Duke, the commissioner of the Big Ten, later visited Luke in Columbus to watch a video of the attack, Luke couldn't watch; he had to turn his head away.

All told, Luke had a scratched cornea, twenty-seven stitches across his face, a cauliflower ear that had swelled and discolored in a grotesque fashion, and the less visible but even more painful after-effects of being kneed in the groin.

Recovery was slow and unsteady. After failing a neurological exam, Luke missed several games, but basketball wasn't the only part of his life affected. Luke went through several "blackout" periods. He once sat through a class without any recollection of what the professor had said. In fact, when the class ended and the students filed out, Luke didn't realize class was over, so he sat through a second class, still not understanding that he wasn't in the right place. It wasn't until a friend walked in for yet a third class and asked Luke, "What are you doing here?" that Luke realized what had happened.

At the time, Luke wasn't a devout Christian. "I classify myself then as a one-hour-a-week Christian," he told me, but he felt God's voice urging him to choose forgiveness over retaliation—this, in spite of the fact that he immediately started being pressed to sue everybody: the school, the players, the coaches, the state, even members of the police force who had exited the building before the end of the game and left the Ohio State players in an extremely vulnerable situation.

Not a single person—not even Luke's dad, who was a pastor—suggested forgiveness. Although Luke wasn't a devout believer, he still heard God's voice telling him that "I needed to drop it, turn the other cheek, and start my process of healing." Luke attributes these thoughts to God, as he says, "I didn't have enough cognitive understanding to come up with that myself."

> **"I can choose to live in anger and hurt, but I can also choose to live in the freedom of knowing that Christ is in charge."**

Luke's decision to forgive was a "thirty-year process" made up of many small choices. "I can choose to live in anger and hurt," he told one sports magazine, "but I can also choose to live in the freedom of knowing that Christ is in charge."[15]

About ten years after the attack, Luke finally got a letter from Corky Taylor, one of the players who had hurt him. Corky was raising two boys and felt that he needed to address his past before he could teach his sons about love, morality, and ethics. Since the incident, Corky had become very involved at his church and was teaching Sunday school.

Luke tried to respond with a letter, but could never get it quite right. Finally, his wife suggested, "Why don't you just call him?"

Luke did, and the reconciliation began.

That reconciliation ultimately led to a visit in which Luke flew into Minneapolis and met not just with Corky, but also with Clyde Turner, who had delivered the original roundhouse across the face. Near the end of their time together, Luke said to Clyde, "We've talked about a lot of stuff; would you mind if I use it when I speak or write?" Clyde, who had become a strong believer, responded, "You know what, Luke? I don't care what you use, except I want you to make sure that, when you use it, you tell the full gospel."

As Luke reached out to the Minnesota players, he realized how God had used that terrible experience to awaken and mature his faith. "I realized God was there, God was moving, God was putting things in my path, taking me around obstacles. I could see that he had led me through this."

Today, one of Luke's ministries as a pastor at the Forest Hills Church in Charlotte, North Carolina, is divorce recovery. "People come in who have been physically and mentally abused. We talk about forgiveness and what it really means," Luke told me. He's learned that forgiveness is separate from the other person's repentance and commitment to reconciliation. Some of the Minnesota players haven't wanted to reconcile, and some see things as having happened very differently, though the news footage is pretty self-explanatory. "It's not our responsibility to make the offender repent," Luke says, "but forgiveness is our part . . . that brings the full freedom of Christ into our life."

A couple months ago, Luke had breakfast with a guy who confessed he was struggling with "really bad feelings" about his dad.

"What kind of relationship do you have with your dad?" Luke asked.

"He's dead."

Luke used his own experience to talk about the difference between forgiveness and reconciliation. "It isn't even about the other person still being alive," Luke assured the man. "Forgiveness is in your heart—that's where your healing comes from. You're being dragged down by a grave, but an empty cross tells us we shouldn't be brought down by a grave."

There has never been a formal "Will you forgive me?" "Yes, I forgive you" session with the Minnesota players. "I don't think forgiveness usually happens like that," Luke says. "For me, it's always been about responding to those sometimes really weird situations that God brings about. He puts this opportunity in front of you, and you have a choice—are you going to follow through, or not?"

Though initially forgiveness seemed like a chore and solely a spiritual obligation, eventually Luke came to see it as the doorway to spiritual freedom. He now views forgiveness as "the start, the beginning of the healing process. Not until we have totally abandoned our hearts to the power of Christ Jesus can true freedom be accomplished. This true freedom and peace come from having a reconciliatory heart, transformed so that we can experience the fruit of the Spirit as Christ intended. The equation begins with the conscious choice of forgiving (again and again), which brings our hearts to be transformed through faith. Then the reconciled heart begins to know the true freedom of trusting in Christ and the peace of knowing and walking with God."

> "The equation begins with the conscious choice of forgiving (again and again), which brings our hearts to be transformed through faith."

David Chadwick, the senior pastor at Luke's church, gave a sermon on forgiveness, and highlighted it by having Luke stand next to a photo of himself lying on the basketball court in 1972, his face a bloodied mess.

In many cases of such abuse, the physical injuries heal long before the spiritual ones. In this case, Luke's healing is nearly complete. "Your heart is free, isn't it?" Chadwick asked Luke.

"It is very free," Luke responded.[16]

The same freedom can be ours if we embrace Christ's call to forgive. In a fallen world, forgiveness is a skill every Christian must master.

eight

mourning's promise

The Discipline of Mourning

Oh, that there were more crying persons, when there are so many crying sins!
Ralph Venning, seventeenth-century Puritan

The Bible was written in tears, and to tears it yields its best treasures.
A. W. Tozer

"**I**'m a Christian because for once I feel pain. For the first time in ten years, I feel sadness. *That's* why I'm a Christian."

Mark's gay friend was incredulous. "Look, Mark, if you want pain, why don't you try S & M instead of Christianity?"

"That's not pain," Mark insisted. "You don't know what I'm talking about."

Mark (not his real name) is a former drag queen (a homosexual who dresses up like a woman). By his own account, he lived a self-indulgent, pleasure-seeking life. His business practices were ruthless, and he could do cruel things without feeling a twinge of guilt. When his heart was finally awakened by faith, he welcomed two elements that had been strangers throughout his life: mourning and sadness. As I heard him tell his story, I was struck by the depth of his comment to his former friend: "I'm a Christian because for once I feel pain."

So often in our evangelism, we want to stress joy, peace, happiness, and the lifting of burdens, but Mark had had enough of self-absorption. His lifestyle was about as self-focused as one could get—and put up with. He wanted to be awakened, to be alive to justice and righteousness and peace and love. The truth is, there is no spiritual sensitivity in this world without a corresponding pain and sadness. Jesus himself was known as a "man of sorrows" (Isaiah 53:3). To Mark, feeling sadness and pain was a great relief, a certain sign of the gospel's reality and ability to literally make him "born again."

> **There is no spiritual sensitivity in this world without a corresponding pain and sadness.**

It was comforting for me to hear this. I was working on this book at the time, wondering if a text on the "hard" truths of the faith would be welcomed by readers, but Mark's testimony was proof that there are Christians who are looking for a real faith that will awaken deadened sensitivity. These Christians want to experience all of life, including heartache. We've heard enough easy answers. We're tired of the pabulum of self-centeredness and want a faith that challenges us to be fully human and fully God's.

Mourning's Horizon

The woman's testimony was a story of many difficulties and heartbreaks. You'd have to be stone-cold not to feel for her, but then she said something that stopped me dead in my tracks. The woman concluded her saga with a picture of God visiting her and telling her that she was done mourning. She would never be sad again. There would be nothing but joy and celebration for the rest of her life. The studio audience clapped, shouted "amen!" and celebrated as vigorously as I was shaking my head in wonder—and dismay.

I wonder how it would be possible to be "done mourning" and still be part of a church. While I suppose, in very rare circumstances, that it's *possible* a person might not have anything personally to mourn over, if a Christian truly wants to be done mourning, she had better not read the newspaper. She had better sit by herself at church. She had better stop her ears when prayer requests are offered. And she had better learn how to achieve a state of moral perfection.

Otherwise, how will she protect herself from stories of couples who love the Lord but are still slammed in the face on a monthly basis with the painful reality of their infertility? How can she love fellow believers who have been praying for their relatives to become Christians for decades, but who watch with anguish as their loved ones pass into eternity without submitting to Jesus Christ? How can she escape sadness when others with whom she is called to fellowship inevitably face the struggles, burdens, and pain of a fallen world? And how will she repent when she does something that grieves our Lord? To be "delivered" from mourning is to be delivered into a lonely existence, cut off from real life, and, even worse, cut off from real love. As we'll see in a moment, there is no real love without real mourning.

> **Mourning invites us to a deeper life.**

The time will come when all of us will be done mourning—but that time is not now; that time doesn't exist on this earth. We need to mourn. Mourning invites us to a deeper life. It takes us beyond the surface to give us a glimpse of the world as God sees it. Biblically speaking, living life without some degree of mourning is worse than naive; it betrays a lack of wisdom. "For with much wisdom comes much sorrow; the more knowledge, the more grief," Solomon tells us in Ecclesiastes 1:18.

In the Wisdom literature, mourning isn't seen as something to *run* from but something to *learn* from:

> It is better to go to a house of mourning
>   than to go to a house of feasting,
> for death is the destiny of every man;
>   the living should take this to heart.
> Sorrow is better than laughter,
>   because a sad face is good for the heart.
> The heart of the wise is in the house of mourning,
>   but the heart of fools is in the house of pleasure.

ECCLESIASTES 7:2–4

I don't want to take this verse out of context. Clearly, it's talking about the reality of death more than it is about the notion of mourning for mourning's sake, but at the very least it points out that there are many sad realities in this world. To live as though the world were a perfectly happy place with no disappointment and pain is foolish and absurd. Wisdom never loses its sobriety. There is a time for celebration and laughter, but laughter loses its depth and sweetness if it is entirely divorced from occasional sorrow. As my friend Jeromy Matkin points out, paintings require both highlights and shadows to create the appearance of depth. So do people.

> According to the biblical witness, being a true believer requires mourning in certain seasons.

According to the biblical witness, being a true believer *requires* mourning in certain seasons. The Lord cried out to the Israelites, "O my people, put on sackcloth and roll in ashes; mourn with bitter wailing as for an only son" (Jeremiah 6:26). Jeremiah confessed, "Since my people are crushed, I am crushed; I mourn, and horror grips me. . . . Oh, that my head were a spring of water and my eyes a fountain of tears! I would weep day and night for the slain of my people" (Jeremiah 8:21; 9:1).

In his classic work *Religious Affections,* the great Puritan writer Jonathan Edwards lists mourning as one of the genuine marks of true faith:

> Religious sorrow, mourning, and brokenness of heart are often mentioned in reference to true religion. These are frequently described as those qualities which distinguish true saints and are a significant part of their character: "Blessed are they that mourn, for they shall be comforted" (Matthew 5:4). "The Lord is near to them that are of a broken heart, and saves such as be of a contrite spirit" (Psalm 34:18). Thus godly sorrow and brokenness of heart is often referred to as one of the great distinguishing traits of saints that is peculiarly pleasing and acceptable to God. "The sacrifices of God are a broken spirit: a

broken and contrite heart, O God, you will not despise" (Psalm 51:17; see Isaiah 57:15; 66:2).[1]

In one of the more provocative passages in the Bible, Ezekiel sees a vision where God tells one of the angels to scour the city of Jerusalem, marking the foreheads of those who "grieve and lament over all the detestable things" (Ezekiel 9:4) done in the city. He then hears God tell another servant, "Follow him through the city and kill, without showing pity or compassion . . . but do not touch anyone who has the mark" (Ezekiel 9:5–6). In this instance, the lack of mourning over a city's wickedness constituted a capital offense. You

> *So often, our culture looks on mourning as something to be shunned and overcome.*

can be sure that Ezekiel duly obeyed when God later instructed him, "Therefore groan, son of man! Groan before them with broken heart and bitter grief" (Ezekiel 21:6).

Yet so often, our culture looks on mourning as something to be shunned and overcome. This is sad, because a preacher who insists on always spouting "sweetness and light" may well miss some of the more substantive truths of God's message. During Joel's time, religious leaders were specifically instructed to lead the nation in mourning: "Put on sackcloth, O priests, and mourn; wail, you who minister before the altar. Come, spend the night in sackcloth, you who minister before my God" (Joel 1:13). While God offered forgiveness, the doorway was not rejoicing, as some would imagine, but mourning: "Return to me with all your heart, with fasting and weeping and mourning" (Joel 2:12).

While many historical traditions leave room for repentance and mourning in their liturgical services, the modern nondenominational Protestant church all too often keeps every service deliberately upbeat and positive. Even though somber issues may be addressed, pastors often feel obligated to wrap everything up at the end so that the service ends in an uplifting way. This lightheartedness is not an accurate reflection of life. I know of one pastor who had to admit this when he sat through a service just after his mom had unexpectedly passed away. Suddenly the focus on celebrating and rejoicing became an assault, not a comfort, and he wondered why today's church sings one hundred psalms of praise for every one song of lament.[2]

celebration and weeping

Mourning is a curious thing. A spiritually deadened person mourns over things that should bring celebration—and often celebrates things that should be mourned. In many ways, what we mourn over is a benchmark of our maturity—or at least, of what we hold dear.

> **What we mourn over is a benchmark of our maturity.**

On the other hand, some mourning can be misguided. Mourning isn't meant to be an absolute, but rather a right response.

Shakespeare had fun with the whole concept of mourning in his play *Twelfth Night*. Olivia feels tremendous grief over the death of her brother, but even more, she resents the fact that the world goes on, which, in her mind at least, dishonors the dead. Consequently, she seeks to prolong the period of grief beyond all natural experience. For seven years, she walks with a veil and continues to shed tears on a daily basis. Because her brother has died, she wants the world to stop, or at least slow down, and she's bitter over the fact that it doesn't. Shakespeare sends the fool Feste to prod Olivia from this prison.

> FESTE: Good madonna, why mourn'st thou?
> OLIVIA: Good fool, for my brother's death.
> FESTE: I think his soul is in hell, madonna.
> OLIVIA: I know his soul is in heaven, fool.
> FESTE: The more fool, madonna, to mourn for your brother's soul, being in heaven.[3]

It is not easy to mourn well, and even more difficult to mourn for the right reasons in the right way.

As Jesus entered Jerusalem prior to his arrest on the Mount of Olives, the crowds gave him an ovation that surpassed those given to the Beatles on the Ed Sullivan show. "Blessed is the king who comes in the name of the Lord!" they sang out, much to the Pharisees' disgust, who begged Jesus to call a halt to such worship (for that is what it truly was). Instead, Jesus said, "If they keep quiet, the stones will cry out" (see Luke 19:38–40).

Yet as Jesus drew closer to Jerusalem, with the crowd's worship and cheers ringing in his ears, he did a curious thing. *He wept.* Jesus cried over the future that was hidden from Jerusalem's inhabitants, a future destined to come to pass, because even now, though the cheers were loud, the city was already in the process of rejecting its Messiah. "[The Romans]

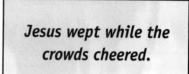

Jesus wept while the crowds cheered.

will not leave one stone on another," Jesus prophesied, "because you did not recognize the time of God's coming to you" (Luke 19:44).

As I put my Bible down the morning I read this, one thought kept running through my head: *Jesus wept while the crowds cheered.* It's a curious picture, ripe for meditative reflection, pregnant with profound meaning. I wonder how often this happens today: God's church, lost in spiritual ecstasy, worshiping enthusiastically, as God weeps about another lost city, longing for us to join him in his sorrow.

Jesus—whom Isaiah prophesied would be called "a man of sorrows, and familiar with suffering" (Isaiah 53:3)—experienced an even deeper sorrow later on, as he entered the Garden of Gethsemane. He told his disciples, "My soul is overwhelmed with sorrow to the point of death" (Matthew 26:38). John Calvin calls this a "deadly wound of grief."[4]

The early disciples shared Jesus' deep and abiding sadness. Paul confessed that he had "great sorrow and unceasing anguish" over those in Israel who had not embraced the Messiah (see Romans 9:2). Paul also grieved over the sins of the Gentiles. "For I wrote you out of great distress and anguish of heart and with many tears," he wrote the Corinthians, "not to grieve you but to let you know the depth of my love for you" (2 Corinthians 2:4). In this case, a sinner needed to be confronted, and though it hurt Paul to have to make such a stern rebuke, he knew it must be done. True community sometimes leads us into true depths of sadness.

Jesus said that those who mourn will be comforted (see Matthew 5:4). Notice that mourning is a precondition of comfort. Wanting one without the other shows a desire to be half-human. If you've

> **True community sometimes leads us into true depths of sadness.**

never been truly thirsty after a run or hike, you have no idea how deliciously refreshing cold water can be. I was hiking with my sister and our two families around Mount Baker one time when we came upon a glacial mountain stream. We had been hiking uphill for about an hour—long enough to get plenty thirsty—and this water was truly heaven-sent.

"This is the best drink I've ever had!" my son Graham proclaimed—this from a kid who thinks Barq's Root Beer and Mr. Pibb are two of history's all-time greatest inventions. His thirst, however, elevated his enjoyment, so that he treasured pure water over any sugary alternative. In a similar reality, we will never learn the full joy of celebration if we have not pierced the depths of true sorrow and mourning.

The apostle Paul spoke of a "godly sorrow," distinguishing it from a "worldly sorrow." Godly sorrow "brings repentance that leads to salvation and leaves no regret." It can produce a healthy earnestness, indignation, alarm, longing, concern, and "readiness to see justice done" (see 2 Corinthians 7:10–11). Because of these results, Paul says he has no regrets about causing the Corinthian church such sorrow. It hurt them, yes, but the hurt lasted only a little while and produced a much greater good, making the short season of sorrow more than worthwhile.

The clear implication is that if we are not genuinely sorrowful in the face of serious corruption and sin, if we blink at scandal rather than risk confrontation, if we act as though sorrow has no place in the Christian life and insist on harmony instead of holiness, we are living a faith that is utterly foreign to the teaching of Paul.

I don't want to overstate this. I still believe joy is the primary mark of a mature Christian. But joy without occasional mourning is naïveté, not wisdom; it's playacting, not true love. As Calvin writes, "Though joy overcomes sorrow, yet it does not put an end to it, because it does not divest us of humanity."[5]

The classical chorus

Mourning certainly played a key role in the faith of the ancients. In his Eastern classic *The Ladder of Divine Ascent* (written around A.D. 640), John Climacus calls mourning a "golden spur within the soul."[6]

When we truly mourn, Climacus says, we become "inordinately compassionate" and nonjudgmental. While most modern readers would take issue with John's assessment of laughter as dangerous to the soul, we can still learn from the insights he discovered while practicing the discipline of mourning. I've found that in my own zeal to grow in righteousness, without a balanced emphasis on mourning, I have a tendency to become critical instead of compassionate, angry instead of gentle, and condemning instead of welcoming.

> **Mourning is a "golden spur within the soul."**

On one occasion, I was having lunch with a pastor who asked me, "I don't know you very well, Gary, but you seem really tired. Is everything okay?"

The pastor was genuinely concerned. Yet, I wasn't able to come up with an explanation. Later that same day, as I carried out various tasks, I felt an anger rising up within me. I couldn't figure out what was causing it, but it was strong.

At the same time, I was completing an article for *Discipleship Journal*. "This is hot!" I said to Lisa, as I e-mailed the final draft to the editor. "I didn't hold anything back! I really let the readers have it." A week later, I received a very gracious and tactful—but equally forceful—reply. Although the editor wasn't this blunt, in essence she said the article was terrible—to her ears it sounded judgmental, cynical, and critical. The editor pointed out that it didn't sound at all like my typical submissions, and she explained in clear detail exactly why she had drawn that conclusion.

She was clearly right. I knew that full well. So my next question was, *What is going on with me?*

I needed to learn that "haughty" rhymes with "naughty" for good reason! Although I was living an outwardly victorious Christian life, my "success" was giving a foothold to poisonous pride. It had been way too long since I had genuinely mourned, and I was correspondingly empty of compassion and empathy. I was skating on the edges of Pharisaism.

Mourning is the handmaiden of repentance, and repentance is the doorway to humility. When my attitudes and actions become marked by pride, it's usually been far too long since I've repented and experienced the essential discipline of mourning.

In addition to defeating haughtiness and pride, mourning is a good antidote to lust, according to John Climacus—but he warns that it must be a consistent mourning: "The man who mourns at

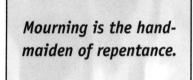

Mourning is the hand-maiden of repentance.

one time and then goes in for high living ... on another occasion is like someone who pelts the dog of sensuality with bread."[7] John is urging us to maintain a certain self-restraint about our actions. If we fail morally, say a quick and glib, "Oh, I'm sorry, forgive me," and immediately return to our former pattern of living without really considering what we've done, we're feeding the sin (pelting the dog with bread) rather than being redeemed from it—and we're using forgiveness as an aid to continue in our sin rather than as a tool to be delivered from that sin. When we fail God, a certain season of mourning is entirely appropriate as we look honestly at what we have done.

This is a practice I've followed in my own life and encourage others to do as well. So often, we rush into wanting to experience God's joy and forgiveness, yet fail to truly mourn our sins—and mourning (as we'll see in a moment) can be an effective deterrent to habitual sins.

Regarding the practice of mourning, John Climacus very practically recognizes that we cannot manufacture tears: "Regarding our tears, as in everything else about us, the good and just Judge will certainly make allowances for our natural attributes."[8] Whether you are a "wailer" or tears come out one by one (or not at all) isn't nearly as important as the disposition of our wills—which includes, but is not limited to, our heart and emotions.

John Calvin assumes the presence of tears in a normal Christian life. When answering the question, "Is weeping requisite in true repentance?" he says, "Believers often with dry eyes groan before the Lord without hypocrisy, and confess their fault to obtain pardon." He adds, however, that "in more aggra-

> *When we fail God, a certain season of mourning is entirely appropriate.*

vated offences" we must be particularly "stupid and hardened" if our sorrow does not lead to tears.[9]

There have been times when I've sat and cried over how I have failed God, forcing myself to face the fact that I've acted despicably and even, at times, played the role of a hypocrite. Alone before God, this is not the "spiritually correct" parroting of Paul's "I am the chief of sinners," but the stark realization that I really *am* the chief of sinners. Given the advantages God has graced me with, there is no excuse for what I have done—or haven't done. I don't rush for consolation, because mourning has a role to play. Particularly with habitual sins or deep-seated character flaws, mourning gets a little more mileage out of our repentance.

Ralph Venning, a seventeenth-century Puritan, urged believers to mourn over other persons' failings, as well as their own. Not to do so, he argued, is tantamount to being an "accessory" to others' sins. "All sin is against God," he wrote, "and for that reason he who truly grieves for his own sin will grieve for other men's too." Venning adds, "Oh, that there were more crying persons, when there are so many crying sins!"[10]

John Wesley also experienced this aspect of mourning. He writes in his journal, "My soul has been pained day by day, even in walking the streets of Newcastle, at the senseless, shameless wickedness, the ignorant profaneness, of the poor men to whom our lives are entrusted. The continual cursing and swearing, the wanton blasphemy of

> *Particularly with habitual sins or deep-seated character flaws, mourning gets a little more mileage out of our repentance.*

the soldiers in general, must needs be a torture to the sober ear. . . .
Can any that either fear God, or love their neighbor, hear this without concern?"[11]

I was studying at a public park one sunny afternoon, the sound
of children playing in a creek providing background noise. The
words they were saying suddenly jumped out at me. Two girls—
neither of whom looked to be over ten years old—were literally
singing, "I'm a bitch, I'm a sinner . . ." It was apparent they were
singing a well-known song, though I had never heard it before and
haven't heard it since. My heart deflated—what has gone wrong,
that ten-year-old girls were singing these lyrics with happy aban-
don? In the face of such loss of innocence, am I supposed to "claim
the joy of the Lord" and move on in happy and silly forgetfulness?
Or am I, like John Wesley, Paul, and Jesus, to be personally grieved
over this offense and implore God to use his church and me to shed
light in this dark world?

I know what Ezra would have done. When he heard about how
the Israelites had disobeyed God by intermarrying with the neigh-
boring peoples, he tore his clothes,
yanked hair from his head and beard,
and "sat there appalled until the
evening sacrifice" (Ezra 9:4). He then
undertook a complete fast (10:6).
When Nehemiah heard about the
state of Jerusalem, he wept, fasted, prayed, and mourned "for some
days" (Nehemiah 1:4).

> **How do we respond
> to news of evil?**

How do we respond to news of evil? Are our lives so full of our
own petty concerns that we have no room to care anymore about the
plight of others? To be a Christian—or even simply to be a sensitive
person—is to mourn when we encounter such sadness. Not to be
moved by such things is the hallmark of a hardened heart and a deadened conscience. We have no right to be deliriously happy when confronted with such evil. There are times to rejoice, by all means; there
are times to celebrate. But there are just as many times to mourn.

The classics encourage us—as Jesus promised—that this
mourning ironically leads to a deeper spiritual celebration. John Climacus writes, "I find myself amazed by the way in which inward

joy and gladness mingle with what we call mourning and grief, like honey in a comb. There must be a lesson here, and it surely is that [mourning] is properly a gift from God, so that there is a real pleasure in the soul, since God secretly brings consolation to those who in their heart of hearts are repentant."[12]

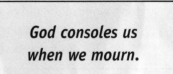

God consoles us when we mourn.

The irony John points to is that God consoles us when we mourn. This consolation isn't a shallow giddiness, but rather a deep, abiding joy, tempered by sobriety, refined by wisdom, strengthened with understanding. It is a strong spiritual state, unassailable by a "bad hair day," a single unkind comment, or a piece of bad news. Forged out of the rock of mourning, it is Gibraltar-like in its constancy—and is a true mark of authentic faith.

mourning's promise

I am struck by how perceptive the ancients were. More than a thousand years before the discoveries of modern psychology, the Christian classics spoke of the importance of mourning in the spiritual life. The clear implication is that if we don't mourn our sins, we can't be holy.

Today, psychologists recognize a mental process called "conditioning." If I do something that brings pleasure or relief from distress, my brain will immediately draw a strong connection between that pleasure (or relief) and the action. If a man finds that a glass of whiskey and soda at the end of a long day relaxes him, it won't be long before his brain starts yearning for that whiskey and soda. Once his shoulders cross that threshold, the mind anticipates the liquid relief. If the whiskey bottle should be empty, the man may feel tremendous stress. Ironically, when something his body has counted on to bring relaxation is withheld, the onetime "antidote" to stress becomes a cause of even greater stress! His body has come to appreciate the routine of the alcohol's effect; now that the routine is broken, his brain has to find a new way to cope, and human brains, by and large, prefer ruts and routines over breaking into new territory.

The danger, of course, is quite obvious—what if the action that brings pleasure or relief is illicit and forbidden by God? In this case, we enter the world Paul wrote of in Romans 7, where we do what we don't want to do and don't do what we want to do. In other words, our spiritual will and our biological conditioning go to war with each other. Our body wants the pleasure or relief, our spirit wants to find that pleasure or relief in God, and a holy war ensues. All of us have experienced the absolute paucity of willpower in the midst of such struggles. It takes more strength than most of us have to overcome neurological patterning with sheer determination.

> **Our body wants the pleasure or relief, our spirit wants to find that pleasure or relief in God, and a holy war ensues.**

Enter the discipline of mourning into the equation, however, and a new patterning may develop. If I allow myself to go through a process of regret and repentance, if I consider why my actions were hurtful and an offense to the power of love, if I contemplate how my evil actions are shaping me into someone I don't want to become, if I make myself face up to the fact that I have dishonored and rebelled against the God who loves me and who saved me—suddenly *negative* conditioning can begin to take place. If I know that an action will lead me through a difficult period of mourning, then the next time I'm faced with that action I will not be solely captivated by its pleasure or relief. Instead, I will remember the consequences, which were decidedly less than sweet.

Embracing the ancients' call to the discipline of mourning has truly been spiritually therapeutic for me. If I'm willing to let myself suffer a little for my sins and mourn over my actions or attitudes long enough to make them a miserable experience, eventually I learn to avoid that sinful action or attitude. There are some sins I now associate with excruciating regret; I no longer look solely at the sin's allure. Instead, I look at what that particular sin cost me, and I say, "I never want to go through that again."

A young seminarian, married just a few years, once shared with me his lapse into pornography. He had developed a habit before marriage, but early on in his marriage he had avoided this behavior. After a couple of years however, he gave in to the temptation once again. Then he did something that some counselors say isn't particularly wise, though it proved very effective in his case: He shared his lapse with his wife. He saw the horror on her face. He experienced her feelings of betrayal, her sense of hurt, and he was covered with a healthy, holy shame. In his wife's face, he was invited to mourn, and he took up the invitation.

"Now, when I think about pornography," he said, "I think about how much I hurt my wife. I don't want to do that again."

He has conditioned his mind to associate pornography with pain instead of pleasure. Most men who talk to me about victory over pornography share one common trait: They've disclosed their actions to their wives. Most men who talk to me about their ongoing struggle with this addiction have kept it secret from those who can most help them, namely, the ones they live with. Sometimes this hiding is spiritualized: "Why should I burden her with my struggle? I don't want her to think she isn't enough for me or that I'm not sat-

> *If spiritual growth is truly a goal in your life, it's okay to make your sins hurt a little.*

isfied with her." Such thinking allows the man to continue looking at pictures of naked women while he continually deceives himself with the promise that "this is going to be the last time."[13]

This is not to suggest that every male reader who has this struggle should immediately, without counsel, make such a disclosure. A wise pastor or counselor can help you determine the time and place for this. What I *am* trying to say is that if spiritual growth is truly a goal in your life, it's okay to make your sins hurt a little. Don't rush so quickly into "peace." James tells us, "Wash your hands, you sinners, and purify your hearts, you double-minded. Grieve, mourn and wail. Change your laughter to mourning and your joy to gloom. Humble yourselves before the Lord, and he will lift you up" (James 4:8–10). If you've sinned, let yourself feel the pain. Experience the negative side of sin before you find solace in the peaceful world of forgiveness. Distress can be a powerful deterrent.

Note, though, that I'm *not* talking about holding on to guilt. Long-term, inappropriate guilt is something much different from true spiritual mourning. Biblical mourning is not even in the same neighborhood as depression, which is a spiritual and mental malady. When I'm mourning as God calls me to mourn, I'm mourning in a secure relationship. My forgiveness is assured. There is no doubt that God's mercy is covering me. I'm mourning as a son who knows he will receive a full inheritance, not as one who fears he will be cut out of the will and disowned. My mourning is focused on the shame I've brought on myself, the hurt I've inflicted on others, and the rebellion I've demonstrated against a God who has shown me only love—but thankfully the story doesn't end there.

> *Holy sadness eventually lifts me up and makes my soul feel lighter.*

Although I am scarred and sobered by my defeat, I am lifted up by God's grace, empowered by God's Spirit, emboldened by God's hope, and comforted by God's presence. I know the future does not depend on me, and I can rest in God's provision. Biblical mourning "washes" me; guilt makes me feel dirty. Holy sadness eventually lifts me up and makes my soul feel lighter; false guilt weighs me down and keeps my head hanging in shame.

Just about any truth can become heresy if it is pushed too far, and this is certainly true of the discipline of mourning. Thomas Aquinas warned against becoming so sad over our sins that we slip into one of the seven deadly sins, namely, sloth. Modern readers tend to think of sloth as physical laziness, but historically sloth carries more a sense of apathetic despair. If our sadness keeps us from living virtuously, doing good deeds, and dedicating ourselves to service (both to God and to others), then it is not helping our Christian life, and it is not holy. Holy sadness is never entirely divorced from a foundational spirit of joy, hope, and even celebration. Divorced from hope, forgiveness, and grace, mourning acts like a wet blanket that holds us back and keeps us entrenched in apathy.

Such distinctions may seem subtle—but that's why the ancients advised us to make use of a good spiritual director who can help us discern what is truly going on in our souls.[14]

Learning to Mourn

In 1998, David Duval was widely considered to be one of the world's best golfers never to have won a major championship. But that looked like it might change when Duval led the Masters at Augusta National by three strokes with three holes to play on Sunday, the final day of the tournament. David figured that as long as he parred each of the final three holes, the worst-case scenario would be a play-off.

He desperately wanted the win because victory in a major is the difference between being considered a "good" player and a "great" player. Even being ranked number one in the world isn't enough to overcome the lack of a major win on a player's résumé.

> *Divorced from hope, forgiveness, and grace, mourning acts like a wet blanket that holds us back and keeps us entrenched in apathy.*

Duval missed his putt on hole 16 by just a few inches, leading to a bogey, but then he parred 17 and 18. The door was opened just a crack, and Mark O'Meara appeared ready to run right through it. Putting together an amazing string of birdies, O'Meara was looking at a very difficult twenty-foot putt with a wicked right-to-left break on the 18th hole. If he sank it, he'd win; if he missed it and tapped it in for par, he'd face Duval in a play-off.

As David Duval sat and watched the drama unfold on television, Jack Stephens, the president of Augusta National, consoled David Duval with the words, "Don't worry about a thing, David. *Nobody* makes this putt."[15] But O'Meara defied the odds. In a heartbreaker for Duval, O'Meara drained the putt and won the Masters in a most dramatic fashion.

To have come so close, and then to have lost, was a difficult blow, the kind that can make a grown man cry months later just thinking about it. Duval's friends did their best to cheer him up, but Duval finally asked them to stop: "Guys," he said, "I know what you're trying to do and I appreciate it. But you know what? There's nothing you can say that will make me feel better. Not a single thing."[16]

There's nothing you can say that will make me feel better. Not a single thing.

So often, when we try to console a friend, we're trying to take away their grief. This can be a highly selfish enterprise, because grief can be very inconvenient—for us! While losing an athletic contest won't mean much in the light of eternity, Duval's story points out something that is true universally: It's not always fair to try to pull someone out of his or her grief. We *need* to grieve, and it's compassionate to let others grieve as well.

> It's not always fair to try to pull someone out of his or her grief.

Almost fifteen years ago now, a close friend of ours miscarried her first child. In a misguided attempt to console her, a number of friends and family members said some things that hurt her even more deeply: "Don't worry. You're young. You can have lots of other children." "It was probably for the best. After all, the baby might have been deformed."

She had just lost a baby. It was right for her to mourn. It would have been unhealthy not to mourn. The spiritually immature try to minimize others' pain, while authentic faith calls us to share others' pain with a sympathetic, compassionate, and loving spirit (see 1 Peter 3:8).

It's uncomfortable to mourn or to be around people who mourn, so sometimes we try to short-circuit the process. Authentic faith and the call to love require us to respect the role that mourning plays and to let people mourn—including ourselves. There is no rush to "get over" something; trying to "talk away" a legitimate grief is naive at best and cruelly superficial at worst. So many times people come up to me and ask me to recommend a book to give to someone who has lost a child or a spouse or who has faced some tragedy, in the hope that the book will comfort them and help them "get over it."

When will we learn that words are limited and so often inadequate? That our call is not to approach grief as something to "talk people out of" as much as it is to share the hurt with them? That we will never "get over" some losses but will in fact carry them to our graves?

I'm suggesting that we gain a new respect for the discipline of mourning— that we let ourselves mourn our sins, mourn our losses, mourn the rebellious state of the world, surely not to the extent that we forget joy and grace and

> *Authentic faith calls us to share others' pain with a sympathetic, compassionate, and loving spirit.*

renewal, but enough so that we recognize the discipline of mourning as a legitimate tool, a true blessing that God provides for us as fallen people in a fallen world.

Let mourning fulfill its function. Don't fear it, but embrace it, use it, and baptize it for God's glory.

Authentic Faith

Twenty years ago, Larry Gadbaugh led one of the most resistant members of his family into the Christian faith. Larry's grandfather was, in Larry's words, "one tough nut." He had run bootleg during Prohibition, owned a tavern, and even spent time as a professional wrestler. He lived the hard life of a logger and had, according to Larry, "three wives that we know of." But before he died, he embraced the Savior.

Larry was asked to sing at his grandfather's funeral. At the end of the service, Larry stood by the casket, watching the mourners file past. His heart almost stopped when his dad finally stepped up to take one last look.

Though Larry's grandfather had embraced the faith, Larry's father was still a self-described "pagan." "I'm not one of you," he had once told a church group. He was highly independent and pragmatic: If faith didn't put food on the table or help you hold down a job, what good was it?

Larry watched as his dad gazed at his grandfather. His dad uttered a few parting words, then softly touched the dead man's hands before moving on. Suddenly, Larry was seized with the future picture of himself standing at his dad's coffin, looking down and saying his final good-bye. He realized that if his dad continued in his unbelief, there would be no hope of heaven, and the parting would be as bitter as it was final.

There, in front of everyone, Larry started to weep. People came up to him to console him, assuming he was crying for his grandfather, but Larry knew his grandfather was in a blessed place. These tears were for his dad.

Over the course of previous years, Larry had slowly stopped praying for his dad. Their relationship had become distant, and sometimes very painful, but as the tears kept pouring from his eyes, Larry realized that he couldn't give up. His mourning gave way to a new determination, and he dedicated himself to renew his prayers on his father's behalf.

After a very hurtful dispute, in which his dad vowed to never set foot in Larry's house again, Larry humbled himself, went over to his dad's house, asked for forgiveness, and listened as his dad admitted his own wrongs. This gave Larry one more opportunity to share the reasons he had for his beliefs.

> *Mourning calls us to plumb the depths of human experience, so that God can raise us to new heights.*

Larry's dad didn't immediately embrace the faith, but he did start attending church, all the while making it clear that "I'm not like the rest of you." One Sunday, one of the pastors invited Larry's dad to lunch. After an hour's talk, Larry's dad finally accepted the invitation to surrender his soul to Jesus Christ. The first thing Mr. Gadbaugh said when he saw Larry was, "Well, I'm one of you now." The next week he gave his testimony to the entire church and was greeted with a standing ovation.

Mourning—so often feared and shunned by our culture—broke up the hardened ground and renewed Larry's efforts and prayers to see his father come to faith. Had Larry insisted on immediate comfort, had he refused to feel the pain or face the agony of the possibility that his father would pass into eternity without salvation, his father might still be lost in his sin, eventually to die apart from grace.

Mourning calls us to plumb the depths of human experience, so that God can raise us to new heights. Mourning is a necessary anchor for our souls to keep us steady amid the reality of a fallen world. It reminds us of our true priorities, and it can be used to compel us into godly action and into profound character growth.

May we not spurn a tool that the ancients found so effective. May we embrace a discipline that marked the life of our Lord. May we weep when God weeps, and join the apostle Paul in the fellowship of sharing in Christ's sufferings.

nine

Tyrannical Expectations

The Discipline of Contentment

The problem with contentment is that I always want more of it.

Matt Atkins

As our family passed by the famous sign, a young cry rang out: "There it is!"

All eyes turned to read the massive inscription: DISNEYLAND: THE HAPPIEST PLACE ON EARTH. There were twenty-two of us on this trip—my parents had generously decided to treat all their children and grandchildren to the extended family vacation of a lifetime.

Five days later, a very tired bunch rode a bus back to the airport. We had enjoyed a wonderful, though exhausting, time. We took a different route back to the airport, one that led us along the back of Disneyland rather than the front. Suddenly, I was shaken out of my slumber by what seemed the irony of all ironies. In the

174

back of Disneyland's grounds, the place where fewer people drive, barbwire stretched from one end of the park to the other.

The world's happiest place . . . surrounded by barbwire.

The incongruity wasn't hard to catch. The fallen world intrudes on all our happiness. No matter how clean we sweep the grounds, no matter how much fun we manufacture within, no matter how full we pack the days, we still need barbwire to keep the "undesirables" from intruding.

When we visited Knott's Berry Farm, an amusement park with a frontier theme, there were virtually no lines, and we went easily from major attraction to major attraction, in many cases walking right on. If the kids really enjoyed the ride, they stayed on and rode again.

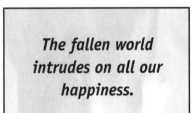

The fallen world intrudes on all our happiness.

My then six-year-old daughter Kelsey was having the time of her life. After about three hours, however, I noticed something curious. She jumped off some little cars; earlier, she had ridden a train, a log ride, a Ferris wheel, a flying school bus—you name it. Her words, however, revealed a spirit that was getting *more* hungry, not less: "What's next?" she asked, with a slightly desperate edge to her voice.

That's when I realized there's never enough excitement to quiet the human heart. We'll never have as much excitement as we want. This has been true from the beginning of time.

poisoned paradise

The Garden of Eden is the definition, literally, of paradise—what we think of as the most blissful state ever known in human experience. Adam and Eve lived unencumbered lives. They were naked, yet there was no lust, no shame. They didn't need to worry about famine, war, cancer, or death. Their relationship with God was something that mystics could only dream about—seeing God face-to-face, talking with him as though he were a next-door neighbor, taking strolls together in the most pleasant part of the day.

Adam and Eve had everything they could want in the Garden of Eden, but contentment was still a stranger. That's what the serpent capitalized on. God held just one experience from history's first couple: They were not to eat from one of the trees. Everything else was provided for their enjoyment.

But there, in the middle of paradise, with no sin or shame present in the world, Eve and Adam weren't . . . content. They wanted more. They wanted what was forbidden.

Eve saw the fruit, and it looked good. It looked as though it would provide something she wanted. Her heart burned within her, blinded to all that she already enjoyed, consumed with the one thing that was forbidden—and suddenly paradise wasn't quite so blissful. It was confining, restrictive, amazingly insufficient.

> **Adam and Eve had everything they could want in the Garden of Eden, but contentment was still a stranger.**

Why can't I eat it? she asked herself. Suddenly, every fruit in the Garden paled in comparison to the one fruit God forbade.

The very first sin, which radically altered the nature of this world and human existence as we know it, wasn't violence. It wasn't lust. It wasn't substance abuse or blasphemy or murder or lying or stealing or even gossip. It was *discontentment.*

If contentment isn't easy in paradise, what hope do we have as we live in a radically fallen world, where even Disneyland is surrounded by barbwire? If we Christians don't address the sickness in our hearts, God will never be able to "bless" us out of our discontentment. The more God gives us, the more we'll want.

Contentment anchors our soul's satisfaction on different shores. C. S. Lewis is quite practical in his approach: "If I find in myself desires which nothing in this world can satisfy, the only logical explanation is that I was made for another world."

soul rest

Contentment is nothing more than soul rest. It is satisfaction, peace, assurance, and a sense of well-being, cultivated by pursuing the right things. Instead of more power, more money, more pleasure, and more control, we seek an "abundance" of grace and peace (see

1 Peter 1:2)—inner qualities of a spiritual nature. Contentment is the opposite of striving, aching, restlessness, and worry. Ask yourself, "Which life would I rather live?"

Contentment	Discontentment
Soul rest	Agitated spirit
Satisfaction	Continual disappointment
Peace	Frustration
Assurance	Anxiety
Sense of well-being	Bitterness

One of the writers of Proverbs very practically surveyed the situation and prayed this prayer:

> Two things I ask of you, O LORD;
>   do not refuse me before I die.
> Keep falsehood and lies far from me;
>   give me neither poverty nor riches,
>   but give me only my daily bread.
> Otherwise, I may have too much and disown you
>   and say, "Who is the LORD?"
> Or I may become poor and steal,
>   and so dishonor the name of my God.
>
> PROVERBS 30:7–9

Solomon understood how much better it is to choose inner tranquility over vain striving: "Better one handful with tranquillity than two handfuls with toil and chasing after the wind" (Ecclesiastes 4:6). If the process we must endure to acquire all the things we want is so loathsome, tiring, and exhausting, Solomon asks us, why would we want it in the first place? Why not decrease our demands and increase our inner satisfaction?

Solomon warns that once the lust for more has captivated us, we will be wretched prisoners indeed: "Whoever loves money never has money enough; whoever loves wealth is never satisfied with his income. This too is meaningless" (Ecclesiastes 5:10).

The biblical writers are clear. We will pay a high price, internally, for being externally based: "The sleep of a laborer is sweet,

> **Discontentment may wear different faces, but it will chase after us our entire lives.**

whether he eats little or much, but the abundance of a rich man permits him no sleep" (Ecclesiastes 5:12). This is as true of food as it is of money: "All man's efforts are for his mouth, yet his appetite is never satisfied" (Ecclesiastes 6:7).

An externally based Christian is ultimately going to be a wretched woman or man. She or he will never be satisfied, never at peace. They will never enjoy the profound tranquility of the restful spirit exhibited by Paul when he wrote these poignant words:

> *I am not saying this because I am in need, for I have learned to be content whatever the circumstances. I know what it is to be in need, and I know what it is to have plenty. I have the learned the secret of being content in any and every situation, whether well fed or hungry, whether living in plenty or in want. I can do everything through him who gives me strength.*
>
> PHILIPPIANS 4:11–13

This state didn't come naturally to Paul, and it won't come naturally to us. Remember, Paul says that he "learned" to be content.

Lusting for more—whether the "more" is a relationship, money, power, or whatever—is something that evolves as we get older. In a book with an unusually provocative title *(Sex and Real Estate: Why We Love Houses)*, Marjorie Garber quips, "When you're 17, you dream of a summer romance. When you're 47, . . . you dream of a summer home."[1]

Discontentment may wear different faces, but it will chase after us our entire lives.

more, more, more

As I flipped through channels on the television, I came across a well-known teacher of "health and wealth" Christianity. He was sitting at a table with a guest, and just as their signal came into my living room, I heard him say, "All right, get ready, this is going to change your life!"

He then looked straight into the camera and said, "Now, before we say this together, I want you to get ready. I don't want you to whisper it. I want you to *shout it out!* I don't care where you are or who can hear you. You just stand with me right now and shout this out. Are you ready? Let's go!"

"Moooooeeeey, come to me now! In Jesus' name.

"Mooooonnnneeeyy, come to me now! In Jesus' name.

"Moooooonnnnneeeeyyy, come to me now! In Jesus' name."

"Whew!" he exclaimed. "Was that a breakthrough or what?"

"I tell you, *I'm* feeling it," the sidekick declared.

I don't mean to be uncharitable, but the two men were huffing and puffing like something amazing had just taken place. They were out of breath and had almost a pseudosexual afterglow. I was embarrassed for them, and my heart grew sick. This was a new one—praying to money. Is money supposed to have ears now? Can we call out to it, and it hears us and comes running?

Biblically, of course, money has no spiritual force we can call out to—*but the love of money does.* The love of money has a force that Scripture says is a root of all kinds of evil. Paul warns Timothy that the love of money will lead some people away from a true faith and cause them to pierce themselves with many griefs (see 1 Timothy 6:10). The writer of Proverbs goes so far as to say that we should "put a knife" to our throats before we crave the delicacies of the rich (see Proverbs 23:1–5).

> **Can we call out to money, and it hears us and comes running?**

There's *never* enough money for a soul-sick heart. In his book *The New New Thing,* Michael Lewis tells the story of Silicon Valley entrepreneur Jim Clark, who has enjoyed a fabulously successful career, including overseeing the invention of a microchip that made three-dimensional computer graphics possible. Before he launched Silicon Graphics, Clark said he'd be happy making $10 million.

When he launched Netscape—building the world's first massmarket Web browser—Clark set his sights a little higher. At that time Clark said he could be happy amassing a fortune of $100 million.

That figure, too, was short-lived, when Clark got "yacht fever" and realized that when you're trying to build the world's biggest yacht, $100 million just doesn't go as far as it used to. But $1 billion, he said—that ought to do it.

Well, not quite. Once he stood on top of Healtheon, a computerized medical clearinghouse, and once he passed the $1 billion mark, Clark told Lewis he'd be happy when he was worth more than software mogul Larry Ellison (who, at the time, was worth $13 billion, but whose wealth has recently climbed to over $50 billion and who may well become the wealthiest man on the planet).[2]

The ante always goes up, doesn't it? Professional basketball player Scottie Pippen was born into a small house crammed with a lot of people. He didn't have much as a boy, but his journey into the NBA changed all of that. In 1999, he was riding a contract that promised him at least $14.7 million a year through the year 2002. Together with endorsements, Pippen is virtually certain to walk into another $50 million over the course of the next three years—and that's after already having enough money to own a 74-foot yacht and a $100,000 Mercedes.

But it's not enough. A feature in *Sports Illustrated* follows Scottie's thoughts during a pregame warm-up:

> Before every game in Portland's Rose Garden, Pippen only has eyes for one. He'll let his gaze drift over to the courtside seat occupied by Paul Allen, cofounder of Microsoft and owner of both the Trail Blazers and the Seattle Seahawks, a man with a personal net worth of $40 billion. Pippen looks at his employer's geeky exterior and wonders, How does he do it? . . .
>
> "He's an amazing guy to look at, man," Pippen says, his voice rising. "What does he have? Forty billion? I want to know: How can I make a billion? I just want one of them! What do I need to do? . . . Tell me how I can make a billion dollars. Tell me how I can become a billionaire."[3]

If you asked most guys earning $65,000 a year if they'd be happy bringing in $15 million annually, 99 percent would think that was enough. Yet Pippen doesn't look at his own salary, he looks at Paul Allen's—and suddenly $15 million a year seems paltry.

In the late 1990s, a well-known titan of business and communications entered divorce proceedings with his wife. At the time, his net worth was estimated at around $5 billion. Wanting to avoid a messy divorce that would disrupt his business, the titan offered his former wife $1 billion if she'd just walk away.

She refused. She wanted half. The lawyers smiled, sharpened their knives, and went to work padding their own firms' ledgers by carving up their respective clients' estate.

I almost laughed out loud when I read this account. What can you buy with $2.5 billion that you can't buy with $1 billion? Think about it! Both partners were in their seventies, and both were willingly bringing untold misery, frustration, and bitterness into their final decades instead of graciously splitting up what was enough money for a small country, let alone two people.

Clark, Pippen, and the billionaires prove true the proverb that reads, "Death and Destruction are never satisfied, and neither are the eyes of man" (Proverbs 27:20).

The Terrible Toll of Tolerance

I suppose it's only fair to Clark, Pippen, and the dueling billionaires to point out that our brain is literally wired toward discontentment. Neurologists talk about a state called "tolerance," which serves as an explanation for how our brain becomes accustomed to what is happening within and without.

The phenomenon can perhaps be best understood by considering substance addiction. If someone puts chemicals into their body, eventually the chemical makeup of our brain learns to tolerate the drugs by achieving a chemical balance that depends on the drug's introduction. Withdrawal, therefore, becomes exceedingly difficult, because withholding the substance upsets the new balance that had been achieved with the drug.

> *Our brain is literally wired toward discontentment.*

Although non-substance addictions are more controversial, many brain researchers believe the same process takes place. We are physically wired, they say, so that we become comfortable with what we have. Our brain gets used to it, which explains why Scottie Pippen, who grew up in a small house with eleven other siblings, can two decades later think his $15 million a year is a pittance next to Paul Allen's $40 billion portfolio.

All of this means, neurologically, that no matter how much money we make, our mind will function in such a way that even vast wealth eventually will feel "normal." Our brain becomes accustomed to a certain standard of living, and once we become accustomed to something, it's only a matter of time until we become bored with it.

> **The discipline of thankfulness keeps God's goodness fresh.**

It is vital to understand this process if we are ever to rid ourselves of this spiritual sickness, which has a fundamental physical foundation. Spiritually speaking, we become sick when we start *tolerating* God's blessings instead of being *thankful* for them. The Bible prescribes thankfulness as the way for us to counteract our growing accustomed to our affluence.[4]

Every time we sit down for a meal, instead of taking the food for granted, we are encouraged to remember God, who provided it, and thank him for its provision. It's helpful to do the same thing every time we enter our houses, namely, thank God for providing shelter from the weather. We should be thankful every time we adjust the thermostat, bringing either the refreshing cool air or the comforting warmth from the furnace. Gratitude should cover us every time we put on a shirt or cover our feet with shoes. We take most of these things for granted, but the discipline of thankfulness keeps God's goodness fresh. We must fight our strong temptation to become merely tolerant of blessings.

This is the clear teaching of Moses in the book of Deuteronomy:

> Be careful that you do not forget the LORD your God, failing to observe his commands.... Otherwise, when you eat and are satisfied, when you build fine houses and settle down, and when your herds and flocks grow large and your silver and gold increase and all you have is multiplied, then your heart will become proud and you will forget the LORD your God, who brought you out of Egypt, out of the land of slavery.
>
> DEUTERONOMY 8:11–14

Tolerance is also the doorway to an even greater sin—the sin of pride: "You may say to yourself, 'My power and the strength of my hands have produced this wealth for me.' But remember the LORD your God, for it is he who gives you the ability to produce wealth" (Deuteronomy 8:17–18). This is a common but particularly sad failing. A friend of mine told me of one man he knows who won't allow his family to say a prayer before meals. "They have no reason to thank God for this food," the man asserts. "I'm the one who went out and earned the money to buy it."

The problem of possessions

In my own life, I've found that greater abundance often invites *more* worry, *more* anxiety, rather than less. When we drove a ten-year-old van, I never concerned myself with where to park it. I didn't worry about someone bumping the side with their car door. I didn't look out at it and wonder if I had remembered to lock it. When a friend or a neighbor kid slammed the sliding door a little too hard, I couldn't care less. But when we bought a new van, suddenly I thought twice about where to park it at church or at the mall. Maintenance demands started eating up my thoughts. When a kid slammed the side door a little too hard, I winced. Upgrading our van, at least initially, took its toll on my psyche. It was embarrassing to admit, but I was attached to a piece of metal.

Jesus was getting at this when he said we can't serve two masters (Matthew 6:24). Notice, Jesus doesn't say it is *hard* to serve both God and Money, but that it is *impossible*. We will inevitably hate one and love the other. In this passage, we are specifically instructed not to worry about physical provisions. Although the pagans run after these things, we are called to seek first the kingdom of God and his righteousness (see Matthew 6:33). Our pursuit should be a spiritual one of character and the advancement of God's kingdom.

Paul's words to Timothy put the bar rather high as far as contentment goes. In Paul's mind, if we have food and clothing—which could reasonably be taken to include shelter—"we will be content with that" (1 Timothy 6:8). The real "getting," in Paul's mind, is spiritual: "But godliness with contentment is great gain" (1 Timothy 6:6).

Throughout Christian history, a number of saints have taken these words at face value. Ambrose wrote, "It is not property which makes rich, but the spirit. . . . For the more a man has gained the more he thirsts for gain, and burns as it were with a kind of intoxication from his lusts." He then adds, "Why do you seek for a heap of riches as though it were necessary? Nothing is so necessary as to know that this is not necessary."[5]

John Wesley gives us a particular challenge in this regard, not only in his words but also in his life. Though he was a wealthy man in his day (his writings brought in about 1,400 pounds annually), Wesley lived on just thirty pounds a year and gave the rest away. (This means Wesley tithed about 98 percent of his income.)

> "It is not property which makes rich, but the spirit."

Wesley held to a rather strict view of Paul's advice to Timothy. He believed that anything beyond the "plain necessaries of life" should be given to the poor or for the propagation of the faith. The fact that this wasn't typically done was merely proof to Wesley that many professed believers are "living men but dead Christians." "Any 'Christian' who takes for himself anything more than the plain necessaries of life," Wesley wrote, "lives in open, habitual denial of the Lord." Such a person has "gained riches and hell-fire!" When Wesley died, he left behind virtually nothing, a goal he had long set out to achieve. "If I leave behind me ten pounds," he wrote, "you and all mankind bear witness against me that I lived and died a thief and a robber."[6]

Let's be honest: Few of us will ever achieve such a spirit, much less such a self-sacrificial lifestyle. An argument could even be made that it is wise and responsible to prepare for emergencies and for retirement with savings accounts, IRAs, and like—otherwise we'd become financial liabilities to the church in our old age. But all of us are obligated—perhaps a better word would be *invited*—to be freed from the endless pursuit of accumulation and instead become a profoundly thankful and uncommonly generous people. Ultimately, it is to our own advantage to receive this spirit from God:

"A heart at peace gives life to the body, but envy rots the bones" (Proverbs 14:30).

contentment in.loss

Contentment is about more than money, of course. It is also about learning to accept God's sovereignty in our lives. Ambrose of Milan (fourth century) had an extraordinary brother named Satyrus, a well-placed man who was himself moving up the ladder of advancement in the church. As soon as Ambrose was appointed bishop, however, Satyrus sacrificed his own career, dedicating himself to serve Ambrose. He didn't want Ambrose to have anything that might distract him from his important duties as bishop.

Ambrose received this sacrifice with great gratitude and plunged into the work of the church. Everything was going fine until Satyrus died, relatively young and quite unexpectedly. Suddenly, Ambrose's world was turned upside down. Not only was he heartsick over the relational loss, but now he had to do the same amount of work without his trusted brother taking up so much of the slack.

> *Contentment is about learning to accept God's sovereignty in our lives.*

It would have been easy for Ambrose to accuse God of unfair play for taking Satyrus away. Instead, Ambrose praised God for the time he was privileged to enjoy with Satyrus. At Satyrus's funeral, Ambrose spoke these words to the gathered people:

> Nothing among things of earth, dearest brethren, was more precious to me, nothing more worthy of love, nothing more dear than such a brother.... I cannot be ungrateful to God, for I must rather rejoice that I had such a brother than grieve that I had lost a brother.
>
> As long as I might, I enjoyed the loan entrusted to me, now He Who deposited the pledge has taken it back.... Who would think that he ought to be excepted from the lot of dying, who has not been excepted from the lot of being born?... Not even in Christ was exception made of the death of the body.[7]

Rather than wail over his loss, rather than wallow in discontentment over how he was forced to carry on without such a trusted brother by his side, Ambrose is thankful for the time that he had with Satyrus. Further, he honestly faces the reality of the human condition: Everyone dies, he says, so why should his brother be an exception? Just because Ambrose "needed" Satyrus didn't mean that Satyrus could escape what each of us must eventually experience. Ambrose remembers Satyrus's life with thanksgiving rather than obsessing over his death with accusations and bitterness.

> **We can choose to thank God for the joy he gave us in the past, or we can wallow in misery.**

What a bishop!

We can adopt the same spirit. When a loved one dies, when a friend moves away, when something in our life changes, we can choose to thank God for the joy he gave us in the past, or we can wallow in misery over the joy we think we will be denied in the future. The choice is ours.

The cauldron of comparison

Sometimes it seems like 90 percent of the world is writing, or planning to write, a book, so I've learned how dangerous it can be to mention what I do for a living, particularly if I'm in a hurry. When I moved back to the state of Washington several years ago, I applied for a membership in a video store. The young woman asked me what I did for a living, and I replied, "I'm self-employed."

Then she asked, "But what is it you do?"

I gritted my teeth and answered, "I'm a writer."

"Oh, really? What do you write?"

I sighed, intuitively knowing what was coming.

"Books, mostly."

"No kidding," she said.

Here it comes, I thought.

"You know, I've been working on a book myself. Think you could read it and give me your opinion?"

I didn't mean to be uncharitable, but I was in a hurry, and all I wanted was a video card so I could rent a movie for the family that weekend; I didn't want to have to read three hundred pages of a novel-in-progress in order to get it!

In this respect, I've come across a number of people who wish they were where I am, vocationally speaking. But does that make me satisfied? Not when I'm sitting on a plane reading *Discipleship Journal* and I come across a *three-page* ad (complete with a response card/coupon!) for Larry Crabb's new book!

I'm not particularly materialistic. You can have your 6000-square-foot home; I can be content with 2,500. You can have your BMW or luxury car; I'd be happy with a five- or six-year-old Ford Bronco. But what I wouldn't give for a three-page ad (including a $2-off response coupon!) featuring one of my books . . .

Wow! I thought to myself. *What do you have to do to get three full ad pages publicizing your book?*

While I've had ads in magazines, I always share the ink with half a dozen other writers. You usually have to use a magnifying glass to make out my name on the cover image. My book is given a one-sentence description that sounds nice—but never nice enough to make me think someone would part with $15 or $20 to read it.

"No wonder Larry Crabb sells so many books," I muttered as I squirmed in my airplane seat. "He gets three-page ads! With a response card!" (Of course, the *reason* he gets three-page ads is because he's already demonstrated an ability to sell a lot of books, but I didn't want to go down that route, lest it destroy my "envy fit.")

I was on my way to Alabama as I read this magazine, and when I arrived, a young man picked me up in an older van that had three car seats in the backseat.

"You've got your hands full," I said.

"I sure do," he responded. In fact, his wife was ready to give birth any day to their fourth child. Their oldest two (twins) were three-and-a-half years old. This couple was hours away from having four children under the age of four.

"Where do you live?" I asked.

"My wife and I have a single-wide trailer out in the middle of nowhere," he laughed.

I quickly did the arithmetic: four children under the age of four, plus two adults, in a single-wide trailer . . .

Suddenly, my own 2000-square-foot house with three children and two adults didn't seem quite so small—even though it had felt like it just a few hours before.

But it's not human nature to compare our lot with those who have it more difficult. No, we are far more likely to compare our circumstances with those who have it demonstrably easier or "better."

It seems that, regardless of how good we have it, we still struggle with envy if someone else has it just a little bit better. In the Old Testament, the Levites had a number of privileges. Instead of having to work the fields, they were supported by tithes given to the Lord. They received spoils from wars in which they didn't have to fight, and they were given forty-eight different cities in which to reside. They were honored with a special place in Israel's religion—a proximity to the ark, and later the tabernacle, which members of the other tribes could not experience except on pain of death.

> It's not human nature to compare our lot with those who have it more difficult.

But the Levites were still one level down from the priests, particularly the high priest, of whom Aaron was the first. And when we're in position number two, we typically don't spend our days being thankful we're not number three. No, we usually think, "I wish I could be number one."

So it's not too surprising that Korah and his followers—Levites—eventually rose up against Moses and Aaron, saying, "The whole community is holy, every one of them, and the LORD is with them. Why then do you set yourselves above the LORD's assembly?" (Numbers 16:2–3).

Moses' response shows the heart of our attachment to envy:

> Now listen, you Levites! Isn't it enough for you that the God of Israel has separated you from the rest of the Israelite community and brought you near himself to do the work at the LORD's tabernacle and to stand before the community and minister to them? He has brought you and all your fellow Levites near himself, but now you are trying to get the priesthood

too. It is against the LORD that you and all your followers have banded together. Who is Aaron that you should grumble against him?

NUMBERS 16:8–11

Instead of being thankful for the privileges afforded them, the Levites became obsessed with the privileges denied them. Ultimately, their dissatisfaction wasn't with Aaron and Moses. In Moses' eyes, at least, their dissatisfaction was with God, who ordained things to be as they were.

One of the side effects of discontentment is that it can blind us to the challenges that a change in our situation might represent. Shortsightedly, we often neglect the truth that sometimes "advancement" can destroy us. William Law, an eminent eighteenth-century Anglican, points out, "[One] clergyman may be undone by his being made a bishop, and that [other one] may save both himself and others by being fixed to his first poor vicarage."[8]

> **Discontentment can blind us to the challenges that a change in our situation might represent.**

Francis de Sales adds another perspective:

> We will soon be in eternity, and then we will see how all the affairs of this world are such little things and how little it matters whether they turn out or not. At this time, nevertheless, we apply ourselves to them as if they were great things. When we were little children, with what eagerness did we put together little bits of tile, wood, and mud to make houses and small buildings. And if someone destroyed them, we were very grieved and tearful at it; but now we know well that it all mattered very little. One day it will be the same with us in Heaven, when we will see that our concerns in this world were truly only child's play.[9]

Francis doesn't trivialize these concerns: "I do not want to take away the care that we must have regarding these little trifles, because God has entrusted them to us in this world for exercise; but I would indeed like to take away the passion and anxiety of this care."[10]

I like Francis's practical approach. To be honest, one of the reasons (from a human perspective) that I was able to make it as a writer is because I was discontented with where I was, and I sought to change it. I worked long and hard. Any man or woman who wants to change their vocational situation may find themselves in a similar position. This isn't necessarily wrong; what can be wrong is the internal desperateness that often accompanies such a pursuit. Thus Francis says that sometimes we need to pay attention to trifles, but "I would indeed like to take away the passion and anxiety of this care."

It sounds like a cliché, but the things we strive for won't bring fulfillment. I once taught a seminary course with Gordon MacDonald. One of Gordon's books has sold over a million copies; for a few years, just about every Christian I knew had that book on his shelf. Yet that success was little comfort during the trials that followed in Gordon's life, and in the wisdom of looking back, he shared that real satisfaction is found in relationships—with God and others. It is shortsighted at best, and misguided at worst, to think that deep soul satisfaction will ever come from achievements alone.

Contentment is about resting, about removing ourselves from the vain strivings of the world and thus finding peace and quiet in God's will. We will never catch up to the incessant desire to better our situation, but we can immediately find satisfaction by accepting it. I'm challenged by the example of the "primitive" Benedictines, known for their vow to a geographical location—which essentially means they agree to stay in one place for their entire lifetime. This is a profound contentment with and appreciation for where you are, an antidote to the wanderlust of "I've got to get out of here." It's taking to heart the words of Scripture, "Like a bird that strays from its nest is a man who strays from his home" (Proverbs 27:8).

> **Contentment is about resting, about removing ourselves from the vain strivings of the world and finding peace and quiet in God's will.**

On the flip side of this, many might experience what Woody Allen confesses to in the documentary *Wild Man Blues:* "I've got the kind of personality where when I'm here in Europe I miss New York, and when I'm in New York I miss Europe. I just don't want to be where I am at any given moment. I would rather be somewhere else. There's no way to beat that problem because no matter where you are, it's chronic dissatisfaction."

Francis de Sales warns that "as long as your spirit looks elsewhere than where you are, it will never apply itself rightly to profiting from where you are."[11]

Joy at the Job

Jim Murphy's job was about as humiliating as it gets: He cleaned up at a sausage factory. According to Jim, being the "cleanup boy" at a sausage factory was a "nothing" job in the minds of most outsiders. Such a job was a little easier to bear for college students who were trying to earn enough money to get through school, but for Jim, who had a wife and a child, this wasn't a part-time, get-through-school venture. This was how he fed his family.

Initially, Jim was thankful for an opportunity to provide for his wife and daughter, even though the work wasn't exactly what he dreamed of. Though Jim was capable of doing more than cleaning, he was doing this job out of principle. In those days, Jim was "antiunion," and he turned down any job offers that would have required him to join one. In a sausage factory, that line of thinking effectively eliminated him from all other positions except management, and since it is a tremendous leap to go from scraping slop off the floors to filling out spreadsheets, Jim certainly limited his prospects for advancement by holding to his principles.

This wasn't a brief experience for Jim: He did cleanup for five years. While Jim accepted his place at the factory, it was still embarrassing, particularly in social settings, when people asked him what he did. Answering the question "What do you do for a living?" was for him an "ongoing lesson in humility and contentment."

On one occasion, that question became a point of acute embarrassment.

When Jim was at the funeral of his wife's father, another relative walked up and introduced himself. Finally, the inevitable question was raised, "So, Jim, what do you do for a living?"

Jim swallowed hard and said, "I'm a maintenance and sanitation engineer."

"No kidding!" the relative beamed. "So am I!"

Jim wilted. What were the odds?

The relative then started talking shop, mentioning equipment and practices that made Jim's eyes glaze over. It was all standard stuff for a real sanitation engineer, but Jim, of course, didn't have a clue what the man was talking about.

After Jim responded "No, I'm not sure what that means" several times, the relative finally caught on. "Well, Jim, tell me," he said, "what exactly *do* you do as a sanitation engineer?"

Jim felt his face grow hot as he confessed, "Basically, I just clean up."

He'll never forget the look of condescension and disgust that covered the relative's face, who excused himself by saying he had to go outside "to get some fresh air."

Jim stood there by himself, "embarrassed before God." But it was a holy embarrassment, because it led Jim to the realization that, at this point in his life, contentment was still a stranger. He saw his relative's question as "the prodding of God," urging him on to the point of vocational appreciation. A committed Christian, Jim took this charge seriously, until he eventually became "as enthusiastic about that job as any job I've ever had." (Jim is now a pastor.) Why? Because he realized he wasn't really working for B & B Sausage—he was working for God. Because of this truth, he knew that he had no need for embarrassment or apology.

> **"God's will is never something to be ashamed of."**

"God's will is never something to be ashamed of," he reminded himself. "I'm happy to have this job, and my words and work should show it."

Does this mean that Jim would have been wrong to ever seek a change in vocation? Not at all. As his family's needs grew, he knew he would have to develop a more marketable skill, since advancement at B & B wasn't likely. He eventually began working for a contractor, became a self-employed plumber, and is now a very effective pastor. I think most people who know Jim would say that his ministry is marked by a refreshing humility. We love to hear his teaching, because we know it will be spoken out of the quiet depths. I'm convinced that Jim's time at B & B was God's way of putting him through "seminary," only this was a character-laden seminary with final exams in contentment and humility, two key virtues for any believer, but especially for a pastor.

For Jim and for all of us, contentment is rarely a onetime choice; it's an ongoing challenge. It's a commitment to being thankful for what we have, even while we may be working toward something better. Contentment has more to do with the attitude and spirit with which we approach our days than with the substance of our days (remember—the apostle Paul learned to be content in any and all situations).

In fact, God can and sometimes does inject us with a degree of restlessness to get our attention and motivate us to move on. Various forms of discontentment have spawned some of history's greatest accomplishments. For instance, God wasn't content to let the world go to hell, so he condescended to become human and to procure our salvation. Our forefathers weren't content to be ruled by a foreign dictator, so they fought valiantly for an experiment known as democracy. A father might not be content to let his family live in poverty, and so he works diligently at night to improve his education so he can secure a better-paying job.

> *Various forms of discontentment have spawned some of history's greatest accomplishments.*

Notice, however, that in each instance, the discontentment is focused on the lot of others. God, our forefathers, and the discontented father had someone else in mind. These were not mere individual pursuits but rather acts of dedication and obedience toward a higher end.

Paradoxically, for our own spiritual health, we must learn how to be content even in our discontentment! That father must learn not to become resentful or bitter about the long hours he puts in as he seeks to create a better life situation for his family. The key is that, wherever we are, we need to adopt a holy attitude of contentment, even while we're working for a change.

Through it all, it's helpful to keep our eyes open and not idealize any future hope, which typically only makes us feel sicker in our present circumstances. Francis de Sales warns that vocational discontentment is a natural and narrow-minded temptation:

> We must consider that there is no vocation that has not its irksome aspects, its bitternesses, and disgusts. And what is more, except for those who are fully resigned to the will of God, each one would willingly change his condition for that of others: those who are bishops would like not to be; those who are married would like not to be, and those who are not married would like to be. Whence comes this general disquietude of souls, if not from a certain dislike of constraint and a perversity of spirit that makes us think that each one is better off than we?[12]

Without contentment, de Sales warns, we will always be restless. "It all comes to the same: whoever is not fully resigned, let him turn himself here or there, he will never have rest." What de Sales teaches us is that discontentment is an inner reality independent of our outward circumstances. A discontented person won't find contentment through any outward change. Put her in a new and bigger house, and she'll still complain. A discontented man can change wives, but if he doesn't address the spiritual cancer within, he'll grow just as weary with the new one. Trying to find contentment in this world without addressing the inner person is no more drastic a change than simply changing cubicles while continuing to work for the same company. Your location may change, but the overall environment is exactly the same.

> **Without contentment we will always be restless.**

Change is sometimes necessary and inevitable in the contemporary business world, but a spirit of surrender will help us face it properly. A good example is Thomas Merton, who, as he approached the Abbey of Gethsemani, eager to become a postulant, encountered curiously mixed emotions:

> It was a strange thing. Mile after mile my desire to be in the monastery increased beyond belief. I was altogether absorbed in that one idea. And yet, paradoxically, mile after mile my indifference increased, and my interior peace. What if they did not receive

me? Then I would go to the army. But surely that would be a disaster? Not at all. If, after all this, I was rejected by the monastery
and had to be drafted, it would be quite clear that it was God's will.
I had done everything that was in my power; the rest was in His
hands. And for all the tremendous and increasing intensity of my
desire to be in the cloister, the thought that I might find myself,
instead, in an army camp no longer troubled me in the least.

I was free, I had received my liberty. I belonged to God, not
to myself: and to belong to Him is to be free, free of all the anx-
ieties and worries and sorrows that belong to this world, and the
love of the things that are in it.[13]

The key is that Merton's dreams were that he would belong to
God; resting in that aim, he could face an uncertain future with a willingness to accept any station in life. Any other spirit will eat us up, as
Ignatius of Loyola noted and wrote about in his autobiography many
centuries ago.

In Ignatius's days, boys didn't dream of throwing touchdown
passes or shooting a three-pointer at the buzzer. Instead, they imagined being a powerful and fierce knight and ultimately winning the
hand of a beautiful woman. As Ignatius allowed his mind to spin
these daydreams, he felt ecstatic and joyful. But later, he discovered
that they inevitably led to feelings of discontentment, a sourness in
his spirit that only depressed him.

When Ignatius changed his focus and began to imagine doing
great exploits on God's behalf, he felt the same joyful and happy
feelings; but in these instances, the feelings didn't fade. They created an undercurrent of joy, a sustainable river of emotional and
spiritual life. Speaking of himself in the third person, Ignatius
writes, "His eyes were opened a little, and he began to marvel at the
difference and to reflect upon it, realizing from experience that
some thoughts left him sad and others happy."[14]

Human imagination is the true garden of contentment. When
C. S. Lewis wrote his fantasy stories, he did so with a well-thought-
out philosophy. Lewis believed that stories based on the desire for
"magic" are healthy for the imagination and spirit—in a way that
stories pandering to the desire to be the most famous, the smartest,
or the most talented sports star are not. Such ego-stroking tales,

Lewis says, are dangerous "flattery to the ego," leaving readers "undivinely discontented."[15] But seeking after the transcendent—which can be found in God alone—points us to the only world where we can be truly satisfied.

Soul rest is found in only one place: seeking first God's kingdom and his righteousness. When we faithfully place our best energies, efforts, and attention on this aim, all other necessities will be added as well (see Matthew 6:33).

chasing contentment

Perhaps you're a realtor. You've just become a member of the "million dollar club" and feel great about it—until you realize that a woman who got her license the same time you did has just hired two more staff people and has bought a huge billboard on the busiest street in town. You think you have the ability to catch her, but your daughter has been asking you to coach her soccer team this spring. You know you make enough money for your family's needs, but the fire of competition still burns ...

Maybe you're facing your twentieth high school reunion with a sense of regret. Everyone thought of you as "most likely to succeed," and, in fact, you did go on to graduate with honors from college. Then you started a family, and you've been a stay-at-home mom ever since. You greet former classmates who were less skilled than you but who now have their own corner offices, and their IRAs are worth more than your house ...

Let's say you're a pastor. God has been moving in your community. A couple marriages have been saved; several individuals have made decisions for Christ over the past few months; you've helped a woman make the difficult transition into widowhood. But you realize you'll never be able to compete with that church just ten miles away that has more staff people than your entire congregation has members. You'll never be asked to speak at your denominational convention, even though you know you have a lot to say ...

> **Contentment is a safe harbor, a true shelter, from the desires that would destroy all that we hold as most precious.**

Social situations often assault our spiritual integrity. We face external and internal pressures every day that ruthlessly challenge our commitment to relationships and mission integrity. Until we value obedience over affirmation, integrity over achievement, and relationships over "success," our souls are literally in peril. Contentment is a safe harbor, a true shelter, from the desires that would destroy all that we hold as most precious.

Authentic Faith

Leo Tolstoy (1828–1910), the great Russian author, wrote his massive novels in virtually illegible handwriting that could be read only by his wife. Sonya diligently typed her husband's scrawling words so that others could read them. Unfortunately, Tolstoy was a bit of a perfectionist, so after his wife had typed his words, Tolstoy wrote corrections on the pages before sending them in to his publisher. The unfortunate printers came to near despair as they tried to make out the famed novelist's changes.

Once the changes were incorporated, the publisher returned the galley sheets to Tolstoy, whereupon he invariably rewrote the book in the same circuitous scroll. Sometimes the changes would be so lengthy that they worked their way out of the margins, up the page, and back down again on the other side. Thus, not only were the words nearly illegible, it was also exceedingly difficult to discern the construction of the sentences and how they fit into various paragraphs.

Since so many changes were made, the publisher sent the corrected galleys back to Tolstoy for his final approval. Contemporary publishers do this as well, but usually with a strong warning that any extensive changes at this point would be too expensive to make. Nevertheless, Tolstoy always took the opportunity to do virtually the same thing, scrawling over the clean pages until they looked like ancient scrolls—and yet again necessitating returning the galleys to Tolstoy to make sure his difficult handwriting was being interpreted correctly.

It began to dawn on his publisher that this could go on forever, especially during the writing of the mammoth novel *War and Peace*.

Tolstoy's publisher finally ran out of patience. He sent a telegram that read, quite simply, "DEAR LEV NIKOLAYEVICH—IN THE NAME OF GOD, STOP!"

Some of us are as obsessive as Tolstoy when it comes to "rewriting" our lives. We say we want a new house; God provides the means for a house, and then we set our sights on a new couch. The couch comes, and we imagine how much better the couch would look if we had new carpeting or a hardwood floor . . .

> *In this blessed place called contentment, ambitious strivings are replaced by firm resolution.*

Or we pray for a new job; we get the job, but then imagine that life would be so much more pleasant if we could get a promotion. Two weeks after the promotion occurs, we realize that the new boss is a bit of a jerk, and think how much better it would be if we could have a new supervisor.

This obsessive rewriting of our desires and expectations can drive us and those around us crazy. There is a place of rest, a time to cool off, snuggle in, and be what God wants us to be. In this blessed place called contentment, ambitious strivings are replaced by firm resolution, daydreams of glory-filled service give way to patient and humble obedience, restlessness transforms itself into peace, and the wormwood of bitterness becomes the life-giving elixir of thanksgiving.

We can always think of ways to improve our lives, but then again, we can also always think of things to be thankful for. Which mental pursuit marks your days? If God were to send you a telegram, would it be, "Well done, good and faithful servant," or would it resemble the one sent to Tolstoy—"In the name of God, stop!"?

Not My Will . . .

The Discipline of Sacrifice

Weaklings are those who know the truth, but maintain it only as far
as it is in their interest to do so, and apart from that forsake it.

Blaise Pascal

My wife startled me with what, at the time, seemed like a bizarre
suggestion. "I think we should let the Smiths borrow our van for
the weekend," she said.

"Where are they going?" I asked.

"Eastern Washington."

"You mean, over-the-mountains-and-across-the-state eastern
Washington?"

"Yeah."

Just weeks earlier, we had purchased our first brand-new vehicle
in almost fifteen years. We had finally secured a minivan that hadn't
been driven halfway into the ground and littered with a previous
family's supply of fast-food wrappers and playground dirt. I was

determined to make the car last—and keep the mileage down—for as long as possible. The thought of someone else dropping a thousand miles on it in three days (when the car had just seven hundred miles on it to begin with) wasn't a pleasant one.

But I knew God had set me up. My devotions that morning had been taken from the book of Acts, and these were the key verses: "All the believers were together and had everything in common. Selling their possessions and goods, they gave to anyone as he had need" (Acts 2:44–45). Sometimes it's safer to schedule your Bible reading in the evening, after all your important decisions have been made!

When I saw that Lisa was clearly serious, I winced. Obviously this was a case where God had provided for us and thus we could help out another Christian couple.

Even so, I was reluctant.

"If money weren't an issue," I protested to my wife, "I wouldn't mind letting them borrow our *brand-new* van. It's just that this is our only vehicle, and I want it to last. We've been trying to keep the mileage down, and now we're going to tell someone else to take it over the mountains?"

Having been married to me for over sixteen years, Lisa knows how to read my face. I wasn't acting nobly, but I was certainly feeling guilty, and guilt usually wins out in me. "Should I call them?" she asked.

"I don't want you to," I confessed. "But I think God wants us to." *Sigh. Deep breath. Second sigh.* "Yeah. Go ahead."

During my run later that day, I began to pray about this discussion. God opened my heart to me, and I saw my words in an entirely new light. I'm simplifying what went on by presenting it in the form of a dialogue, but I know of no other way to capture God's persistent but still, small voice.

It was as though God had asked me, "You said if money weren't an issue, you'd be happy to lend your van to the Smiths."

"That's absolutely right," I replied. "If we had two or three vehicles, and if we weren't worried about paying for the maintenance, it wouldn't bother me at all to see someone else get behind the wheel of that van."

"So what you're really saying," God seemed to reply, "is that you're willing to act like a Christian only as long as it doesn't cost you anything."

Those words hit me so hard I almost fell off the road, which is a tough thing to do when you're plodding along at *my* jogging speed. But they were true. If God "blessed" me so much that I wouldn't even miss my car if I were to loan it out, I was willing to do it. But if it might mean that our one car would wear down a little faster or that maintenance costs would go up, suddenly I was eager to disprove my wife's clear leading.

My reluctance points back to the very heart of why we believe in God in the first place. I asked a friend of mine about her impression of a Christian conference she had attended. This friend is by no means a critical woman, but I

> *If any of these blessings become the focus, or even worse, the purpose, of our faith, we have slipped from practicing an authentic faith.*

could hear her heart's sadness as she said, "Virtually every emphasis was on how to become more fulfilled, more successful, healthier, you name it. It just seemed like a very self-centered approach to me."

It's a fine line to walk, because, in general, we *will* prosper when we listen to God's wisdom for handling money. Our relationships and families *will* be stronger when we adopt the attitudes and virtues of Jesus Christ. We *will* experience more joy as we walk in obedience, and God *does* bless us in many ways—but if any of these blessings become the focus, or even worse, the purpose, of our faith, we have slipped from practicing an authentic faith and substituted instead a gross distortion.

Christianity was birthed in sacrifice—Jesus faced a torturous death, even crying out, "My God, my God, why have you forsaken me?" (Matthew 27:46). *And he is the model for how life is to be lived.* Paul tells us to offer ourselves as living sacrifices (see Romans 12:1). Both Scripture and the ancients present a faith motivated not just by how much we are blessed and how far we are catapulted into affluence, but also by our willingness to sacrifice all those blessings, to literally give up everything, for the pearl of great value (see Matthew 13:45–46).

The cost of commitment

You don't have to know much Scripture to see just how far from an authentic faith I had strayed when my attitude was, "I'm willing to act like a Christian as long as it doesn't cost me anything." After a great failure in his life, King David adopted exactly the opposite attitude.

King David's life had many highlights, but sometimes he really blew it—and this was, at least initially, one of those times. (The story is told in 2 Samuel 24.) His disobedience had resulted in a terrible plague that was pulverizing the nation. People began to drop dead by the thousands. David watched from the roof of his palace and knew it was all his fault.

Finally, the angel of death stopped right at the threshing floor of Araunah the Jebusite, who must have been sweating bullets. Araunah saw the devastation and knew his family was just one house away from becoming just another statistic, so when David came running up and said he intended to sacrifice to God on that very spot, Araunah couldn't have been more accommodating.

"By all means!" Araunah told David. "Here, take whatever you need. You need wood? Cut up the threshing sledges and ox yokes. You need animals? Take my oxen. They're yours!"

Some enterprising believers might have adopted the line, "Wow, God really does provide!" but David had a different perspective. He refused Araunah's offer, saying, "No, I insist on paying you for it. *I will not sacrifice to the LORD my God burnt offerings that cost me nothing*" (2 Samuel 24:24, emphasis added). In David's mind, if it didn't cost him something, it wasn't an acceptable sacrifice. What a contrast this is to my own way of thinking, which wants to serve God only when it *doesn't* cost me something!

This willingness, and even desire, to sacrifice was a lesson that was passed from father to son. As soon as the kingdom was "firmly established in Solomon's hands" (1 Kings 2:46), Solomon offered a *thousand* burnt offerings in sacrifice to God as an act of worship. It's important to remember that burnt offerings were wholly consumed by the fire (except for the skin)—the benefit of these animals was completely lost to the king. Solomon's gesture really was extraordinary, even for a wealthy ruler.

Abraham, the father of all who believe, defined sacrifice as "worship." To this spiritual forefather, worship wasn't merely about emotional satisfaction or personal blessing. On the contrary, when he headed up the mountain, intending to sacrifice his only son, he told his servants, "Stay here with the donkey while I and the boy go over there. *We will worship* and then we will come back to you" (Genesis 22:5, emphasis added).

> *Our faith is about what we are willing to give up, not what we are able to coax God into giving us.*

Clearly, Abraham, David, and Solomon had the viewpoint that our faith is about what we are willing to give up, *not* what we are able to coax God into giving us. Abraham was seen as a mature Christian not because he was wealthy, but because he was willing to obey God at a profound cost. Sacrifice, not affluence, was the mark of his maturity.

Many times throughout Scripture, God calls his people to a deliberate sacrificial act on behalf of his kingdom. God told Jeremiah to buy a field in Anathoth (Jeremiah 32), even as the Babylonian army was besieging Jerusalem. The reasoning was that God wanted Jeremiah to provide a "picture prophecy" that, although Babylon would successfully conquer the nation of Israel, the time would come when a remnant would return—and it was in anticipation of that future remnant that Jeremiah was to purchase the land. Jeremiah himself would never benefit from his purchase. Indeed, buying a piece of land that is soon to be conquered is about as ridiculous a financial investment as you can make, but Jeremiah forked over the seventeen shekels of silver anyway.

The implications are clear: God told Jeremiah to make a costly financial investment for the sake of God's kingdom. If we think that serving God always leads to greater prosperity, we're selectively reading our Bibles.

The New Testament continues this same line of thinking. Jesus commended the widow for giving up all she had, even though what she gave was a relatively small gift (see Luke 21:1–4). It is clear that God looks not at the size of the gift, but at the size of the sacrifice.

As Christians, we no longer sacrifice animals as burnt offerings, but we can offer financial gifts, food for the poor, and good deeds toward others. The writer of Hebrews tells us, "Do not forget to do good and to share with others, for with such sacrifices God is pleased" (Hebrews 13:16). We will never even think about this aspect of faith, however, if we continue to define our faith in terms of God being obligated to bring blessings to *us*.

Where are you today? Consider these two attitudes, and ponder which one marks where you are right now:

Gary's Attitude: "I'm willing to act like a Christian as long as it doesn't cost me anything."

David's Attitude: "I will not sacrifice to the Lord my God something that costs me nothing."

What have you given to God in recent days that cost you something? Are you willing to be a member of your church—as long as they don't ask you to start serving (or work with the young people)? Are you willing to give a few dollars to God's work—as long as you won't really miss them? Are you willing to pray—but not willing to fast? Are your daily decisions based on what brings you the least amount of discomfort and the greatest amount of affluence (which we have grown to conveniently call "blessing")?

If you are dissatisfied with your faith or disillusioned with your God, try this: Instead of accusing or blaming God, ask yourself what *you've* been holding back. Instead of waiting for God's blessing, ask him where you can begin serving. Rather than becoming disillusioned by what God seems to be withholding, or by how life isn't working out just the way you planned it, remember that we are called to follow the example of our Lord, presenting our bodies as *living* sacrifices to accomplish God's work on earth.

> **What have you given to God in recent days that cost you something?**

In fact, the most accurate picture of Jesus, and therefore the most accurate description of what we are to be, is on display in the Garden of Gethsemane. There Jesus prayed, "Not my will, but yours be done" (Luke 22:42). This prayer is at the heart of true Christianity—but that *doesn't* mean it's an easy prayer.

NO EASY conflict

What a night it must have been as Jesus struggled with the reality that was about to take place. He knew what must happen—but the road was so severe, so terrible, so devastating, that of course he had to have been thinking, *If there's an acceptable way out of this, let me know. But if not, I'll move forward.*

John Calvin saw Christ's prayer—"Not my will, but yours be done"—as a revelation of the conflict in Christ's soul, a conflict that all of us experience as we seek to align our will with God's. Sacrifice, though an essential element of true faith, is never easy. Calvin explains:

> The prayers of believers do not always flow on with uninterrupted progress to the end . . . but, on the contrary, are involved and confused, and either oppose each other, or stop in the middle of the course, like a vessel tossed by tempests, which, though it advances towards the harbor, cannot always keep a straight and uniform course, as in a calm sea.[1]

Have you ever experienced this? Perhaps your prayers have had the same chaotic confusion. You begin to pray one way, then stop yourself: "Am I *really* willing to do that? Do I really mean what I'm praying?"

Calvin is quick to point out that Jesus didn't have "confused emotions" as he prayed about his upcoming sacrifice, but "he was struck with fear and seized with anguish, so that, amidst the violent shocks of temptation, he vacillated—as it were—from one wish to another."[2]

There is no vacillation in our prayers when we pray for affluence or blessing. It's easy to agree with God that he should step in and help us! But if we dare to enter the true arena of Christianity, if we accept the cross of

> *If we accept the cross of sacrifice, then prayer becomes a tempest as we seek to die to our own wills.*

sacrifice, then prayer becomes a tempest as we seek to die to our own wills so that God's will and purpose might reign supreme and uncontested—even though we know a price must be paid. It is not a lack of maturity that causes this tempest—remember, Jesus himself walked through it! As fallen, sinful people, naturally selfish and self-centered, we will only too regularly resist God's will, finally settling into it only with a struggle.

Francis de Sales, author of the renowned *Introduction to the Devout Life,* prepared a close friend of his, Jane de Chantal, by warning her that this call to sacrifice will continually wage war in her soul. "Self-love never dies until we die," he admits. "It has a thousand ways of rooting itself in our soul.... It has a legion of soldiers with it, of movements, actions, and passions. It is cunning, and knows a thousand subtle turns."[3]

The call to sacrifice, to self-resignation, is a lifelong battle, waged on newer and deeper levels. As parents, we learn to sacrifice by giving up some of our favorite activities so that we can spend more time with our children. As employees, it might mean staying late so that a single mom can go home to care for her sick child. As church members, it could mean calling a halt to complaining about the building fund and actually contributing to the fund in a way that may hurt our checkbooks.

> **The call to sacrifice, to self-resignation, is a lifelong battle.**

These quiet sacrifices don't carry the air of nobility about them. There are no heroics, no applause, sometimes not even an acknowledgment that they've been made, but that's the nature of sacrifice. One of the "subtle turns" of self-love is turning sacrifice into a stage instead of a cross. De Sales makes this perceptive observation:

> Some are unwilling to suffer any tribulations but those that are honorable; for example, to be wounded in battle, to be a prisoner of war, to be persecuted for religion . . . now these people do not love the tribulation, but the honor wherewith it is accompanied; whereas he that is truly patient suffers, indifferently, tribulations, whether accompanied by ignominy or honor.[4]

De Sales reminds us that once we become willing to sacrifice, we must remember that the nature of the sacrifice is not our choice. "You are quite willing to have a cross," de Sales pointed out to

Jane, "but you want to choose it yourself. . . . The more a cross is from God, the more we should love it."[5]

I remember listening to my former seminary professor Klaus Bockmuehl as he shared the pain of living so far apart from his grown children. "Elizabeth [his wife] and I always prayed that our children would serve God," he said, "and all of them are—in separate countries." His sacrifice was living apart from his children. Others—with mentally or physically challenged children—sacrifice by living with their children for decades beyond the "normal" duration.

What makes sacrifice so difficult is that we don't get to choose our crosses. There is only one man who could die for our sins—Jesus Christ, the perfect one—so his destiny was written in stone from the day he was born. In the same way, God has placed us in settings where certain sacrifices are necessary. The only thing that can make these sacrifices precious is recognizing where the sacrifice is pointing. To repeat the wisdom of de Sales, "The more a cross is from God, the more we should love it." We're not masochists; we don't enjoy pain for its own sake, but we value obedience to God and the intimacy it builds over any pleasure that takes us further away from enjoying his presence. In this light, God's invitations to sacrifice are not April Fool's pranks; they are February's Valentines, if we receive them in this spirit. They become precious because of the One who sent them to us. They mark us as his, and thus we wouldn't trade them for anything in the world.

> *What makes sacrifice so difficult is that we don't get to choose our crosses.*

The human-centered faith so frequently embraced today leads to great disillusionment when life doesn't turn out perfect. The truth is, no life turns out perfect, at least not in this sense. All of us will be called to give up something. When Christians are told up front that the Christian life is a life of sacrifice, they will be better equipped to live out an authentic faith.

In fact, by its nature, sacrifice makes our faith more precious. Jonathan Edwards wrote, "These trials, then, are a further benefit to true religion because they not only manifest its truth but they also enhance its genuine beauty and attractiveness. True virtue is loveliest when it is oppressed. The divine excellency of real Christianity is best exhibited when it is under the greatest trials."[6]

This makes sense, doesn't it? It's human nature to value most that which has cost us something. If you don't highly value your faith, perhaps you've never sacrificed for it.

crazy about sacrifice

In the mid-1990s, Lance Armstrong, a professional cyclist with great promise but not much to show for it, was diagnosed with testicular cancer. After doctors discerned that the disease had spread to Lance's lungs and brain, they gave him a 40-percent chance of surviving—but even that, Lance found out later, was optimistic. The truth is, the physicians didn't want to tell him the sad news that he probably wouldn't live to be thirty.

Somehow, Lance beat the odds. After chemotherapy and the cancer's remission, Lance went back to riding his bike, but his 1998 comeback was short-lived. He placed a very respectable fourteenth in the Ruta del Sol, but then he pulled over to the side of the road in the middle of the Paris-Nice race and told his teammates he was through with racing.

Lance writes, "Back home in Austin, I was a bum. I played golf every day, I water-skied, I drank beer, and I lay on the sofa and channel-surfed. I went to my favorite Mexican restaurant, Chuy's, for Tex-Mex, and violated every rule of my training diet. I intended never to deprive myself again."[7]

Part of this is understandable. To be a top bicycle racer requires tremendous sacrifice—diet, physical training, mental conditioning to endure hours of grueling pain and exertion, all of which grows old in time. Besides, Lance had just come through a harrowing medical experience and had met the woman, Kristin Richard (nicknamed Kik), who would become his wife. As a former professional athlete, his finances were such that he could afford to not work for a while. His life seemed settled. He could bag the sacrifice of the training, the diet, and the ultimate physical test, and instead relax and enjoy himself. Surely he had earned it.

Yet it was with no small measure of pain that Kik watched her future husband become a golf bum. Lance tells the story in his own words:

> After several weeks of the golf, the drinking, the Mexican food, [Kristin] decided it was enough—somebody had to get through to me. One morning we were sitting outside on the patio having coffee. I put down my cup and said, "Well, okay, I'll see you later. It's my tee time."
>
> "Lance," Kik said, "you need to decide something. You need to decide if you are going to retire for real and be a golf-playing, beer-drinking, Mexican food-eating slob. If you are, that's fine. I love you, and I'll marry you anyway. But I just need to know, so I can get myself together and go back on the street and get a job to support your golfing. Just tell me.
>
> "But if you're not going to retire, then you need to stop eating and drinking like this and being a bum, and you need to figure it out, because you are deciding by not deciding, and that is so un-Lance. It is just not you. And I'm not quite sure who you are right now. I love you anyway, but you need to figure something out."[8]

Kik's words hit home. One week later, Lance was back on his bike, training hard. About a year later, he did something that nobody thought he could do: Within two years of beating cancer, he won the most grueling sporting event in the world, the Tour de France. He repeated that remarkable feat in July 2000 and 2001, putting together one of the great comeback stories of the century.

Today, Lance actually credits his cancer with helping him to win the tour: "There is no question in my mind that I would never have won the Tour if I hadn't gotten cancer. The truth is, it was the best thing that ever happened to me, because it made me a better man, and a better rider."[9]

Before he had cancer, Lance wanted to be a good biker, but he wasn't willing to put in the extra degree of sacrifice necessary to truly excel. Now, Lance cherishes that sacrifice. "What is a sacrifice?" Armstrong said to a *Sports Illustrated* reporter. "You suffer a little during a training ride, you suffer during a race, and I like that. I would be really upset if I never had the opportunity to suffer. I would go crazy."[10]

Lance hits on a profound truth here: We pay a price when we become leisure-oriented, self-serving, pleasure-seeking people. Something within us dies. We lose a certain nobility and self-respect, for we know we are becoming less than we could be. Sacrifice sharpens our character and refines our faith.

> *We pay a price when we become leisure-oriented, self-serving, pleasure-seeking people.*

I think many Christians stand at the same crossroads Lance encountered. In years past, we were excited about our faith. We sacrificed for it, disciplined ourselves to cultivate a prayer time, risked our reputation by engaging in evangelism, and generally did the things Scripture calls us to do. But now we've reached a plateau. We think we've passed through sacrifice and come out on the other side, but I think we'll find, as Lance did, that sacrificing for our faith is something *we need to do*. The reason we feel disillusioned about our life and faith is not because Christianity isn't fulfilling, but because we've stopped thinking and acting like a Christian—someone who has sold all she has for the pearl of great value, someone who considers everything a loss compared to the greatness of knowing Jesus Christ. Without this opportunity to suffer we will, like Lance, "go crazy," becoming undisciplined robots who think that relief is found in leisure and irresponsibility when in fact it comes from being wholly devoted to God's kingdom.

The sweet side of sacrifice

Ironically, sometimes sacrifice brings its own rewards. I was in a business setting a number of years ago, and a woman was receiving what I perceived to be very unfair treatment. She was being challenged by several people on several levels. Those who work in business know how these situations can snowball into a free-for-all where everyone builds camaraderie, not to mention job security, by taking on a common enemy.

Because I believe that Scripture describes love as an active verb—standing up for others, actively becoming involved—I couldn't sit back. With a lump in my throat and with some risk to my own financial situation, I spoke up to defend this person and to take her side. Part of me thought I was being incredibly stupid. *You don't have to join in the harpooning,* one side of me was saying, *but why stick your neck out to defend her?*

Immediately afterwards, I called my wife and told her to be prepared—we might be facing a tight financial situation in the very near future. Eventually, things settled down.

A number of years later, this woman entered a completely different vocational setting, and in this position, she has sent literally tens of thousands of dollars' worth of work my way. I thought I was sacrificing. I knew I'd have to pay a price with my colleagues for taking a very unpopular position—which would cause some to resent me. I was prepared to do it because I thought it was the right thing to do—but I had no idea how well rewarded I'd be for speaking just a few words! Of course, I couldn't anticipate what would happen in this woman's future, or that she would even remember me.

But she did. And my "sacrifice" brought, ironically enough, tremendous blessing.

It doesn't always work out that way, of course. I wrote in an earlier book *(The Glorious Pursuit)* about how Lisa and I became frustrated when we couldn't sell our home in Virginia. We had prayed earnestly for wisdom before we had made the purchase, and God seemed to open every door. So we felt somewhat betrayed when we tried to sell the house six and a half years later and realized that the market had gone south and that selling the house would cost us many thousands of dollars.

"Why didn't God stop us?" we wanted to know.

Lisa was praying one morning and sensed God asking her, "Has it ever occurred to you that I wanted you in that neighborhood to reach other people rather than to enhance your financial situation?" Lisa and I were led to raise the question, "Does our theology leave room for serving a God who would lead us toward what might turn out to be a poor financial situation but a profitable spiritual one?"

The story doesn't end there, unfortunately. In that book, I mentioned that we eventually "sold" our house (at a loss), but the sale was a bit complicated as we continued the financing. In fact, we have had to make additional payments, and this ongoing burden made purchasing a new home very difficult. Each thousand-dollar check hurts, but Lisa and I remind ourselves, "God wanted us in that neighborhood. It cost us plenty, but we sought his direction, and he gave it."

> **Does our theology leave room for serving a God who would lead us toward what might turn out to be a poor financial situation but a profitable spiritual one?**

When I grow in understanding that the Christian life involves sacrifice, I find it a little easier to let things go rather than to stew about them. I *expect* my faith to cost me something. Besides, our sacrifice is minuscule compared to what saints in days gone by and many people today have given and are giving.

Little things, like forgoing your three-mile run in order to take a person with a disability to the store or sacrificing a leisurely Sunday afternoon in order to take a hurting couple out to lunch can either derail your joy or deepen your faith, depending on the attitude you have toward Christian sacrifice. This insight can literally slice through the deepest bout of disillusionment.

Such an attitude is all the more important as an entire generation of baby boomers become what sociologists now call "the sandwich generation." In this generation, parents are often conflicted over spending time and money on elderly parents, while still trying to put kids through high school or college—leaving little time for themselves. Because people now tend to live longer than ever, and kids often leave home later than they once did, the "sandwich generation" often gets caught in the middle. According to one *USA Today* reporter, "the Sandwich is getting bigger every day. About 64 million boomers will turn 50 in the next 14 years—which comes out to one boomer turning 50 every seven seconds."[11] One financial planner told the reporter, "I hardly know anybody who doesn't have some of these pressures at my age unless their parents died very young." Another boomer confesses, "Sometimes it seems like you're taking care of everybody but yourself."[12]

Life can call us into places where we feel as though we're being poured out on behalf of others. If we don't build a spirit of surrender and sacrifice, we're liable to grow resentful and bitter during such seasons. John

> *Life can call us into places where we feel as though we're being poured out on behalf of others.*

Calvin urges Christians to find comfort in Jesus' words to the sons of Zebedee: "Can you drink the cup I drink or be baptized with the baptism I am baptized with?" (Mark 10:38). Calvin makes this observation:

> These words contain no ordinary consolation for alleviating the bitterness of the cross, when in the cross Christ associates himself with us. And what could be more desirable than to have everything in common with the Son of God? For thus are those things which at first sight appear to be deadly made to yield to us salvation and life.[13]

In many ways, Calvin is summarizing the message of this book you hold in your hands: *Those truths that at first glance appear to be heavy, even "deadly," burdens actually are given to us as a gift that we might yield to God's plan for our salvation and life.* This is "no ordinary consolation," for it means we are invited to share in Christ himself—but even this consolation doesn't completely annul the fact that there is still "the bitterness of the cross."

Calvin goes on to write this:

> On the other hand, how shall he be reckoned among the disciples of Christ, who desires to be wholly exempted from the cross? For such a person refuses to submit to the baptism of Christ, which is nothing else than to withdraw from the earliest lessons. Now whenever baptism is mentioned, let us recollect that we were baptized on this condition, and for this purpose, that the cross may be attached to our shoulders.[14]

Calvin's words—*we were baptized on this condition, and for this purpose, that the cross may be attached to our shoulders*—

weighed heavily in my mind when my youngest daughter, Kelsey, was baptized. As soon as she came up out of the water, I placed a new cross necklace around her neck. Her eyes lit up at the sign of this ornament (which she wasn't expecting), but I was praying that she would learn to yield to this profound Christian truth: We are baptized on this condition and for this purpose, that the cross of Jesus Christ may be attached to our shoulders. Jesus is mercifully giving my daughter salvation; in return, he is going to ask her to drink his cup and to be baptized with his baptism, a baptism that includes the discipline of sacrifice.

I needed to remind myself of this, because part of me wants Kelsey to have a really easy life. Part of me hurts at the thought of Kelsey ever really suffering or sacrificing. But in order for her to mature in Christ, God will have to break her. He'll humble her, as he has humbled me and as he has humbled my wife, and he'll teach her the joy of obedience and surrender. It's not a pleasant process, but ultimately it's a glorious one.

Many of us casually approach God with a spiritually gluttonous attitude: "God, where's my next blessing? How come you didn't resolve this? What's up?" We're like a teenager with a bag of potato chips. We keep popping the chips into our mouth, but all it does is make us crave more.

> **"We were baptized on this condition, and for this purpose, that the cross may be attached to our shoulders."**

Scripture and the Christian classics call us to an entirely different orientation: Are we in the Christian faith for what it gives us, or is our chief purpose to glorify God? Until we resolve this question and get our priorities straight, we will at times resent God, occasionally become bitter at God, and even, perhaps, become disillusioned with the Christian faith. But once we adopt a heart of sacrifice, a mind-set that we are here to serve at God's good pleasure, everything else tends to fall into place.

I'd like to make one other point here. Ninety-nine percent of this book was written before *The Prayer of Jabez* was published. My editor returned the manuscript to me with a few suggested changes, but almost all of the text was completed before Bruce Wilkinson's fine work hit the book-buying public with a storm. This book is not an attack on, or a response to, *The Prayer of Jabez,* which I have read and benefited from. Clearly, God does call us to pray for blessing. Just as clearly,

> *Once we adopt a heart of sacrifice, everything else tends to fall into place.*

God does bless us. Blessing is one of Scripture's precious truths, but it is not the *only* truth, and I'm sure Bruce Wilkinson would agree. God blesses us so that we can bless others, and sometimes (not always), blessing others requires sacrifice on our part.

Authentic Faith

Platoon medic Sp4c. Brad Lawrence was the son of an active-duty army colonel.[15] His home life became potentially explosive when Brad developed antiwar sentiments during the Vietnam conflict. As a compromise with his father, Lawrence agreed to serve in the military as a medic—by definition a noncombatant.

One night, the Vietcong attacked Lawrence's platoon, unleashing, in the words of his platoon leader, a "carnival of sound and color: the whistling, flickering flares; the bright explosives; the screaming wounded; cries for help, cries for more fire, and cries for ammunition; machine guns beating out a deafening staccato; the wire snapping under the harsh bite of lead bullets."

Out of the darkness a Vietnamese woman bolted toward the American platoon, aiming for a break in the wire. She had a "bulky object" in her arms, but the platoon leader noted that "in the flickering light of the flares it was impossible to identify it."

The Vietnam War was full of treacherous acts—on both sides. Men would befriend little children, only to have those children deliver death a few days later by carrying a bomb or explosive right into their waiting arms, or by helping the VC set up an ambush. Many soldiers helped the Vietnamese people on a sacrificial level; a very few tragically murdered some civilians for sport.

Never really knowing who was "on your side," the soldiers had no guarantee that this woman wasn't also delivering a fatal charge, but in the chaos of the night, Lawrence shouted out, "Don't fire."

James McDonough, the platoon leader, hesitated. "I was not sure I agreed," he wrote. "If it was a satchel charge the woman was carrying, she would be able to fling it at us in another few steps. The explosion would rip that part of the perimeter wide open, allowing the enemy to rush through unimpeded."

As McDonough hesitated, VC rounds forced the woman down. Lawrence made a harrowing and life-risking dash for the wire at the camp's perimeter, then dropped into a low crawl, slowly inching his way toward the woman, ducking bullets along the way. Once he reached her, he discovered that the woman was carrying her seven-year-old daughter, who had taken a round through the chest. A lung had collapsed, and the child was bleeding heavily.

Lawrence's "job" was to serve the platoon, but his comrades watched as this conscientious objector "placed his body between the enemy fire and the mother and child and proceeded to treat the wound."

Sucking chest wounds are difficult to treat under the best of circumstances. They are almost impossible to care for when lying down, so in the midst of enemy fire, Lawrence rose to one knee in a desperate attempt to seal off the two holes, front and back, and get the child's chest cavity properly pressurized so that she could breathe again.

Finally another solider approached Lawrence and helped him drag the mother and child inside the platoon's perimeter. The Vietcong thanked them for their heroics by charging the platoon at precisely that point, trying to follow them into the perimeter.

The fight was finally brought to an end in typical Vietnam fashion: The Americans held on long enough until a pair of Cobra gunships (helicopters with immense firepower) chased the Vietcong away.

The little girl was evacuated to an American hospital, but her wounds were too severe. She died on the operating table. In all honesty, Lawrence knew there was probably little hope for a girl who had suffered such a massive wound—but he had risked his life anyway.

McDonough gives us no reason to believe that Lawrence was a man of faith; in fact, he suggests that Lawrence was the biggest drug user in the entire platoon. Yet this man risked his life for a woman who approached him from the very village that was attacking him and his comrades. Not only did he welcome the woman in, but he got up on his knees, clearly risking his life when people from this woman's village tried to shoot him down.

I don't know where such heroics come from or why this soldier was willing to make the ultimate sacrifice on a hunch that the woman really was in need and not carrying a bomb. The truth will probably never be known, but I wonder how infrequently we match such fortitude in our own churches.

I wonder this not because of cynicism but because my vocation takes me to so many different churches a year. Thankfully, most of the pastors I've met offer godly, almost heroic care to their congregations. I have met numerous believers who typify the love of Christ. But I have also heard the "war stories" of an entirely different kind. Some church members seek a new congregation solely because a pastor referred to an R-rated movie from the pulpit. We quibble over whether raising hands is a theological statement or whether a drum set is an appropriate instrument with which to worship our God. We get into a vigorous congregation-splitting debate over whether to enlarge the church kitchen or the children's nursery. Giving the pastor a $150-a-month raise takes weeks of discussion and creates mountains of acrimony. Consumed with these crucial "battles," waged as vigorously and enthusiastically as though they were a matter of life and death, I wonder if it's possible to lose the meaning of true courage, sacrifice, and faith for the things that really matter.

> **Will we, in childlike faith, surrender and choose to walk in obedience?**

On a personal level, sacrifice means this: *All* of us will eventually come across something we want that is contrary to the will of God. Here is the crossroads of sacrifice: Will we follow *our* heart, or will we, in childlike faith, surrender and choose to walk in obedience?

It is naive and immature to suggest that such a decision is easy—remember Calvin's words about seriously wrestling in prayer, at times even vacillating between one option or the other. But this alignment is an integral part of our faith, the "great duty" (in the words of Jonathan Edwards) of the believer.

Sacrifice is the heart of authentic Christianity.

Eleven

well Done . . . Depart from me!

The Disciplines of Hope and Fear

Our imagination so magnifies the present, because we are continually thinking about it, and so reduces eternity, because we do not think about it, that we turn eternity into nothing and nothing into eternity.

Blaise Pascal

If the righteous receive their due on earth,
how much more the ungodly and the sinner!

Proverbs 11:31

In 1999, the Hollywood-based entertainment industry handed out 3,182 trophies to itself at 332 ceremonies. While most everyone is familiar with the Academy Awards, Hollywood apparently isn't content to wait for an annual event, so there are many smaller ceremonies (in fact, at 332, there is one for almost every night of the year), such as the Tiger Film Awards, the Golden Rams, the Guldbagges, and the Trumpets, to name just a few.[1] In fact, in a clear case of the ridiculous becoming absurd, there are now awards given to award shows! In 1999, the Oscars, Grammys, and Tonys all won Emmys.

Obviously, we are a culture that values rewards. We also believe in appropriate punishment. When Indiana University football coach Cam Cameron was talking with the Hoosiers' controversial and fiery head basketball coach Bobby Knight (infamous for his chair-throwing incident and alleged physical attacks on players—which ultimately contributed to his dismissal), Cameron mentioned that he was looking forward to heaven so that he could tell the deceased legendary football coach Paul Brown how much he appreciated his numerous contributions to football.

"Well, what if he's not in heaven?" Knight asked.

Cameron's reply is a classic: "Then I guess I'll let *you* tell him."[2]

In the long scheme of things, however, the rewards—even the coveted Oscars—we so highly value on this earth are but trinkets.

> *This hope of heavenly rewards, as well as the sobriety that comes from knowing there are divine punishments, will help us persevere.*

The Bible talks about rewards of a more lasting kind. It also mentions punishments that go far beyond the tongue-in-cheek way we so often joke about hell.

Throughout this book, we have reminded ourselves that we live in a fallen world. Perfect justice does not exist in this corrupt environment. But the time will come when perfect justice and perfect mercy will reign, side by side. This hope of heavenly rewards, as well as the sobriety that comes from knowing there are divine punishments, will help us persevere through difficulty, persecution, selfless service, and the other disciplines of the faith that we've been talking about.

The choice

The teaching of the Old Testament is based on a choice. One choice—to follow the will of God—will bring generous reward, long life, and God's favor; the other choice—to disobey God's commands—will bring devastating punishment.

The bulk of the law is predicated on the blessings and curses listed in Deuteronomy 27 and 28. God wants his people to make the right choice, for they will be rewarded in doing so. On the other hand, disobeying his precepts means inevitable disaster:

> *See, I set before you today life and prosperity, death and destruction.*
> *For I command you today to love the LORD your God, to walk in his ways,*

and to keep his commands, decrees and laws; then you will live and increase, and the LORD your God will bless you. . . .

But if your heart turns away and you are not obedient. . . , I declare to you this day that you will certainly be destroyed.

DEUTERONOMY 30:15–18

Obedience, scripturally speaking, is not without its fringe benefits: "I the LORD search the heart and examine the mind, to reward a man according to his conduct, according to what his deeds deserve" (Jeremiah 17:10). And the consequences of disobedience, though checked by grace, are nevertheless quite fierce: "The LORD is slow to anger and great in power; the LORD will not leave the guilty unpunished" (Nahum 1:3).

> **The message was obvious: Do good, and be blessed; forsake God, and be destroyed.**

The message was obvious: Do good, and be blessed; forsake God, and be destroyed. This thought forms a foundation for the collection of Psalms as well:

Trust in the LORD and do good;
dwell in the land and enjoy safe pasture. . . .
Evil men will be cut off,
but those who hope in the LORD will inherit the land.

PSALM 37:3, 9

Consider the blameless, observe the upright;
there is a future for the man of peace.
But all sinners will be destroyed;
the future of the wicked will be cut off.

PSALM 37:37–38

Today, sadly, few Christians think about God's blessings and punishments as being even remotely connected to our actual behavior. I've talked to people who, because they have "prayed the sinner's prayer," believe that they are somehow immune to the consequences of their actions. For those who walk in this "easy believism" (which in some forms is virtual superstition, as though the believer's prayer were an incantation with magical power)—

ascribing to the tenets of faith but living a different life—Moses is very strict:

> When such a person hears the words of this oath, he invokes a blessing on himself and therefore thinks, "I will be safe, even though I persist in going my own way." This will bring disaster. . . . The LORD will never be willing to forgive him; his wrath and zeal will burn against that man. All the curses written in this book will fall upon him, and the LORD will blot out his name from under heaven. The LORD will single him out from all the tribes of Israel for disaster, according to all the curses of the covenant written in this Book of the Law.
>
> DEUTERONOMY 29:19–21

If neither Moses (who was refused admission into the promised land) nor David (who lost a child) escaped severe consequences for their sins, why should *we* expect to escape?

> **Jesus is by no means silent about the continuing realities of rewards and punishments.**

Today's Christian, of course, is all too quick to turn this around and say, "But that's the Old Testament, the *old* covenant. It doesn't apply to today's believer, at least not with rewards and punishments. After all, we're saved by grace through faith, aren't we? We're living in the new covenant!"

Indeed we are. But that's not the end of the story. Jesus is by no means silent about the continuing realities of rewards and punishments.

Jesus and rewards

The one thing that may shock modern sensibilities is that, according to Jesus, the *last* word that applies in either heaven or hell is "equality." On the contrary, Jesus teaches that some will experience great level of rewards, even above others (see Matthew 5:12). He specifically refers to those who are called "least" and those who are called "great" in the kingdom of heaven (see Matthew 5:19), and in context this declaration is clearly based on earthly obedience.

While no one earns their way into heaven, within heaven itself we will receive various degrees of honor. As Jesus calls his disciples to a higher way of living, he freely uses reward terminology to do so, though most of these rewards are dispensed in eternity. Jesus explicitly tells his disciples to "store up for yourselves treasures in heaven" (Matthew 6:20) and assures them that "no one who has left home or brothers or sisters or mother or father or children or fields for me and the gospel will fail to receive a hundred times as much in this present age . . . and in the age to come, eternal life" (Mark 10:29–30).

Jesus uses the thought of rewards to teach his disciples to love beyond the ordinary. In Matthew 5:46 he asks, if we reserve our love for only those who love us, what kind of reward can we expect to receive? Jesus uses the same motivation in urging us to do our good deeds in secret. He warns us in Matthew 6:1–4 that if we do "acts of righteousness" to be seen by others, we won't receive a reward from our heavenly Father, but if we do these good deeds in secret, our Father will reward us in secret. If Jesus uses rewards to motivate us, they *must* be real!

In the same way, hell has various degrees of punishment. Some in hell will be "beaten with many blows" while others will be "beaten with few blows" (Luke 12:47–48). Judas, who betrayed Jesus, will face such severe punishment that he will wish he had never been born (see Matthew 26:24). Jesus specifically says that "it will be more bearable for Tyre and Sidon on the day of judgment" than for Korazin and Bethsaida (Matthew 11:21–22). We should not assume that Adolf Hitler (who was responsible for the deaths of over six million Jews—not counting the soldiers who died promoting and fighting for his imperialistic aims) and someone who just never got around to turning from his sin and yielding to Christ will receive exactly the same punishment. They may share the same address, but they will not share the same rooms.

Jesus has particular antipathy for those who prey on the disenfranchised. The teachers of the law, he said, who "for a show make lengthy prayers" but who nevertheless "devour widows' houses" will be "punished most severely" (Mark 12:40). Here Jesus is challenging a common practice. Since teachers of the law were not allowed to receive payment for their teaching, the well-meaning faithful went out of their way to support the most visibly devout.

Some teachers exploited the hospitality of people who had very little means themselves. Their showy religion was calculated primarily to produce a financial response (the equivalent practice today hardly needs to be pointed out). Jesus doesn't pull any punches with this group: Their praying will never excuse their preying. These crafty teachers will suffer in a particularly hot place in hell for their thievery.

> **Jesus has particular antipathy for those who prey on the disenfranchised.**

The Sermon on the Mount, *the* central teaching for the Christian church, mirrors the blessings and curses imagery presented through Moses and Joshua. Jesus says that when we act with his character and attitudes, we will be "blessed." Conversely, "anyone who breaks one of the least of these commandments ... will be called least in the kingdom of heaven," while "whoever practices and teaches these commands will be called great in the kingdom of heaven" (Matthew 5:19).

That's why, when James and John seek a heavenly favor from Jesus—the privilege of sitting at his right and left hand (see Matthew 20:20–21)—the sons of Zebedee are not faulted for wanting to receive such a great honor. Jesus never says, "Shame on you for seeking a glorious place in heaven!" Instead, Jesus tells them that they're going about it the wrong way. Whoever wants to be great, he says, must be a servant. Jesus uses his disciples' desire for greatness *as motivation*, not as something that is shameful. He's not telling his disciples that their problem is that they are desiring the wrong ends, but rather that they are adopting the wrong means to that end. If we really want to be great in heaven, we must become the servant of all on earth.

This thought of rewards continues in the book of Revelation: "My reward is with me, and I will give to everyone according to what he has done" (Revelation 22:12). The beauty of it is this: These rewards will last—unlike many of the rewards we receive on this earth.

paul: pressing on for the great reward

In 1965, Lieutenant Colonel Robert Haldane was especially surprised when he heard that General William Westmoreland, commander of the American forces in Vietnam, was coming to his unit to hand out Silver Stars, an exceptionally high decoration. "Well, just who do we give them to?" Haldane wondered. "I don't remember recommending anyone for Silver Stars."[3] Some of the officers surmised that Westmoreland had decided to upgrade other decorations.

> *These rewards will last—unlike many of the rewards we receive on this earth.*

The general arrived exactly on time, news personnel scurrying behind him to shoot their pictures. The troops were lined up, as Westmoreland, smiling all the while, passed out the highly coveted medals. Almost as fast as they had come in, Westmoreland and the cameras were gone, at which point a major walked back through the line and collected all the medals—"an awards ceremony in reverse."[4] The entire ceremony had been for show, nothing more than a grand photo opportunity.

The apostle Paul assures us that the rewards God promises to us will not be taken back. While earthly runners (and apparently soldiers as well) receive a "crown that will not last," we run "to get a crown that will last forever" (1 Corinthians 9:25).

These words are particularly significant in that Paul—the undisputed champion of salvation by grace through faith—takes up Jesus' motivation of rewards, apparently seeing no contradiction in the two truths of *salvation by grace through faith* and *rewards and punishments*. In fact, Paul commends those who seek a reward, provided it's the *right* reward, namely, "glory, honor and immortality" (Romans 2:7). Paul uses the thought of heavenly rewards to help those in all life situations, from the wealthy (see 1 Timothy 6:17–19) to slaves (see Colossians 3:23–24).

The writer of Hebrews continues Paul's line of thinking. He stresses that not accepting the reality of heavenly rewards has dire consequences for our faith, because "anyone who comes to [God] must believe that he exists and that he rewards those who earnestly seek him" (Hebrews 11:6). This writer tells us that Moses was able to turn his back on the "treasures of Egypt, because he was looking ahead to his reward" (Hebrews 11:26).

Paul speaks of punishment as well. When writing to the Colossian believers, Paul makes it clear that they will be called to account for their actions: "Anyone who does wrong will be repaid for his wrong, and there is no favoritism" (Colossians 3:25). Sin's punishment is not always immediate, however. Sometimes we can get away with loose living for awhile, but ultimately we will pay a price for our transgressions: "The sins of some men are obvious, reaching the place of judgment ahead of them; the sins of others trail behind them" (1 Timothy 5:24).

The ultimate punishment, being barred from heaven and banished to hell, is the lot of unbelievers (see 2 Thessalonians 1:8–10), but Christians shouldn't be misled into thinking that because we have salvation by grace through faith that we will not face some type of punishment or, at the very least, experience the consequences of our sinful actions. When Paul wrote to the Thessalonians, he left the door wide open for Christians to be punished in some way for their sins. "The Lord will punish men for all such sins," Paul writes, "as we have already told you and warned you. For God did not call us to be impure, but to live a holy life. Therefore, he who rejects this instruction does not reject man but God, who gives you his Holy Spirit" (1 Thessalonians 4:6–8). If believers were beyond all sense of punishment, Paul would have no reason to warn the believers in Thessalonica.

Lest some readers assume that these words are directed only toward unbelievers, I urge you to read this passage in context. This section begins with Paul saying, "Finally, *brothers*, we instructed you how to live . . ." (1 Thessalonians 4:1, emphasis added). He then observes that "it is God's will that you should be sanctified" and that the Thessalonian believers shouldn't have "passionate lust like the heathen, who do not know God" (4:3, 5). Clearly, the warning of verses 6–8 is directed at Christians.

Paul is adamant when he writes to the Corinthians that "we must *all* appear before the judgment seat of Christ, that each one may receive what is due him for the things done while in the body, whether good or bad" (2 Corinthians 5:10, emphasis added). The Greek in this passage is precise in that the phrase "we must all" is universal—meaning, "without exception"—and is contrasted with "each one," which is rendered in a stark singular form. Nobody will escape this judgment. Everyone together will come before the judgment seat, but then there will be a time when each life is reviewed and either rewarded or punished on an individual basis.

Clearly, Paul is teaching here that *even for the Christian* there must be a day of reckoning. We are saved and justified solely by grace, but the work we did while in our bodies will still be reviewed and will still result in a judgment by God. Some scholars have taken the aorist tense (which refers to a single incident rather than an ongoing action) of the Greek in this passage to mean that rather than making individual judgments about everything we've done

> *An overall judgment will still be made regarding the character we allowed God to develop in us.*

(which are covered by the mercy and the blood offering of Jesus Christ), it is our *character* that will be judged. In other words, rather than God going through every day of our life and adding up the pluses and minuses, he pronounces one judgment, based on our character—the habitual action of our life, our whole life seen as a unit. Viewed this way, we can see how the reality of judgment still fits within a theology of justification by grace through faith. While our individual sins are washed away by Christ's sacrifice, an overall judgment will still be made regarding the character we allowed God to develop in us. Although our salvation is not hanging in the balance, God may well ask *what we did* with our salvation.

Rather than letting the thought of the judgment seat of Christ cast a shadow over our hope of heaven, we should instead use it as motivation to live a godly, active, generous, and productive life. It would be a grave mistake to let this truth lead us into mere moralism or cause us to forget grace (more on this later). It would be just as tragic to assume that Christianity is all about do's and don'ts— as though one sin will equal one "spiritual whack" and one act of obedience will result in one "spiritual blessing." That's a gross reduction of God as Father to God as a lower-level Judge who is limited to mere judicial pronouncements.

What the reality of rewards and punishments can do, however, is remind us, as Peter says, that we are "aliens and strangers in the world," pilgrims in a foreign land (1 Peter 2:11). Not every account will be settled before we die, but every account will be settled in eternity. It can also motivate us to reach the lost, for we know the punishment they face is both real and severe; and it can help us endure persecution, give sacrificially, become more selfless, wait more patiently, and accept mourning, knowing that the day is coming when we will be given comfort and blessing.

Although we'll touch on this in more detail later in this chapter, we need to state here that while Paul freely talks about punishments and rewards, he is very careful to point out that women and men can never put God in their debt (see Romans 9:16).

The Three faces of punishment

Punishment takes on three faces in the life of the Christian. The first is God shaping our character through discipline; the second is God compelling us to face the consequences of our actions; and the third is God turning our hearts back toward him. All of these can have a powerful impact on our lives when we realize just how much God loves us and what he's willing to walk through with us in order to complete his work in us.

Let's look at each in turn.

Discipline

The psalmist writes, "You rebuke and discipline men for their sin" (Psalm 39:11), and the writer of Hebrews makes it clear that this discipline is also relevant for today's church: " 'The Lord disciplines those he loves, and he punishes everyone he accepts as a son.' Endure hardship as discipline; God is treating you as sons" (Hebrews 12:6–7). These references to discipline don't mean we will be damned for our sins—Jesus took care of that. But it does mean God may mete out some temporal punishment to remind us of the need to walk in holiness and may prune us so that we bear good fruit (see John 15:1–17). Whatever shape this discipline takes, it is not pleasant: "No discipline seems pleasant at the time, but painful"—but if we receive it, "it produces a harvest of righteousness and peace for those who have been trained by it" (Hebrews 12:11).

Clearly, God is not averse to allowing us to suffer, if that suffering might refine our character. One time, not long ago, I got a bit short-tempered with my wife for planning a dinner party between two speaking engagements. I had spoken at a father-son retreat from Friday through Sunday afternoon and hadn't gotten much sleep. Worse, I knew I'd have to get up at 4:00 A.M. on Monday to catch a flight out to Omaha, Nebraska. After I had gotten home from the retreat, I still had to unpack, mow the lawn,

> **God is not averse to allowing us to suffer.**

repack my suitcase for another five days on the road, and gather my notes for the next engagement—before getting ready for a houseful of guests.

When Lisa told me our guests wouldn't be coming until 7:00 P.M., I fell into a self-pitying mood. Although Lisa had discussed this with me, and I had agreed to it, I wasn't too pleased with her. As I had suspected, I got to bed late that night, frustrated that I was going to have to get up early and yet still look energetic for my speech the next night in Omaha. I expressed my frustration to Lisa but still had a difficult time letting it go. My attitude was petty and immature.

The next morning I endured one of the worst travel days of my life. Due to cancellations and a host of airline errors, it took me sixteen hours to get from my home in Bellingham, Washington, to my hotel room in Omaha (causing me to miss my first scheduled talk). After standing in a line for almost two hours, I was five persons from the front when a manager closed the line down and said, "We're moving to Gate N3. Everybody will have to get in that line."

He can't be serious, I thought—but he was. I walked over to N3 and saw, to my great dismay, another thirty-minute line.

As I stewed, God's voice broke through my frustration. It wasn't audible, but you probably know what I mean when I say that God has a way of making a thought known to our hearts: *"If yesterday is indicative of how you're going to act when Lisa 'inconveniences' you, I'm going to show you how you can really be inconvenienced."*

God was true to his word. Because the airline was determined to fill every seat on this already-delayed-by-four-hours flight, we were slower getting out of the gate than they had anticipated, and I missed my next already-rescheduled connection by fifteen minutes, requiring me to spend *another* three hours in Denver (with more lines, of course). Once I finally made it to Omaha, I then had an unusually long, thirty-minute wait for the hotel shuttle bus (the driver was "in the middle of something else" when I called). Two other shuttle drivers came up to me and said, "Boy, you've been waiting a long time!"

I finally just gritted my teeth and tried to assure God that I had gotten his message loud and clear. I then sought his grace to help me be a little less demanding of my wife. In this instance, I truly believe God was disciplining me, working to refine my character

> **I truly believe God was disciplining me, working to refine my character.**

and treating me as his son. Call it coincidence, but the very next morning my devotions took me to Proverbs 12:1 ("Whoever loves discipline loves knowledge, but he who hates correction is stupid") and to Proverbs 15:10 ("Stern discipline awaits him who leaves the path; he who hates correction will die"). I am consistently amazed at how often God seems to "time" my Scripture reading to put an exclamation point on the previous day's insights and experiences.

The drive behind God's discipline is his love—"that we may share in his holiness" (Hebrews 12:10). The aim is to produce "a harvest of righteousness and peace for those who have been trained by it" (Hebrews 12:11). I want to learn how to cooperate with this work in my soul—not resenting it, but leaning into it, recognizing that I am a work in progress, amazed at the incredible privilege we share through being given individual attention by so wonderful a pruner as God himself.

Consequences

Solomon tells us that much of the punishment we receive from committing sin is simply the consequences that follow foolish living:

> For the waywardness of the simple will kill them,
>   and the complacency of fools will destroy them;

but whoever listens to me will live in safety
and be at ease, without fear of harm.

Proverbs 1:32–33

The prophets taught a similar message. Consider Jeremiah, for instance:

"Your wickedness will punish you;
your backsliding will rebuke you.
Consider then and realize
how evil and bitter it is for you
when you forsake the Lord your God
and have no awe of me,"
declares the Lord, the Lord Almighty.

Jeremiah 2:19

A young man once asked me for advice regarding a risky vocational choice he was making. He was convinced God wanted him to become a full-time writer—*right now*. Having some experience in this field, I asked him how he planned to feed his family during the time when he would have little or no income. "God will provide if he's behind this," this man assured me, then proceeded to reveal his true plan. "Besides, my wife and I figure we can get by on about $2,000 a month until I start selling my work."

"And where will that $2,000 come from?" I asked.

After hemming and hawing, he finally admitted, "Visa."

I've seen so many people presumably step out in faith, doing something ridiculously presumptuous, and then get angry at God when the consequences hit—18-percent-interest-rate credit card bills come due, for example, and they're never able to get out of debt.

Others must pay a bitter price for their momentary disobedience. Unfortunately, there is no mathematical precision to these consequences. I know of a young woman who had been pestered by her boyfriend to have sex for quite some time. She finally gave in and slept with that man one time, and through that *one occurrence* she became pregnant *and* contracted HIV. Others might practice a promiscuous lifestyle and never catch anything that a few antibiotics can't cure. It is precisely because this world is not equitable in its distribution of rewards and punishments that heaven

presents such a wonderful hope. There, God represents both ultimate mercy and ultimate justice.

But here on earth we are faced with the fact that sin comes with
certain consequences—never certain, but always potential. Whenever we cross the line, we are opening
the door to negative repercussions.

> **This world is not
> equitable in its
> distribution of rewards
> and punishments.**

The saddest part is that, after we face
the consequences of our sin, we are
sometimes tempted to blame God for
allowing us to suffer the results of our
foolishness: "A man's own folly ruins
his life, yet his heart rages against the
LORD" (Proverbs 19:3). We have only ourselves to blame. One of
the primary reasons God warns us to avoid sin is precisely because
what he forbids in Scripture is ultimately harmful to our own well-
being. We can pretend that sin isn't sin, but our pretending won't
stop the consequences of sin from following in sin's path.

This is very much a New Testament concept as well. In an epistle devoted to lifting up salvation by grace through faith, Paul is nevertheless greatly concerned that this grace-filled offer not be used to
deny the reality of sin's bitter aftertaste. "Do not be deceived," Paul
wrote to the Galatian believers. "God cannot be mocked. A man
reaps what he sows. The one who sows to please his sinful nature,
from that nature will reap destruction; the one who sows to please
the Spirit, from the Spirit will reap eternal life" (Galatians 6:7–8).

The apostle Peter uses consequence teaching to back up a long
list of moral teaching, as he cites this conclusion:

> Whoever would love life
>   and see good days
> must keep his tongue from evil
>   and his lips from deceitful speech.
> He must turn from evil and do good;
>   he must seek peace and pursue it.
> For the eyes of the Lord are on the righteous
>   and his ears are attentive to their prayer,
> but the face of the Lord is against those who do evil.

1 PETER 3:10–12

In commenting on this passage, theologian Wayne Grudem points out that "one proper motive for righteous living is the knowledge that such conduct will bring blessings from God in this life." There is a difference in emphasis in Old and New Testament teaching in this regard. Grudem rightly suggests that in the larger context of 1 Peter, "such blessings do not include freedom from opposition or suffering—the blessings of the New Testament age generally are more spiritual, psychological, and interpersonal, and less material or physical than in the Old Testament."[5]

> *Our pretending won't stop the consequences of sin from following in sin's path.*

Grudem adds that, although Peter reminds us that we have an imperishable inheritance, kept in heaven for us (see 1 Peter 1:4), Peter nevertheless presents "a bold affirmation of the relation between righteous living and God's present blessing in this life. As such it provides a needed corrective to careless, half-hearted Christians living in any age, and a powerful motivation to the kind of holy living to which Peter says all Christians have been called."[6]

What all this comes down to is this: Sin is still profoundly consequential for the Christian. We deceive ourselves if we think we sin with impunity. A cavalier attitude toward blatant wickedness is entirely incompatible with authentic faith. Becoming bitter toward God when we face these consequences is even more foolish: "Why should any living man complain when punished for his sins?" (Lamentations 3:39).

Turning Us Back to God

The book of Amos shows us that God can be rather creative in designing ways to turn our hearts back toward him. Speaking to the people of Israel, God testifies that he gave them "empty stomachs in every city and lack of bread in every town, yet you have not returned to me" (Amos 4:6.) Next, he withheld rain, "yet you have not returned to me" (4:8). He then struck their gardens and vineyards: "I struck them with blight and mildew. Locusts devoured your fig and olive trees, yet you have not returned to me" (4:9).

At this point, God upped the ante. He sent plagues among his own people, as well as unleashing the conquering armies of other nations: "'I filled your nostrils with the stench of your camps, yet you have not returned to me,' declares the LORD" (4:10).

God was allowing hardship not to maliciously tinker with the people of Israel, but to save them—that is, to turn them back to their spiritual home and salvation. He was jealous for their affection and eager to get their attention.

The prophets Hosea[7] and Haggai[8] tell the same story. The book of Revelation contains this warning: "I have given her time to repent of her immorality, but she is unwilling. So I will cast her on a bed of suffering, and I will make those who commit adultery with her suffer intensely, unless they repent of her ways" (Revelation 2:21–22).

> **God puts greater value on his relationship with us than on our comfort and affluence.**

One thing is abundantly clear: God puts greater value on his relationship with us than on our comfort and affluence. If we get too comfortable and complacent in our disobedience, he is not shy to withhold his blessing and even bring trouble into our lives in order to turn our eyes, hearts, and minds back to him.

The classical chorus

With so much biblical attention given to punishments and rewards, it's no surprise that the great classical Christian writers carried this same message in their writings. Like every idea expressed in this book, the idea of rewards and punishments represents classical Christian teaching; it's certainly not a new concept. Ambrose of Milan, a bishop who served as Augustine's spiritual director, wrote, "Is it not plain from this [Luke 16:19–31] that rewards and punishments according to deserts await one after death? And surely this is but right. . . . Is the palm ever given or the crown granted before the course is finished?"[9]

Thomas à Kempis, a medieval monk, said, "Truly, when the day of judgment comes, we shall not be examined as to what we have read but what we have done, not how well we have spoken but how well we have lived."[10] Before you simply dismiss this as "Roman Catholic theology," compare it to Jesus' words in Matthew 7:21: "Not everyone who says to me, 'Lord, Lord,' will enter the kingdom of heaven, but only he who does the will of my Father who is in heaven."

Ralph Venning, a popular seventeenth-century Puritan preacher, also taught about rewards and punishments. In his book *The Sinfulness of Sin*, Venning writes, "There will be degrees of torment. Though it will be intolerable for all, yet it will be more tolerable for some than others (see Matthew 11:21–24). In certain cases, the torments will be aggravated."[11] According to Venning, the cases for increased torment include those who have lived longer in sin, those who have had easy access to the gospel's message but refused it, and those who had knowledge and even conviction of the gospel but rejected it.

Because even Christians will be judged, John Chrysostom (a fourth-century patriarch in the Eastern church) urges us to use the teaching of future judgment for contemporary motivation:

> Let us then imagine Christ's judgment-seat to be present now, and reckon each one of us with his own conscience, and account the Judge to be already present, and everything to be revealed and brought forth. For we must not merely stand, but also be manifested. Do you not blush? Are you not dismayed?[12]

This is a key point, as some Christians may well read this book and think, *What does it matter anyway? Can't I get into heaven if I live a selfish life and don't care for the downtrodden? Do I really have to forgive? Is materialism really all that bad?*

When heavenly rewards and punishments come into play, our perspective on what really matters will undergo a radical, life-changing shift. We'll be willing to persevere where before we might have given up at the first sign of discomfort. This teaching will also help us cultivate a mature and full relationship with God—which must include a reverent awe and fear.

NO FEAR

One of the great challenges of modern-day Christian service is that we live in a society in which so many have lost virtually all sense of the fear of the Lord, leaving the concept of heavenly rewards and punishments sounding meaningless and outdated, if not bizarre and anti-intellectual. Such a society is bound to include those such as Ted Turner, who is arguably one of the most accomplished men of our generation. He reshaped television news by founding CNN and its 24-hour Headline News sister channel. As a sportsman, Turner has won yachting's America's Cup, and as a team owner, his Atlanta Braves won the 1995 Major League Baseball World Series. As a philanthropist, he's certainly near the top of the list, at one time pledging a gift of one billion dollars to the United Nations. He's also the largest individual private landowner in the entire United States. Few people could match this résumé in just one area; taken together, his accomplishments are truly phenomenal.

> *We live in a society in which so many have lost virtually all sense of the fear of the Lord.*

And yet Turner would have little patience with what I've previously written in this chapter. He told one reporter, "I'm not looking for any big rewards. I'm not a religious person. I believe this life is all we have. I'm not doing what I'm doing to be rewarded in heaven or punished in hell. I'm doing it because I feel it's the right thing to do. Almost every religion talks about a savior coming. When you look in the mirror in the morning, when you're putting on your lipstick or shaving, you're looking at the savior. Nobody else is going to save you but yourself."[13]

Am I being unfair by characterizing Turner as having a secular mind-set? I don't think so! Clearly, he would revel in the label "secularist." Now watch where such a mind-set leads. Without this fear of the Lord, our *public* lives may prosper, but our *private* lives will surely suffer. Ted confessed to the same reporter that, after having accomplished all that he's accomplished, "I feel that I can do just about anything. Except have a successful marriage." In fact, after going through two previous divorces, Turner's most recent marriage (to Jane Fonda) has now ended in divorce as well.

When we live only for this world, we will lack the character to tackle difficult relationships with any moral comprehension. We have to be happy *right now,* or we assume the struggle isn't worth it. After all, if all we're living for is today, and today isn't "happy," we'll want to make an immediate change. With this belief, few marriages would survive.[14]

Even the mere mention of "the wrath of God" makes one sound hopelessly outdated. Although this is a foundational truth of Scripture that has served Christians well for centuries, it is seen as anachronistic today. But what was essential for Jesus cannot be nonessential for us:

> The Spirit of the Lord will rest on [Jesus] —
>> the Spirit of wisdom and of understanding,
>> the Spirit of counsel and of power,
>> the Spirit of knowledge and of the fear of the Lord —
> and he will delight in the fear of the Lord.

Isaiah 11:2–3, emphasis added

The Israelites were aided in their devotion to God by cultivating and maintaining an attitude of awe at his presence:

> The mountains quake before him
>> and the hills melt away.
> The earth trembles at his presence,
>> the world and all who live in it.
> Who can withstand his indignation?
>> Who can endure his fierce anger?
> His wrath is poured out like fire;
>> the rocks are shattered before him.

Nahum 1:5–6

The fear of God's wrath also served as a *positive* motivator, to encourage the Israelites to do right:

> Administer justice every morning;
>> rescue from the hand of his oppressor
>> the one who has been robbed,
> or my wrath will break out and burn like fire
>> because of the evil you have done —
>> burn with no one to quench it.

Jeremiah 21:12

Although this fear was terrible, it had a positive end: "I will give them singleness of heart and action, so that they will always fear me *for their own good* and the good of their children after them" (Jeremiah 32:39, emphasis added).

Sadly, our fear of God has too often been replaced by the less noble fear of man. By this I mean that many of us sometimes fear exposure of our sin more than we fear facing God's wrath. Rather than living in genuine concern that we might offend the powerful God of the universe, we are more concerned that other people will discover and disclose our moral failings and thus embarrass us. We know we've fallen into this trap if we spend more time covering up our sin and keeping our tracks hidden than we do mourning over and confessing our sin, and making plans to cooperate with God's Spirit so that we can be rid of our sin.

> *Our fear of God has too often been replaced by the less noble fear of man.*

The fear of man is a prideful, self-centered, soul-shrinking fear. It is a desire to remain in sin, but to not have that sin become known. Such an attitude will never lead to repentance but rather to deceit and hypocrisy.

The fear of God, on the other hand, makes known to us the insanity of continuing in disobedience. The allure of that action or attitude is burned up in the light of God's grace, favor, mercy, and love. Only the fear of God can truly challenge our souls. There has been more than one occasion in my own life when I've sensed God's strict warning that I needed to address a moral failing in my life more seriously—or else. I never knew what the "or else" would be, but I've found it comforting to take shelter in God's warning, as it was born out of love and given to protect me, guide me, and help me grow in maturity. I praise God that he loves us enough to get tough with us at times.

You'll know that you are more concerned with offending God than being exposed publicly by whether you are choosing to engage in Christian confession, thereby revealing your sins to another brother or sister in the Lord. The Bible is clear that we need to be in fellowship with each other in order to live a holy life. Keeping habitual sins secret reveals hearts that are more concerned about our image or reputation than about real obedience.

It is inevitable that once we lose the fear of the Lord, private holiness will become a veritable stranger. Although believers have renewed hearts, they are still wayward hearts. None of us is noble enough to say no to our temptations out of the "goodness" of our hearts (see Romans 7:14–25). In fact, we are all rebellious sinners, with hearts that deceive us. If we do not have any fear of God, there is little to restrain us from doing whatever we want to do. Moses made this principle distinctly clear: "The fear of God will be with you to keep you from sinning" (Exodus 20:20).

> *Keeping habitual sins secret reveals hearts that are more concerned about our image or reputation than about real obedience.*

Having said this, it's important to point out that the biblical notion of "the fear of the Lord" cannot be defined solely by using the words *terror* or *dread*. It also encompasses

- a passionate love.
- the positive desire to please God.
- a worshipful awe.

Viewing it in this way, the fear of God is relationally based: "I will inspire them to fear me, so that they will never turn away from me" (Jeremiah 32:40).

Old Testament scholar Bruce Waltke points out that "the heart that both fears and loves God at one and the same time is *not divided but unified in a single religious response to God.*"[15] *Fear* and *love,* in fact, can be considered religious synonyms. This is a thoroughly Hebrew concept. Other world religions might have feared their gods (that is, related to their gods in superstitious terror), but the people of Israel were unique in loving and trusting their God. One scholar has explained, "The confident trust which constantly prevails as the basic note in Israel's fear of God has no parallel in the other religions of the ancient Near East."[16]

This isn't the place to discuss a theological concept in great detail,[17] but in summary (read this paragraph slowly—it's loaded with meaning), the fear of the Lord involves a *moral understanding*, a *trust* in God's commands and goodness, a *willingness* to accept his higher understanding, and a corresponding *surrender* to his will. It is underscored by a genuine *love* and *affection*, tempered by *awe* and *reverence*. To fully fear God, we must practice all of the above.

> **The people of Israel were unique in loving and trusting their God.**

The fear of the Lord is something that can be taught ("Come, my children, listen to me; I will teach you the fear of the LORD" [Psalm 34:11]) as well as rejected (Abraham bemoaned his perception that "there is surely no fear of God in this place," [Genesis 20:11]). But remember: "fear of God" always has two poles: awe and love. The complete Christian response to God is one that entails not just personal trust and affection (we're very good at stressing this) but also awe and reverence—even terror at the thought of offending him (this is what sometimes gets ignored in modern teaching). While we don't want believers to wallow only in dread and terror of God, it is just as much a theological error to teach them to have affection for God without a corresponding attitude of reverence and awe.

Even Jesus had an attitude of "reverent submission" (Hebrews 5:7), the same attitude Paul tells us to cultivate in our approach to our heavenly Father and to Jesus Christ (2 Corinthians 7:1 and Ephesians 5:21, respectively). Early Gentile believers were known as "God-fearing" (Acts 10:2), and Paul urges an active reverence (fear) toward God in Philippians 2:12.

It's my belief that our rejection of the idea of rewards and punishments has undercut our teaching of the fear of God. It reminds me of the summer track meets my hometown holds for children and adults. Our kids have taken part in many of these, and as is common these days, everybody who participates in an event gets a ribbon. There are the traditional blue ribbons for first, red for second, white for third, and green for "participants." My youngest daughter used to refer to these green ribbons as "good job anyway" awards. That's the way some people assume God to be as well: "Ah, yes, you lived as my enemy for eighty years. You never sought shelter in my grace. You died in rebellion—but good job anyway. Enter into my kingdom."

The Bible directly, consistently, and definitively refutes any such wishful thinking. Such a view turns God into a "gift machine" who mechanically answers prayers without asking for allegiance. God is not a "machine." The Bible depicts him as a passionate personal Being who is moved by compassion but who also possesses his share of righteous wrath.

> *Our rejection of the idea of rewards and punishments has undercut our teaching of the fear of God.*

Although the above thought focuses mostly on nonbelievers, in a different sense it also applies to believers who have started the race well, but who are now slacking off. In their pastoral care, the disciples frequently urged Christians, *You've begun well, now finish well.* For example, the apostle John writes, "And now, dear children, *continue in him,* so that when he appears we may be confident and unashamed before him at his coming" (1 John 2:28, emphasis added). Paul urges the Philippian believers to "continue to work out your salvation with fear and trembling" (Philippians 2:12).

A certain degree of fear, properly defined, is more than appropriate; it is essential for a right response and attitude toward God. Yet, of course, it's important to point out that while God's rewards and punishments are certain, both can have a delayed reception.

Delayed reception

The Dutch Postimpressionist painter, Vincent van Gogh (1853–1890), was the son of a Protestant pastor. Greatly influenced by the works of Thomas à Kempis, John Wesley, and John Bunyan (author of *Pilgrim's Progress*), Vincent dabbled in theology and even spent time as an evangelist among Belgium miners. His somber portrayal of peasants is to art what Tolstoy's writings are to literature.

Although van Gogh began life well, his troubled psyche resulted in tempestuous relationships, perhaps the most famous of which was his friendship with fellow painter Paul Gauguin. The two men quarreled violently, and on one occasion, van Gogh actually chased Gauguin away by threatening him with a razor. Later that night, deeply affected by the departure of his friend, van Gogh severed part of his own ear. Thus began a series of stays in mental asylums, which culminated in his grisly suicide on July 27, 1890. It took two days for van Gogh to die of his self-inflicted gunshot wounds.

Vincent van Gogh left behind an impressive body of work, not just in quality, but sheer quantity as well—approximately 750 paintings and 1,600 drawings. A single van Gogh painting has sold for as much as $50 million, but the poverty-stricken artist sold just two paintings during his lifetime. On one occasion, he was so saddled by debt that he packed a number of works into a wheelbarrow and carted them over to a creditor.

> **True rewards are often slow in coming.**

"Would you be interested in accepting these paintings in fulfillment of my debt?" van Gogh asked.

The man, not realizing that the paintings he was looking at would one day bring in enough money to buy an entire town, scoffed and turned van Gogh away. When the creditor told his wife about it, she scolded him, "You could have at least kept the wheelbarrow!"

Art historians love to tell this story, chortling about the shortsightedness and poor judgment of van Gogh's creditor. But the same thing is happening today. Saints often go unnoticed in the wake of a world that screams more loudly for its own heroes. That is, true rewards are often slow in coming.

One of my favorite Christian writers, C. S. Lewis, died the same day the 35th president of the United States, John F. Kennedy, was assassinated. The entire world seemed focused on the shocking events in Dallas, Texas, with the result that only a few people attended Lewis's funeral at Holy Trinity Church in Headington Quarry, England, on November 26, 1963. According to George Sayer, Lewis's close friend for three decades, those who did come were nearly all personal friends.

Sayer's description of the funeral is moving, if not a little sad: "A lighted church candle was placed on the coffin, and its flame did not flicker. For more than one of us, that clear, bright candle flame seemed to symbolize Jack. He had been the light of our lives, ever steadfast in friendship. Yet, most of all, the candle symbolized his unflagging pursuit of illumination."[18]

Lewis's estate was valued at just 37,772 pounds. He had given away most of his literary earnings and never owned a house. Consequently, he left just a small legacy of 100 pounds to his caretaker, Paxford. When asked about the paltry gift, Paxford said, "Werl, it won't take me far, wull it? Mr. Jack, 'e never 'ad no idea of money. 'Is mind was always set on 'igher things."[19]

That such an influential man should die so humbly and so quietly, with such little fanfare, is almost disturbing. Yet, in a way, it is appropriate, considering everything Lewis stood for, his mind "always set on higher things." Because he didn't live solely for this world, he had to look to a new world in which to receive his full reward.

> **What we do as Christians today will have value chiefly in another time.**

What we do as Christians today will have value chiefly in another time. To some, our accomplishments, such as they are, won't be worth the gasoline spent in transporting us from place to place. But in another context, according to Scripture, these heavenly works, performed with the right motivation, will be eternally golden. We are reminded to expect our rewards in another age. Ambrose tells us, "Do not . . . as a child claim those things now which belong to a future time. The crown belongs to the perfect. Wait till that which is perfect is come."[20]

The discipline of endurance and the expectation of rewards and punishments need to be combined with the spiritual discipline of waiting. As we wait, I pray we are overcome with joy at the sheer mercy and wonder of a God who would deign to reward such sinful human beings.

rewards, punishments, and grace

It's so easy for us to become overwhelmed with busywork on behalf of the kingdom, and then to forget what incredible mercy God shows us by allowing us to be on his team. As I was praying one busy morning a while back, thinking about the manuscript that needed to be completed, the articles I had to write by a certain deadline, a talk I was scheduled to give the next day, and a rapidly approaching seminary class I needed to prepare for, I was tempted to cut short my morning time with God. Prayer had become something of a necessary "prelude" for me, but I wanted to get into the "real" work of the day.

Spiritually, it was a dangerous state, to be sure, and I was duly chastened by God's Spirit. I was made to realize that *every single act* of that day—the fact that I was given the tasks of working on a book, or writing an article, or speaking at a retreat, or teaching a seminary class—*is there by God's mercy*, and God's mercy alone. If God had acted "justly" with me, giving me what I deserve, I wouldn't be allowed to do *any* of it.

This is not just some pious rhetoric. It is only by God's grace that I am allowed to be a part of his kingdom, much less to serve in it. If somebody prepared a video of my ten worst moments in life, and people saw me in my lowest depths, would anyone really care what I have to say? Could *any of us* survive such a showing?

Every demand on my time is in reality an amazing marker of God's mercy, a God-gift of the highest order. I don't know that I'll ever look at a busy schedule or my numerous "obligations" in the same way again.

> **It is only by God's grace that I am allowed to be a part of his kingdom, much less to serve in it.**

I stress this because I don't want any of the above to ever be interpreted that I'm suggesting we critique salvation by grace through faith. The clear teaching of Scripture is that all of us deserve "capital punishment." The wages of sin—any sin—is death. There are certainly different degrees of punishment in hell, but, undeniably, all of us deserve to end up there. The fact that anyone will be saved is an act of sheer mercy and compassion on God's part. We all deserve a spot on death row, spiritually speaking.

Nothing we do can force or coerce God's hand. God is never in any person's debt. We can't give away enough money, suffer enough pain, or die a brutal enough death to ever merit God's favor. There is no inherent merit in any spiritual or practical service, *apart from the merit that God chooses out of his mercy to bestow on it.* We will cross over into heresy if we start teaching that there is a direct, forced, necessary correlation between our deeds and God's action on our behalf.

However, there is a *promised* correlation, based on God's mercy and compassion, which has been made possible through the sacrifice of his Son. Because of Jesus' work, not only can we be saved from the ultimate punishment, but our response to God's grace will result in heavenly blessings and rewards. This is not, I stress again, because we *deserve* these rewards—we will never do enough to erase the fact that we deserve hell—but because God in his mercy chooses to reward those who are faithful to his commands. Thus, the rewards are free gifts, given out of God's great mercy.

We can (and should) use these promised rewards as our motivation to continue in good deeds and obedient living, but we must wait for them through faith, not demand them through impertinence. Why? Because apart from Jesus Christ we are all objects of God's wrath. The man who spends sixty hours a week ministering to the terminally ill through hospice care deserves hell no less than the man who sells drugs to adolescent kids. The faithful

> **There is no inherent merit in any spiritual or practical service.**

wife who homeschools three kids and cares for her elderly mother-in-law deserves to go to the same place as the prostitute who never married and underwent two abortions. The enthusiastic and dedicated pastor who faithfully serves his flock deserves hell just as much as a Mafia lawyer who makes his living by covering up crime. That *anyone* will experience heaven is nothing short of a miracle. That there will be further rewards in heaven is really beyond our comprehension. It is too wonderful to behold, yet another amazing testimony to the absolutely incredible love and mercy of our heavenly Father.

Authentic Faith

It's a sad, sad picture. Solomon built the kingdom of Israel to unparalleled heights. He achieved a wealth and notoriety that would stagger even a Bill Gates or a Warren Buffett. But he broke a lot of rules along the way, and his family paid dearly for those transgressions.

Rehoboam, Solomon's son, lost the kingdom within days of his father's death. Rehoboam still maintained rule over a small splinter group, represented by Jerusalem in Judah, but the wealth, the power, and the aura of invincibility were gone. King Shishak of Egypt ransacked Solomon's famous gold-laden temple and carried off *everything*—all the gold utensils, the fixtures, the sacred furniture. He left nothing but holes in the walls and a demoralized king in his wake.

Having abandoned his father's God, Rehoboam was powerless to stop Shishak, so he learned to settle for pitifully less. After the king of Egypt departed, Rehoboam ordered that bronze shields be cast to replace the gold shields that had been stolen. There had been two hundred of these gold shields, each of which had about 7-1/2 pounds of gold in them. An additional three hundred shields had about 3-3/4 pounds of gold in them (see 1 Kings 10:16–17). All of these were taken away by Shisak. In their place, Rehoboam settled for bronze. The darker metal couldn't be made to look like gold, but maybe, if he squinted, it would allow him to forget . . .

The Bible tells us that wherever Rehoboam went, "the guards bore the [bronze] shields, and afterward they returned them to the guardroom" (1 Kings 14:28). Rehoboam no longer felt safe, and his punishment was bitter indeed, for in that insecurity, he was constantly reminded of how far he had fallen. Those bronze shields confronted him with the fact that he had lost the gold—and that he was still afraid of losing the bronze. Back in his father's day, "nothing was made of silver, because silver was considered of little value" (1 Kings 10:21). But now, Rehoboam had to settle for something even less than silver. Worse, those shields followed him every time he ventured outside, until the day he died.

> **Obedience is never quite as costly as disobedience.**

Why did God allow this to happen? According to the author of 2 Chronicles, it was so that Rehoboam and Israel would "learn the difference between serving [God] and serving the kings of other lands" (2 Chronicles 12:8).

There are truths to the duty of following God that may, indeed, initially taste bitter in our mouths, but obedience is never quite as costly as disobedience. Though God may seem hard and unyielding, he is a benevolent Master, especially when we consider the alternative.

It is not fashionable today to talk about rewards and punishments, but you cannot read the Bible—either Old or New Testament—with an objective eye and draw any other conclusion except that those who disobey God will be punished, and those who faithfully serve him will be richly rewarded. These punishments and rewards may not all be rendered in this life, but they are certain. The punishments are as severe as we might fear; the grace-filled rewards are beyond human understanding. The choice is ours: gold shields, or bronze.

epilogue

"**I**t is difficult to fast in this country."

Stephen is from Nigeria. He enrolled in a D.Min. (Doctor of Ministry) class I taught at Western Seminary in Portland, Oregon. Western is particularly kind to its students. The schedule is intensive and grueling—8:30 to 5:00, Monday through Friday—but staff people do their best to make it palatable. Every mid-morning we were treated to coffee and a snack—muffins, cookies, or fruit. The same thing occurred every afternoon. Since we also had a lunch break, none of us had to go more than ninety minutes without food.

That's when Stephen bit into a cookie, smiled, and said, "It is difficult to fast in this country."

Our affluence is both a blessing and a challenge that often threatens to sweep us away from the disciplines and lifestyles that previous generations of Christians knew were essential for spiritual growth and maturity. Although our affluence provides much leisure time, a certain degree of security, and perhaps increased freedom, it also tempts us to adopt a pseudofaith that fits our culture, rather than encouraging us to shape our lives in such a way that we can live out our faith.

Perhaps that's why, in an early act of evangelism, I told one of the biggest lies of my life. I was only about twelve years old at the time, working in the cucumber fields outside Sumner, Washington. A Korean man in his twenties worked alongside me. He had been in the country for just a few months, and we began discussing such things as faith. I repeatedly urged him to become a Christian.

> *Our affluence tempts us to adopt a pseudo-faith that fits our culture, rather than encouraging us to shape our lives in such a way that we can live out our faith.*

"But why should I become a Christian?" he asked me.

"Because it makes life a lot easier!" I explained.

Back then, I was ensnared in a simplified faith. In the words of Paul, I talked like a child, I thought like a child, and I reasoned like a child (see 1 Corinthians 13:11). I had yet to learn the lessons that Harry Schaumburg mentions in his fine book *False Intimacy,* when he writes, "A quick reflection on the first-century church reveals that New Testament Christians never attempted to validate the truth of Christianity by the way in which their experiences in life improved. For them, becoming Christians meant real sacrifice and sometimes death."[1]

Had I continued in my childish line of thinking, I no doubt would have become disillusioned with my faith. But now comes the time to "put childish ways behind me" (1 Corinthians 13:11) and to embrace a more mature faith that more authentically mirrors the actual Word of God.

The New Jerusalem

Throughout this book, I've tried to show how, at its very root, the pursuit of an ideal life this side of heaven is going to be frustrated and will result in terrible disillusionment. We live in a fallen world where terrible things happen, even to faithful believers. In

this world, contentment will always be a struggle. At times, the only
proper response to this world is to mourn. We must not be caught
by surprise when we face difficulty, disease, and even death. These
are to be expected. We have been
warned about their reality.

But that's not the end of the story.
In fact, the message of this book finds
its fulfillment in the final chapters of
Revelation. There we are introduced
to the new Jerusalem: "Then I saw a
new heaven and a new earth, for the

> **The pursuit of an ideal
> life this side of heaven
> will result in terrible
> disillusionment.**

first heaven and the first earth had passed away.... I saw the Holy
City, the new Jerusalem, coming down out of heaven from God,
prepared as a bride beautifully dressed for her husband" (Revelation 21:1–2).

In this new Jerusalem, these hard truths of which we have spoken will be with us no more: "Now the dwelling of God is with
men, and he will live with them. They will be his people, and God
himself will be with them and be their God. He will wipe every tear
from their eyes. There will be no more death or mourning or crying or pain, for the old order of things has passed away" (Revelation 21:3–4).

The writer of Revelation captures our heart's desire—a world
with no more mourning, no more difficulty, no more suffering, no
more persecution. God himself will make sure there are no widows,
no orphans, and no aliens. Contentment, finally, will no longer be
a stranger. Rewards and punishments will be meted out—the faithful will inherit this wonderful place, while "the cowardly, the unbe-
lieving, the vile, the murderers, the sexually immoral, those who
practice magic arts, the idolaters and all liars" will be thrown "in
the fiery lake of burning sulfur" (21:7–8)—and everything we've
spoken about will have reached its end. There will be no more curse
(22:3), no more waiting (22:17), no problems with contentment
(22:17). Everything we need will be laid out for us.

What a day that will be!

This is truly our hope—what Peter describes as a *living* hope
(1 Peter 1:3), an invigorating, life-changing belief and trust. Hope

> *Hope is a dynamic virtue that feeds us, strengthens us, encourages us, and carries us through many a dark day and many a long night.*

is a dynamic virtue that feeds us, strengthens us, encourages us, and carries us through many a dark day and many a long night. If we will but endure the "harder" realities of life on this fallen earth for a relatively short time—eighty to one hundred years, at most—there will be eternal rewards waiting for us on the other side. But if we ignore these difficult truths, resent them, refuse them, or think ourselves too important to humble ourselves under their reality, we will become profoundly disillusioned people.

The choice is quite simple. How we define faith, and what we expect from it, will lead either to a hope that is based in eternity or to a disillusionment that is based on ever-changing earthly circumstances. Disillusionment is born when we expect this world to be like the next, or when we try to live in this world without regard for the next. Self-centeredness shrinks our souls; even blessings can get boring. We need meaning, purpose, a mission, and a hope.

Authentic Christianity, I believe, provides all this—and more.

familiar footsteps

I was driving home from speaking at a church late one Sunday evening. I had promised then seven-year-old Kelsey earlier in the day that I'd be home in time to tuck her in to bed. As the clock crept past 8:30, I started to get anxious and called Lisa to tell her to keep Kelsey awake.

"She's spending the night at Laura's house," Lisa said.

"But I promised I would tuck her in!"

I thought for a second and added, "I've got an even better idea. Call Jennie and Tim [Laura's parents] and tell them I'll be there about 9:00. Ask them not to tell Kelsey, though. I want it to be a surprise."

Thirty minutes later, Tim welcomed me into his house and silently pointed toward Laura's bedroom. I walked down the hallway, opened the door, and saw Kelsey's face peeking out of Laura's bed.

"Hi there, Pop-tart!"

Kelsey giggled but didn't look the least bit surprised.

"Did you know I was coming here?" I asked her.

"No, but I heard your footsteps coming down the hall, so I figured you came here to tuck me in."

How did Kelsey know it was me, when she had no reason to expect my arrival? Apparently she had become so familiar with the cadence of my steps that she would know them anytime, anywhere. May we also become so familiar with God's footsteps, and may our hearts be so used to the cadence of his approach and the gentle footfall of his shoes, that when he breaks into our lives, we'll know it's him, regardless of what environment we're in or where we're sleeping.

> *"I heard your footsteps coming down the hall."*

If we have this kind of relationship with God—if we're this captivated by his love—we won't be surprised if he meets us in mourning. We won't be caught off guard if we find his footsteps guiding us through difficulty and even suffering; we won't feel abandoned if his footsteps take us through persecution, or if in following him we know we must learn to forgive others and serve the sick, the imprisoned, or those with disabilities.

Listening for God's footsteps in even the most difficult circumstances will lead to a fire-tested life, to a truly authentic faith. Although some may call it a hard life, I believe it is the most joyous, the richest, and the most meaningful life possible.

notes

chapter 1: severe gifts

1. This is not true of forgiveness, of course, but even here, forgiveness requires a prior act that someone else has done before we have anything to forgive. Even social mercy requires the presence of someone else who needs our help.

2. Because all of my books incorporate the Christian classics, I'm often asked to define just what a Christian classic is. In a time when the average shelf life of any book is somewhere between milk and yogurt, a Christian classic is a book that has been recognized as helpful and is still being read decades or even centuries after its first publication. There is no "definitive" canon (though I list several classics on my Web site, www.garythomas.com), but there is a generally accepted grouping that includes writers such as Augustine, John Climacus, Teresa of Avila, John of the Cross, Jeanne Guyon, Francis de Sales, John Calvin, William Law, and many, many others.

chapter 2: living beyond your self

1. See Romans 12:1–13; 1 John 3:16–20.

2. Augustine, "Enchiridion," chap. 31, in *St. Augustine: On the Holy Trinity, Doctrinal Treatises, Moral Treatises*, vol. 3, *A Select Library of the Nicene and Post-Nicene Fathers of the Christian Church,* ed. Philip Schaff (1887; reprint, Grand Rapids: Eerdmans, 1998), 248, emphasis added.

3. Augustine, *The City of God*, bk. 10, chap. 6, trans. Henry Bettenson (New York: Penguin Books, 1972), 380.

4. Cited in George B. Sayer, *Jack: C. S. Lewis and His Times* (San Francisco: HarperSanFrancisco, 1988), 170–71.

5. Sayer, *Jack: C. S. Lewis and His Times,* 161.

6. J. I. Packer, "Sin," *Systematic Theology B,* Tape Series 2645 (Vancouver, B.C.: Regent College, 1996).

chapter 3: That Excruciating Exercise

1. Marco R. della Cava, "The Price of Speed," *USA Today,* 3 August 2000, 10D.

2. William Burr, ed., *The Kissinger Transcripts: The Top-Secret Talks with Beijing and Moscow* (New York: The New Press, 1999).

3. I'm indebted to Dr. Bob Stone at Hillcrest Chapel in Bellingham, Washington, who used this phrase during a morning sermon on September 10, 2000.

4. Francis de Sales, *Introduction to the Devout Life* (Rome: Frederick Pustet, n.d.), 307–8.

5. De Sales, *Introduction to the Devout Life,* 307.

6. De Sales, *Introduction to the Devout Life,* 131.

7. John of the Cross, "The Dark Night of the Soul," in *John of the Cross: Selected Writings,* ed. Kieran Kavanaugh (New York: Paulist, 1987), 173.

8. Jeanne Guyon, *Experiencing the Depths of Jesus Christ* (Auburn, Maine: SeedSowers, 1975), 27.

9. Guyon, *Experiencing the Depths of Jesus Christ,* 28, emphasis added.

10. Guyon, *Experiencing the Depths of Jesus Christ,* 29, emphasis added.

11. The story is found in Exodus 3–14.

12. John Climacus, *The Ladder of Divine Ascent,* trans. Colm Luibheid and Norman Russell (New York: Paulist, 1982), 289.

13. Account taken from Tom Callahan, "Don't Ever Grow Old. No, Do," *Golf Digest,* October 2000, 51–52.

14. Sam Lacy was honored for his work as a sportswriter, winning the J. G. Taylor Spink Award in 1997.

chapter 4: Fragments of Frustration

1. See also 2 Chronicles 21:14–15; 2 Chronicles 26:20; Isaiah 10:16; and Daniel 8:27 for four other accounts of God sending illnesses.

2. Quoted in Merrell Noden, "Marty Liquori, Dream Miler," *Sports Illustrated,* 5 June 2000, 18.

3. Basil, "Letter CCXXXVI," para. 3, in *St. Basil: Letters and Select Works,* vol. 8, *A Select Library of Nicene and Post-Nicene Fathers of the Christian Church,* 2d series, ed. Philip Schaff and Henry Wace, (1887; reprint, Grand Rapids: Eerdmans, 1989), 279.

4. Cited in Joseph Paul Kozlowski, *Spiritual Direction and Spiritual Directors* (Santa Barbara, Calif.: Queenship, 1998), 187.

5. Cited in Kozlowski, *Spiritual Direction and Spiritual Directors,* 253.

6. Cited in Kozlowski, *Spiritual Direction and Spiritual Directors,* 298.

7. I've written an entire chapter on the virtue of detachment, which appears in *The Glorious Pursuit: Embracing the Virtues of Christ* (Colorado Springs: NavPress, 1998).

8. See Gerald May, *Addiction and Grace* (San Francisco: HarperSanFrancisco, 1988), 54–55.

9. Thanks to my friend Evan Howard for this clever thought.

10. George B. Sayer, *Jack: C. S. Lewis and His Times* (San Francisco: HarperSanFrancisco, 1988), 187.

11. Sayer, *Jack: C. S. Lewis and His Times*, 194.

12. Sayer, *Jack: C. S. Lewis and His Times*, 203.

13. Cited in Sayer, *Jack: C. S. Lewis and His Times*, 160.

14. Cited in Sayer, *Jack: C. S Lewis and His Times*, 200.

15. Cited in Sayer, *Jack: C. S Lewis and His Times*, 225.

16. Cited in Sayer, *Jack: C. S Lewis and His Times*, 225.

17. Jon Kent Walker, "Sanctity of Life." This article originally appeared in *HomeLife* magazine. Copyright © 1999 by Lifeway Christian Resources. Used with permission.

18. Cited in Jon Meacham, "The Flying Pope," *New York Times Book Review*, 14 November 1999.

chapter 5: titanic testimony

1. Cited in John Calvin, *Calvin's Commentaries: The Gospels* (Grand Rapids: Associate Publishers and Authors, Inc., n.d.), 68.

2. The following accounts are taken from the sixteenth-century classic known today as *Foxe's Book of Martyrs*. Although we can't be sure about all that tradition teaches, at the very least we know what the church believed—and thus what their expectations for their own lives were.

3. John Foxe, *Foxe's Book of Martyrs* (1563; reprint, Springdale, Pa.: Whitaker House, 1981), 12.

4. Foxe, *Foxe's Book of Martyrs*, 18.

5. See Paul Marshall, *Their Blood Cries Out* (Nashville: Word, 1997); and James Hefley and Marti Hefley, *By Their Blood* (Grand Rapids: Baker, 1995).

6. Cited in Martha Aldrick, "Baptist Leader Blasts Clinton," *USA Today*, 23 December 1999, 2A.

7. Letter dated November 27, 1999, from the Council of Religious Leaders of Metropolitan Chicago to Paige Patterson, president of the Southern Baptist Convention.

8. George Sayer, *Jack: C. S. Lewis and His Times* (San Francisco: HarperSanFrancisco, 1988), 173–74.

9. Blaise Pascal comments on this in *Pensées* (New York: Penguin, 1966), 272.

10. Pascal, *Pensées*, 272.

11. Pascal, *Pensées*, 314.

12. John Ashcroft with Gary Thomas, *Lessons from a Father to a Son* (Nashville: Nelson, 1998); rereleased in 2001 as *On My Honor*.

13. Wayne Grudem, *1 Peter*, Tyndale New Testament Commentaries (1988; reprint, Grand Rapids: Eerdmans, 1999), 131.

14. Grudem, *1 Peter*, 130.

15. Grudem, *1 Peter*, 131.

16. I talk about the need to defend ourselves at times for the sake of ministry in a section titled "Humility in Ministry," in *Seeking the Face of God* (1994; reprint, Eugene, Ore.: Harvest House, 1999), 128 and following.

17. All these citations and the events from the following story are found in George and Karen Grant, *Best Friends* (Nashville: Cumberland House, 1998), 110.

18. Grant and Grant, *Best Friends*, 115–16. I highly recommend this book for a fascinating study of friendship.

19. Cited in Grant and Grant, *Best Friends*, 118.

chapter 6: the people of god's heart

1. Franklin Graham, *Living Beyond the Limits: A Life in Sync with God* (Nashville: Nelson, 1998), 146.

2. I was introduced to the Tabors's story through an unsigned article in *Psychology for Living*, July/August 2000, 17.

3. Summary of article by Doug Saunders, "You Wouldn't Wish It On a Dog," *Globe and Mail*, 23 June 2001, F1.

4. Note that I'm *not* saying their biblical writings contradict one another, but only that they occasionally had personal disagreements.

5. Cited in Martin Hengel, *Property and Riches in the Early Church: Aspects of a Social History of Early Christianity* (Philadelphia: Fortress, 1974), 45.

6. Ambrose, "On the Duties of the Clergy," bk. 1, chap. 11, in *Ambrose: Select Works and Letters*, vol. 10, *A Select Library of Nicene and Post-Nicene Fathers of the Christian Church*, 2d series, ed. Philip Schaff and Henry Wace (1887; reprint, Grand Rapids: Eerdmans, 1989), 39.

7. Cited in Joseph Paul Kozlowski, *Spiritual Direction and Spiritual Directors* (Santa Barbara, Calif.: Queenship, 1998), 235.

8. Noted in George Sayer, *Jack: C. S. Lewis and His Times* (San Francisco: HarperSanFrancisco, 1988), 175.

9. Basil, "Letter CL," para. 3, in *St. Basil: Letters and Select Works*, vol. 8, *A Select Library of Nicene and Post-Nicene Fathers of the Christian Church*, 208.

10. These and other details taken from David Guterson, "The Kingdom of Apples," *Harper's Magazine* October 1999, as well as the story "Sunshine, Not Shadows" in the December/January 2000 issue of the *Washington Citizen* (the newsletter of Washington Family Council).

11. Cited in William A. Barry & William J. Connolly, *The Practice of Spiritual Direction* (1982; reprint, San Francisco: HarperSanFrancisco, 1986), 126.

12. J. I. Packer, "Sin," *Systematic Theology B*, Tape Series 2645 (Vancouver, B.C.: Regent College, 1996).

13. The conversation with Gary Haugen can be found in *Beyond* magazine, no. 12. It can be viewed online at http://www.beyondmag.com/backiss/issue%2012/IJM.htm

chapter 7: giving up the grudge

1. David McCullough, *John Adams* (New York: Simon & Schuster, 2001), 643.

2. McCullough, as quoted in "Adams vs. Jefferson," *USA Today*, 5 July 2001, 2A.

3. Noted in McCullough, *John Adams,* 582.

4. Noted in McCullough, *John Adams,* 584.

5. Noted in McCullough, *John Adams,* 607 and following.

6. Quoted in McCullough, *John Adams,* 603.

7. Quoted in McCullough, *John Adams,* 632.

8. Augustine, "Enchiridion," chap. 74, in *St. Augustine: On the Holy Trinity, Doctrinal Treatises, Moral Treatises,* vol. 3, *A Select Library of Nicene and Post-Nicene Fathers of the Christian Church,* ed. Philip Schaff, (1887; reprint, Grand Rapids: Eerdmans, 1998), 261.

9. Except where otherwise noted, the following quotes in this chapter are taken from personal interviews conducted by the author, as well as research quoted in his article, "The Forgiveness Factor," *Christianity Today,* 10 January 2000, 38–45.

10. Sydna is now the president of Ramah International (www.ramah-international.org) and the author of *Her Choice to Heal.*

11. William Law, *A Serious Call to a Devout and Holy Life* (New York: Paulist, 1978), 157.

12. Law, *A Serious Call to a Devout and Holy Life,* 308–9.

13. John Calvin, *Genesis,* trans. John King (1554; reprint, Grand Rapids: Baker, 1984), 376.

14. Calvin, *Genesis,* 484.

15. Ken Garfield, "The Season of Forgiveness," *Sports Illustrated,* 27 March 2000, 32.

16. Cited in Garfield, "The Season of Forgiveness," 34.

chapter 8: mourning's promise

1. Jonathan Edwards, *Religious Affections: A Christian's Character Before God* (1851; reprint, Minneapolis: Bethany House, 1996), 13.

2. I want to thank Jeromy Matkin for our discussion that led me to this point.

3. William Shakespeare, *Twelfth Night, or What You Will,* act 1, scene 5.

4. John Calvin, *Calvin's Commentaries: The Gospels* (1555; reprint, Grand Rapids: Associate Publishers and Authors, Inc., n.d.), 515.

5. John Calvin, *Hebrews and 1 and 2 Peter* (1549, 1551; reprint, Grand Rapids: Eerdmans, 1994), 234.

6. John Climacus, *The Ladder of Divine Ascent,* trans. Colm Luibheid and Norman Russell (New York: Paulist, 1982), 136.

7. Climacus, *The Ladder of Divine Ascent,* 138.

8. Climacus, *The Ladder of Divine Ascent,* 138.

9. Calvin, *Calvin's Commentaries: The Gospels,* 532.

10. Ralph Venning, *The Sinfulness of Sin* (1669; reprint, Carlisle, Pa.: Banner of Truth, 1993), 276.

11. John Wesley, *John Wesley's Journal* (London: Isbister and Company, 1902), 144 (entry for 26 October 1745).

12. Climacus, *The Ladder of Divine Ascent*, 141.

13. I discuss the role of repentance in sexual impropriety in *The Glorious Pursuit: Embracing the Virtues of Christ* (Colorado Springs: NavPress, 1998), where I suggest that men shouldn't just repent over what the sin may do to *them* but also over how they are perpetuating a harmful livelihood for the women who are involved in the sex industry. If men didn't purchase pornography or hang out at strip clubs or visit prostitutes, fewer women would submit themselves to such a degrading environment. I make this observation: "Lust is a self-centered sin, and it is not overcome by a self-centered repentance. The solution is to consider others—not merely to be a little thoughtful, but to ask God to give you a respectful reverence for the people He has made.... A life that reverences others has fewer regrets, deeper relationships, and ultimately much more satisfaction" (*The Glorious Pursuit*, 102–3).

14. I discuss the role of spiritual directors in my book *Seeking the Face of God* (Eugene, Ore.: Harvest House, 1999).

15. Cited in John Feinstein, *The Majors* (New York: Little, Brown, and Company, 1999), 9.

16. Cited in Feinstein, *The Majors*, 176.

chapter 9: Tyrannical Expectations

1. Quoted in Ariel Kaminer, "Shelter Porn," *The New York Times Book Review*, 23 July 2000, 26.

2. Noted in Kurt Anderson, "Valley Guy," *The New York Times Book Review*, 31 October 1999, 10–12.

3. S. L. Price, "No Babe in the Woods," *Sports Illustrated*, 13 December 1999, 83–84.

4. I cover the discipline of offering thanks in my book *The Glorious Pursuit* (Eugene, Ore.: Harvest House, 1998).

5. Ambrose, "Letter LXIII," para. 89–91, in *Ambrose: Select Works and Letters*, vol. 10, *A Select Library of Nicene and Post-Nicene Fathers of the Christian Church*, 2d series, ed. Philip Schaff and Henry Wace, (1887; reprint, Grand Rapids: Eerdmans, 1989), 470.

6. Cited in Ron Sider, *Rich Christians in an Age of Hunger*, 20th anniversary revision (1977; reprint, Nashville: Word, 1997), 190.

7. Ambrose, "On the Decease of His Brother Satyrus," bk. 1, para. 2–4, in *Ambrose: Select Works and Letters*, vol. 10, *A Select Library of Nicene and Post-Nicene Fathers of the Christian Church*, 161.

8. William Law, *A Serious Call to a Devout and Holy Life* (New York: Paulist, 1978), 291.

9. Francis de Sales, *Thy Will Be Done: Letters to Persons in the World* (Manchester, N.H.: Sophia Institute Press, 1995), 48.

10. De Sales, *Thy Will Be Done*, 48.

11. De Sales, *Thy Will Be Done*, 16.

12. De Sales, *Thy Will Be Done,* 9–10.

13. Thomas Merton, *The Seven Storey Mountain* (New York: Harcourt Brace, 1948), 370.

14. Cited in Luis Goncalves da Camara, *The Autobiography of St. Ignatius of Loyola,* trans. Joseph F. O'Callaghan, ed. John C. Olin (New York: Harper Torchbooks, 1974), 23–24.

15. Cited in Gregory Maguire, "Lord of the Golden Snitch," *The New York Times Book Review,* 5 September 1999, 12.

chapter 10: not my will . . .

1. John Calvin, *Calvin's Commentaries: The Gospels* (Grand Rapids: Associate Publishers and Authors, Inc., n.d.), 515.

2. Calvin, *Calvin's Commentaries: The Gospels,* 515.

3. Francis de Sales, *Thy Will Be Done: Letters to Persons in the World* (Manchester, N.H.: Sophia Institute Press, 1995), 160.

4. Francis de Sales, *Introduction to the Devout Life* (Rome: Frederick Pustet, n.d.), 128.

5. Francis de Sales, *Thy Will Be Done,* 160.

6. Jonathan Edwards, *Religious Affections: A Christian's Character Before God* (1851; reprint, Minneapolis: Bethany House, 1996), 3.

7. Lance Armstrong with Sally Jenkins, *It's Not About the Bike* (New York, Putnam, 2000), excerpted in "Tour De Lance," *Vanity Fair,* 120.

8. From *It's Not About the Bike,* excerpted in "Tour De Lance," *Vanity Fair,* 120.

9. From *It's Not About the Bike,* excerpted in "Tour De Lance," *Vanity Fair,* 120.

10. Quoted in Ian Thomsen, "Heavenly Ascent," *Sports Illustrated,* 24 July 2000, 48.

11. Sandra Block, "50 Not So Nifty for Baby Boomers," *USA Today,* 20 September 2000, 1B.

12. Cited in Block, "50 Not So Nifty for Baby Boomers," 2B.

13. Calvin, *Calvin's Commentaries: The Gospels,* 395.

14. Calvin, *Calvin's Commentaries: The Gospels,* 395.

15. This account is true, but the author notes that some names have been changed. See James McDonough, *Platoon Leader* (Novato, Calif.: Presidio Press, 1985, 1996), 85 and following.

chapter 11: well done . . . depart from me!

1. Noted in Cesar Soriano, "Award Overdose," *USA Today,* 6 January 2000, D1.

2. Cited in Jon Saraceno, "Keeping Score," *USA Today,* 4 August 2000, 3C.

3. Noted in James Parker Jr., *Last Man Out: A Personal Account of the Vietnam War* (New York: Ballantine Books, 2000), 167.

4. Cited in Parker, *Last Man Out,* 168.

5. Wayne Grudem, *1 Peter*, Tyndale New Testament Commentaries (1988; reprint, Grand Rapids: Eerdmans, 1999), 149.

6. Grudem, *1 Peter*, 150. Grudem is specifically referring to 1 Peter 3:8–12.

7. See Hosea 13:1–16.

8. See Haggai 2:17.

9. Ambrose, "On the Duties of the Clergy," bk. 1, chap. 15, para. 57–58, in *Ambrose: Select Works and Letters*, vol. 10, *A Select Library of Nicene and Post-Nicene Fathers of the Christian Church*, 2d series, ed. Philip Schaff and Henry Wace (1887; reprint, Grand Rapids: Eerdmans, 1989), 11.

10. Thomas à Kempis, *The Imitation of Christ*, bk. 1, chap. 3, para. 5.

11. Ralph Venning, *The Sinfulness of Sin* (Carlisle, Pa.: Banner of Truth, 1993), 89.

12. Cited in Philip Hughes, *The Second Epistle to the Corinthians* (Grand Rapids: Eerdmans, 1962), 180.

13. Jill Lieber, "He Wants to Save the World," *USA Today*, 17 February 2000, C1.

14. I explore this issue much more thoroughly in my book *Sacred Marriage* (Grand Rapids: Zondervan, 2000), especially pages 127–52.

15. Bruce Waltke, "The Fear of the Lord," in *Alive to God: Studies in Spirituality*, ed. J. I. Packer and Loren Wilkinson (Downers Grove, Ill.: InterVarsity Press, 1992), 25, emphasis added.

16. Walther Eichrodt, cited in Waltke, "The Fear of the Lord," in *Alive to God*, 27.

17. For a more thorough discussion, I highly recommend Waltke's essay in *Alive to God*, cited above.

18. Cited in George Sayer, *Jack: C. S. Lewis and His Times* (San Francisco: HarperSanFrancisco, 1988), 252.

19. Cited in Sayer, *Jack: C. S. Lewis and His Times*, 252.

20. Ambrose, "On the Duties of the Clergy," bk. 1, chap. 16, para. 62, in *Ambrose: Select Works and Letters*, vol. 10, *A Select Library of Nicene and Post-Nicene Fathers of the Christian Church*, 11.

Epilogue

1. Harry Schaumburg, *False Intimacy: Understanding the Struggle of Sexual Addiction* (Colorado Springs: NavPress, 1997), 84. I receive numerous questions and E-mails from individuals and couples who are struggling with sexual addiction. This is one of the books I frequently recommend.

For more information about Gary Thomas or the Center for Evangelical Spirituality, visit his Web site at www.garythomas.com. Please refer speaking requests to Martin Culpepper, Interact Agency, 615-446-0087.

Sacred Pathways
Discover Your Soul's Path to God
Gary Thomas

Some Christians effortlessly spend hours in contemplative prayer. Just being around them makes you wish you were that way. Or maybe you *are* that way, but others are far better at showing God's love in practical ways, or courageously standing up for God's kingdom. Why can't you be like them?

Maybe you weren't designed to be.

Sacred Pathways unfolds nine distinct spiritual temperaments—their traits, strengths, and pitfalls. Illustrated with examples from the Bible and from the author's life experience, each one suggests an approach to loving God, a distinctive journey of adoration. In one or more, you will see yourself and the ways you most naturally express your relationship with Jesus Christ. You'll also discover other temperaments that are not necessarily "you" but that you may wish to explore for the way they can stretch and invigorate your spiritual life.

Perhaps you are a Naturalist. Prayer and praise well up within you when you're walking a forest path or drinking in a mountain's jagged beauty. Or maybe you're an Activist. Taking a stand for God's ways is your meat and drink. Whatever temperament or blend of temperaments best describes you, rest assured it's not by accident. It's by the design of a Creator who knew what he was doing when he made you according to his own unique intentions.

If your spiritual walk is not what you'd like it to be, you can change that, starting here. *Sacred Pathways* will show you the route you were made to travel, marked by growth and filled with the riches of a close walk with God.

Pick up a copy today at your favorite bookstore!

Hardcover 0-310-23092-6
Softcover 0-310-24284-3

ZONDERVAN™

GRAND RAPIDS, MICHIGAN 49530

WWW.ZONDERVAN.COM

Sacred Marriage

What If God Designed Marriage to Make Us Holy More Than to Make Us Happy?

Gary Thomas

What if God's primary intent for your marriage is not to make you happy, but to make us holy? What if marriage is not so much about husband and wife, but about each person and God? The Bible is filled with images of the bridegroom and bride—and marriage is filled with the prophetic potential for enabling each partner to discover and reveal Christ's character. In this revolutionary book, author Gary Thomas focuses not so much on how to love a spouse, but on how each person can reflect the character of Jesus.

Gary Thomas writes, "The ultimate purpose of this book is not to make you love your spouse more—although I think that will happen along the way. It's to equip you to love your God more and to help you reflect the character of his Son more precisely."

Historically, the "deeper walk" has been considered the province of the celibate, of saints and ascetics, monks and nuns. But the Bible, in depicting God's passionate, holy relationship with his people, is filled with images of the bridegroom and the bride and of a husband with his wife. Everything about your marriage—everything—is filled with prophetic potential, with the capacity for discovering and revealing Christ's character.

Pick up a copy today at your favorite bookstore!

Hardcover 0-310-22796-8
Softcover 0-310-24282-7

ZONDERVAN™

GRAND RAPIDS, MICHIGAN 49530
WWW.ZONDERVAN.COM

Spiritual Formation Bible

Growing in Intimacy with God through Scripture

Timothy Jones, general editor;
Gary Thomas, contributor

An invitation to intimacy with God

If you hunger for greater depth in your relationship with God, the *NIV Spiritual Formation Bible* offers you the feast you're searching for. Designed to satisfy spirit, mind, and emotions, this unique Bible helps you turn your Scripture reading into a transforming encounter with God.

On each page of Scripture you'll find an "Entry Point" reflection based on spiritual disciplines that have been practiced by Christians throughout the centuries. Five different kinds of "Entry Points," highlighted by beautiful woodcut-style icons, include:

1. LECTIO DIVINA invites you into a time of two-way conversation with God
2. IGNATIAN reading engages all your senses as you explore the passage
3. FRANCISCAN reading helps you encounter God through practical and creative acts such as writing and art
4. FIVEFOLD QUESTION prompts you to consider what the Biblical passage means to you
5. QUOTATIONS from respected Christians, historic and contemporary, illuminate the power of Scripture.

Besides the over 1,500 "Entry Points," this Bible also features:

- Seven articles on the spiritual disciplines to guide you in meeting God in Scripture, Prayer, Worship, Service, the Created Order, Everyday Life, and Community
- Sixty-six book introductions
- Articles on "Getting Started in Spiritual Formation"
- Twenty pages of classic quotations in beautiful calligraphy
- Easy-to-use-single-column, side-margin format
- An index to "Entry Points" and "Meeting God" articles to help you focus on topics of special interest
- New International Version—today's most popular modern translation
- A "How to Use" feature on page v to help you get the most benefit from your Spiritual Formation Bible

Pick up a copy today at your favorite bookstore!

Softcover 0-310-90211-8
Hardcover 0-310-90210-X
Port Premium Leather 0-310-90212-6

ZONDERVAN | NIV

MOST READ. MOST TRUSTED.